T0317042

Participation
and
Atonement

Participation and Atonement

An Analytic and Constructive Account

Oliver D. Crisp

B
Baker Academic
a division of Baker Publishing Group
Grand Rapids, Michigan

Published by Baker Academic
a division of Baker Publishing Group
PO Box 6287, Grand Rapids, MI 49516-6287
www.bakeracademic.com

Printed in the United States of America

Library of Congress Cataloging-in-Publication Data
Names: Crisp, Oliver, author.
Title: Participation and atonement : an analytic and constructive account / Oliver D. Crisp.
Description: Grand Rapids, Michigan : Baker Academic, a division of Baker Publishing Group,
    [2022] | Includes bibliographical references and index.
Identifiers: LCCN 2021048811 | ISBN 9780801049965 (cloth) | ISBN 9781493432219 (ebook) | ISBN
    9781493432226 (pdf)
Subjects: LCSH: Atonement.
Classification: LCC BT265.3 .C75 2022 | DDC 232/.3—dc23/eng/20211118
LC record available at https://lccn.loc.gov/2021048811

Baker Publishing Group publications use paper produced from sustainable forestry practices and post-consumer waste whenever possible.

22   23   24   25   26   27   28   7   6   5   4   3   2   1

To the scholarly community of St. Mary's College,
University of St. Andrews,
with great affection

For in him all the fullness of God was pleased to dwell, and through him God was pleased to reconcile to himself *all things*, whether on earth or in heaven, by making peace through the blood of his cross.

Colossians 1:19–20 (NRSV, emphasis added)

He brought me to the banqueting house, and his banner over me was love.

Song of Songs 2:4 (KJV)

Contents

Acknowledgments

This book has been a long time in gestation. It began life in the University of Bristol in England around 2007, traveled across the Atlantic with me when I moved to Fuller Theological Seminary in Los Angeles in 2011, where it grew and developed, and then returned back to Great Britain via the University of Notre Dame in 2019, finally coming to land in the University of St. Andrews in Scotland, where the last chapters were added in the years 2019–21. In pursuing some of the issues that inform this work, I ended up writing an LLM thesis on punishment theory under the supervision of Dr. Elizabeth Shaw at the University of Aberdeen, though none of that work made it into the final volume. (It was a case of having to do the work to be clear that it did not need to be included in the volume.) All in all, it has been quite an adventure.

Perhaps unsurprisingly for a work this long in preparation, its composition has generated many debts. I gladly acknowledge them here. In particular, the following friends and colleagues gave of their time and expertise to assist me as I have worked on this project: Rev. Dr. James Arcadi, Professor Jc Beall, Dr. Kutter Callaway, Rev. Dr. Joshua Cockayne, Dr. Aaron Cotnair, Professor Ivor Davidson, Professor Gavin D'Costa, Dr. Christopher Eberle, Dr. Joshua Farris, Professor Thomas Flint, Jesse Gentile, Dr. Tommy Givens, Professor Joel Green, Dr. S. Mark Hamilton, Professor Paul Helm, Dr. Daniel Hill, Rev. Dr. Stephen Holmes, Dr. Joseph Jedwab, Dr. Kimberley Kroll, Professor Anthony Lane, Professor Brian Leftow, Dr. Joanna Leidenhag, the late Professor Howard Marshall, Dr. Christa McKirland, Dr. Steven Nemes, Dr. Meghan Page, Professor

Michael Rea, Dani Ross, Dr. Jonathan Rutledge, Rev. Dr. Bill Schweitzer, Professor Eleonore Stump, Professor Douglas Sweeney, Dr. Andrew Torrance, Dr. J. T. Turner, Dr. Jordan Wessling, Dr. Garry Williams, Professor Judith Wolfe, and Dr. Christopher Woznicki. I am sure I have overlooked some people who have helped along the way, and I can only apologize for any omissions I may have made.

Thanks are also due to the members of the Christian Doctrine Study Groups of the 2004 and 2006 Tyndale Fellowship Summer Conferences, and participants in research seminars in the Theological Faculty, University of Cambridge; the Joseph Butler Society, Oriel College, Oxford; St. Mary's College, University of St. Andrews; Bristol Theological Society; and the Department of Theology at the University of Exeter. In each of these places I tried out material that has fed into the project. Support for the final phase of the work was given by the Center for Philosophy of Religion in the University of Notre Dame, where I was the Frederick J. Crosson Research Fellow for the second semester of the academic year 2018–19. My thanks to Professor Samuel Newlands and Professor Michael Rea as directors of the Center for this honor.

Earlier iterations of a number of the chapters have been published in journals or symposia as the book developed. Each of these chapters has been substantially revised for the present volume. Grateful acknowledgment is extended to the editors and publishers of the following essays for permission to use parts of this earlier work here (in order of publication):

- "The Logic of Penal Substitution Revisited." In *The Atonement Debate: Papers from the London Symposium on the Atonement*, edited by Derek Tidball, David Hilborn, and Justin Thacker, 208–27. Grand Rapids: Zondervan, 2008.
- "Salvation and Atonement: On the Value and Necessity of the Work of Christ." In *The God of Salvation: Soteriology in Theological Perspective*, edited by Ivor J. Davidson and Murray A. Rae, 105–20. Farnham: Ashgate, 2010. Reproduced with permission of the Licensor through PLSclear.
- "Is Ransom Enough?" *Journal of Analytic Theology* 3 (2015): 1–11.
- "Methodological Issues in Approaching the Atonement." In *T&T Clark Companion to the Atonement*, edited by Adam Johnson,

315–34. London: Bloomsbury, 2017. By kind permission of T&T Clark/Bloomsbury Publishing.

- "A Moderate Reformed View" and "A Moderate Reformed Response." In *Original Sin and the Fall: Five Views*, edited by J. B. Stump and Chad Meister, 5–54 and 140–49, respectively. Downers Grove, IL: IVP Academic, 2020. Used by permission of InterVarsity Press, Downers Grove, IL. www.ivpress.com.

- "Moral Exemplarism and Atonement." *Scottish Journal of Theology* 73, no. 2 (2020): 137–49.

Finally, but most importantly, thanks to my family: Claire, Liberty, Elliot, and Mathilda. Without you none of this would have seen the light of day.

Introduction

Often theologians are formed through apprenticing themselves to the work of one or more past masters in the great tradition of Christian doctrine. It is a good way to develop and refine one's theological sensibilities. Working closely with the texts and thought of a historic theologian leaves an indelible impression upon the work of those who follow in their footsteps. That is true even when the apprentice strikes out to become a practitioner in her or his own right.

For better or worse, I am an apprentice of several such past masters on the doctrine of atonement, and my work reflects their influence. From Athanasius and Irenaeus I have learned that the incarnation is as important to the notion of human reconciliation to God as the cross. From Anselm of Canterbury I have learned about the shape of atonement theology and the structures that underpin it, as well as much besides that about the nature and purposes of God, and of theological method. From Thomas Aquinas, John Calvin, and Karl Barth I have learned about the overall shape of Christian doctrine, and about the substitutionary nature of Christ's saving work. But it is the great New England pastor-theologian Jonathan Edwards who has, in many respects, shaped my thinking more deeply than any other thinker in this regard.

When I was a doctoral student in philosophy of religion working through Edwards's views about the metaphysics of sin, I ended up thinking about his understanding of the relationship between Adam and Christ in a way that reflects the Pauline "Adam Christology" of Romans

1

5:12–19.[1] As I was engaged in this task, I noticed that Edwards thought about the relationship between Adam and his progeny and between Christ and his elect in a manner that was very different from the sort of forensic doctrine that I had imbibed from the other Reformed theologians to whom I had been exposed up to that point. Rather than thinking of Adam and his progeny as united by means of a kind of moral and legal arrangement according to which God imputes Adam's sin to his offspring and imputes the sin of Adam's offspring to Christ and Christ's righteousness to the elect, Edwards drew a different lesson. He taught that the real union between Adam and his offspring, and between Christ and his elect, is the foundation for any legal union. The real union between the two is more basic than the forensic.

This simple claim is at the heart of Edwards's thinking about the nature of salvation. By means of this concept one can unlock much of the often convoluted and difficult things Edwards says about atonement, justification, and union with Christ. This in itself was interesting to me as a young scholar and apprentice of the Northampton Sage (as Edwards is often called). But what was more important was the fact that this set me off in search of other resources to try to spell out what Edwards had intimated in his thinking about Adam Christology and its relation to the atonement.

This quest led me to the work of other Reformed thinkers who held to a similar view about the fundamentality of union with Christ and notions of participation in their thinking about Adam Christology. I ended up writing a book in search of some of these answers in dialogue with another Reformed divine from the century after Edwards's death, William G. T. Shedd.[2] He shared many theological sensibilities with Edwards on the matter of the relation between Adam and Christ, but he cast his account in the idiom of an Anglicized German idealism rather than that of the empiricist-imbued immaterialism of Edwards. Other interlocutors I encountered at this juncture included John Williamson Nevin, one of the leaders of the Mercersburg Theology. Among other things, he directed me back to the study of John Calvin.[3] In the *Institutes* I found more grist to the mill in Calvin's emphasis on union with Christ and participation in

---

1. The results of this rumination can be found in Crisp, *Jonathan Edwards and the Metaphysics of Sin*.
2. See Crisp, *American Augustinian*.
3. See Crisp, "John Williamson Nevin on the Church."

the divine life. Thomas F. Torrance provided a bridge from Calvin and the Scottish theology I had imbibed as an undergraduate to patristic accounts of the atonement. Kathryn Tanner's work on incarnation and atonement, which drew deeply from similar sources as Torrance, underlined the importance of the patristic witness to notions of participation in the divine life.[4] Through these theologians I found my way back to the theology of Athanasius and Irenaeus. What I discovered there was electrifying. They too had a sense that through participation in Christ we are united to God.[5] From there it was a short but crucial step to the recent literature on the notion of theosis, or divinization, and its recovery in recent Western theology (with particular thanks to my friends Julie Canlis and Carl Mosser). This was also a notion to be found in Edwards.[6] I had come full circle.

This outline of my own intellectual journey in pursuit of a better understanding of the saving work of Christ is far too neat, of course. There were many dead ends and frustrations along the way, and not a few missteps on my part as well. However, I think it is worth narrating this at the outset of a work like the present one because more often than not what the reader holds in his or her hands in a published work is the product of a great deal of intellectual struggle, though this is often not declared by the author. The work you hold in your hands, dear reader, is one such product. In writing it, I had to revise and rethink a number of key issues over the course of more than a decade. This has not been easy, and has certainly delayed publication. But research projects have a habit of taking us in directions we had not anticipated, perhaps especially if we are existentially invested in the outcome.

In this work, I set out to give an account of the nature of the atonement. The central question that drives this volume is as follows: *What is the mechanism by means of which Christ's work reconciles fallen human beings to God?* In the course of the volume, I give some account of various traditional ways of thinking about this topic, and I offer a constructive, participatory account of my own—which I call the *representational account of atonement*. This volume is, in important respects, a companion and sequel to my previous work entitled *The Word Enfleshed*. There I

4. The produce of such engagement can be found in the essays in Crisp, *Revisioning Christology*.

5. I have discussed the work of Athanasius and Irenaeus in Crisp, *Approaching the Atonement*.

6. I worked on this aspect of his thought in Crisp, *Jonathan Edwards on God and Creation*.

sought to provide a joined-up account of the work of Christ that took seriously the fact that it included the incarnation as well as the death and resurrection of Christ. The atonement is not just about the cross, though this is a crucial component of it—or so I sought to argue. *The Word Enfleshed* was, in many respects, a bridge project that connected my previous work on the doctrine of the incarnation with my current concern with the atonement.[7] In *The Word Enfleshed*, I also provided a sketch of a view of the atonement that I called the *realist union account*, and which I develop in important respects here. The current work is more narrowly focused on the nature of the atonement than was *The Word Enfleshed*. Although it can be read independently of my earlier work, the two books are really two phases of one work, or two installments of a single research project.

In the present volume, I try to give a rather different and hopefully more thorough, nuanced, and carefully worked out account of atonement, setting it into a broader context of soteriology, or the doctrine of salvation. In the intervening period between the two works on atonement, my views have changed somewhat so that the version of the doctrine set forth here is different from that given in *The Word Enfleshed*. Not only do I offer a new treatment of the nature of atonement, but I also distinguish between the mechanism of atonement and the consequences of atonement in union with Christ brought about by the Holy Spirit. I think these represent important developments in my thinking. They are connected to the way in which my views about the nature and transmission of original sin have developed in the last decade as well. Thus, the constructive section of the book tackles original sin and the nature of atonement as well as regeneration and union with Christ through the Holy Spirit—all in pursuit of an answer to the central research question that motivates the work. Of course, just how significant a development in my work this constitutes is for others to judge.

Outline of the Book

With the central thesis of the book made clear, let me turn to outline the chapters that follow. The work is divided into three sections. Part 1 is

7. I have also written a short introductory textbook on the atonement, *Approaching the Atonement*, which presents various historic attempts to articulate the doctrine of atonement along with a brief constructive chapter at the end.

entitled "Approaching the Atonement" and deals with preliminary matters. Chapter 1 begins with a ground-clearing exercise, focused on methodological issues. It tackles how we should think about the nature of atonement as a central component of Christ's reconciling work and what language we should use in talking about it.

Having set some conceptual parameters, chapter 2 considers the two related questions of the value and necessity of atonement. It is often said that Christ's saving work has an infinite value because it is the work of someone who is both divine and human. But what does that mean? It is also often said that the atonement is in some sense necessary for human salvation. But necessary in what sense? Why must God bring about atonement in this costly way, if indeed he must bring about reconciliation at all? This chapter considers these important preliminaries.

The second section of the work turns to consider some of the most important historic treatments of atonement in the Christian tradition. These are often rehearsed in textbooks on the subject, and frequently the way in which they are showcased takes a fairly traditional, even well-worn, shape. In the chapters of this section, I try to address some of the major historic models of atonement while also problematizing the way in which they are often presented in textbooks on the topic. Nevertheless, I shall argue that these historic accounts of atonement, as they are usually presented today, are all incomplete or mistaken in various respects. They need some corrective, or some additional component; something seems to be missing. It is just this missing component that I seek to provide in the final constructive section of the book.

Chapter 3 looks at the doctrine of moral exemplarism. This is the idea that Christ's moral example should motivate fallen human beings to live a life that reflects God's love for us. Sometimes this is (mistakenly) associated with the medieval Parisian theologian Peter Abelard. More often than not, the version of the doctrine that is set out is a kind of caricature rather than the most sympathetic or charitable version of it. In this chapter, I set out two versions of moral exemplarism, drawing on the recent work on transformative experience by philosopher L. A. Paul. It is tempting to think that moral exemplarism does not, in fact, present us with a doctrine of atonement at all but rather with a way of thinking about the work of Christ that is nonredemptive. For, so it might be thought, a moral example may motivate us to live a particular kind of life. But that is quite different from being saved by some act on our behalf. It is the difference between being told to be brave like the firefighter who plucks people from burning buildings and actually being rescued by the firefighter from the midst of a blaze. However, I shall argue in this chapter that there is a version of moral exemplarism that does amount to a doctrine of atonement—just a rather conceptually thin one. This is a somewhat surprising result. Nevertheless, it seems to me that the doctrine is appropriately thought of as one aspect of a richer account of Christ's reconciling work rather than as a stand-alone doctrine. This should become clear in the third part of the volume.

Chapter 4 takes up the ransom account of atonement. This has become one of the most talked-about accounts of the work of Christ in contemporary theology, and it is often—mistakenly—thought to be the default option in patristic doctrines of atonement. This chapter provides an account of the conceptual shape of the doctrine and its shortcomings. I argue that it is an important motif in thinking about the atonement but that it does not amount to a complete doctrine of atonement because it does not provide a clear understanding of the mechanism involved. Instead, it is an incomplete but potentially helpful way of thinking about one aspect of Christ's reconciling work.

Chapter 5 considers the doctrine of satisfaction, particularly with reference to the works of Anselm of Canterbury and Thomas Aquinas. Today this is a much-maligned account of Christ's work, though it is arguably the most influential account of atonement in the Christian tradition. I attempt a partial defense of the doctrine as a coherent—though, in Anselm's case, incomplete—account of atonement. It provides a helpful way of framing Christ's reconciling work as a satisfaction of divine honor, not as a punishment. In the course of the chapter, I also deal with some recent criticism of the doctrine raised by Eleonore Stump.

The last chapter in this section is chapter 6. In it, I give some account of penal substitution and its shortcomings. This is by far the most criticized historic account of the atonement, though it is not without its defenders. I shall recount some of the most significant traditional objections to the doctrine. Although I think there are some serious shortcomings to the doctrine, as there are to the doctrine of satisfaction, I think it does raise important issues that may be transposed into a different key as part of a richer union account of atonement that is the subject of the succeeding chapters of the volume.

This brings us to the heart of the volume, the constructive third part. This part gives a complete account of the nature of atonement, drawing on the work of the previous chapters, especially with respect to the understanding of God's action in reconciliation reflected in the various models and motifs of atonement previously considered.

Chapter 7 sets the scene by considering the relationship between sin and atonement. The traditional claim that we are saved from sin by Christ's reconciling work needs some explanation. For what is sin and original sin, and how do they relate to Christ's atonement? Here I set out what I have elsewhere called a *moderate Reformed account* of original sin, or what Thomas McCall calls a "corruption-only" account.[8] On this way of thinking, we bear the corruption of human nature called original sin, but we do not bear original guilt. Rather, the state of sin with which we are generated inevitably gives rise to actual sin if we live long enough to commit such acts.

This leads into the first of two chapters on the nature of atonement and its consequences. Chapter 8 begins by rehearsing the iteration of the union account of atonement I previously published in *The Word Enfleshed*, an iteration that depends on a four-dimensionalist metaphysics to make sense of the relationship between Adam and Christ in reconciliation, as per the Adam Christology of Romans 5:12–19 and 1 Corinthians 15. This I call the *realist union account*. It is "realist" because, somehow, I am really a part of fallen humanity (which has Adam as its first member) and I am really a part of redeemed humanity (which has Christ as its first member). However, there are certain conceptual costs to that version of the argument. So the next part of the chapter is concerned to set out a revised version of the union account that does not depend on the four-dimensionalism I used in the realist version of the union account. Instead, I use some ideas from recent discussion of social ontology, especially group theory, to articulate an understanding of Christ's work as vicarious, reparative, penitential representation. We may call this the *representational union account*. Importantly, on my current understanding of these things, Christ's reconciling work is not a version of penal substitution. It is closer to satisfaction, though it is not exactly that either. Instead, Christ is accountable but not responsible for human sin, and he performs an act of vicarious penitence on behalf of fallen humanity that begins with his

8. See Crisp, *Analyzing Doctrine*, chap. 7; and McCall, *Against God and Nature*.

incarnation and culminates in his death and resurrection. In this way, it includes elements of an Anselmian way of thinking as well as elements of the vicarious penitence view espoused by the nineteenth-century Scottish pastor and theologian John McLeod Campbell.

Chapter 9 then takes up the issue of union with Christ consequent upon atonement. Because Christ's work makes it possible for all of humanity to be reconciled to God, a natural question arising from consideration of the mechanism of atonement is this: How can one be united to Christ so as to enjoy the benefits of his work? This can be done through the secret work of the Holy Spirit in regeneration and union with Christ. Although traditionally regeneration is classed as dogmatically distinct from atonement, being a part of the order of salvation (*ordo salutis*), it is perhaps better thought of as a consequence of atonement within the broader category of soteriology. This chapter explores the notion of regeneration and union with Christ, set into the context of eternal justification. On this way of thinking, God eternally justifies the elect because of the reconciling work of Christ. This is actualized in time through the regenerating act of the Holy Spirit, who unites the believer to Christ on the basis of Christ's work of atonement. This precipitates the process of sanctification in which the believer becomes ever more like Christ in union with him by the Spirit, a process that goes on everlastingly. I adopt a broadly Edwardsian and supralapsarian understanding of these concepts, so that the believer is transformed by the infusion of the Holy Spirit in regeneration according to God's eternal purpose in salvation brought about by Christ in atonement.[9] This leads into a discussion of the way in which the believer is a member of the church, which is the mystical body of Christ. Thus, atonement theology and ecclesiology are intimately related.

Chapter 10 rounds out the whole with a synthesis chapter in which I draw the dogmatic threads of the foregoing together into one summary statement on the shape of soteriology, setting the question of the nature of atonement into the broader theological context of God's work of reconciliation in creation. In this way, those wishing to get a quick overview of the whole might turn to consult this final chapter as a capstone that expresses in short compass the overall shape of the work, set into this larger dogmatic context—a context that can properly be thought of as a species of theosis.

9. I discuss the question of supralapsarian Christology in Crisp, *Analyzing Doctrine*, and regeneration in Crisp, "Regeneration Reconsidered."

Approaching the Atonement

I n approaching the doctrine of atonement it is important to give some sort of conceptual context. How should we think of this doctrine? Are there particular methodological issues that need to be addressed? Such matters are important, and it behooves us to begin by thinking about them. That is the task of part 1, which deals in successive chapters with general methodological issues of terminology and concepts (chapter 1), followed by a discussion of the value and necessity of atonement (chapter 2). This paves the way for part 2, where some influential models of atonement are discussed in more detail. Then, furnished with these methodological considerations and with some theological context for a discussion of atonement as a doctrine, part 3 takes up the constructive task of providing an account of atonement.

Throughout the work, the emphasis is on the historical, theological, and philosophical dimensions of the doctrine. The biblical traditions are discussed as they bear on particular issues, and they inform the argument that follows. But this is not primarily a work of biblical scholarship. My view is that theology is informed by the biblical *and post-biblical* traditions of Christianity, and that the Bible has a particular normative place in making theological judgments.[1] Nevertheless, it is not the only norm in making such judgments, and in the case of atonement, what the Bible says is theologically underdeveloped. It is subsequent discussion of the reconciling work of Christ in the post-biblical theological tradition that has been more important in shaping the sort of views we have of the theology of atonement today. However, lest I be misunderstood, I am not suggesting that we should simply do our theology independent of Scripture and then impose it on the biblical data, or cherry-pick which passages we think will best fit our pet model of atonement. Rather, I am suggesting that the biblical traditions should *inform* the sort of constructive theological account we give of a particular doctrine. That seems appropriate, given the shape of historic Christianity, which looks to Scripture as the primary site where God continues to speak today. But in addition to this, I am also saying that Scripture does not give us a prepackaged doctrine of atonement that just needs to be unwrapped and assembled, much less a full-orbed understanding of the nature of atonement. Scripture is full of hints, intimations, motifs, metaphors, narratives—things from which doctrine can be fashioned, though it does not contain a ready-made account of the doctrine.

As we shall see in the first chapter, this is not as controversial as it at first seems. But it is important to point out at the beginning of a work like this because some readers may come looking for a particular kind of book, one that provides an account of "the biblical" view of atonement. Such readers will be disappointed because there is, in my view, no such thing as *the* biblical view of atonement. Rather, there are biblical building blocks that may be used for the construction of atonement doctrine. In a similar manner, there is no biblical view of the Trinity much less *the* biblical view of the Trinity—indeed, the word "Trinity" is not even in the Bible. But most theologians have thought that the Bible contains the conceptual building blocks needed to fashion a doctrine of the Trinity. Even then, there is not one biblical account of the Trinity: models proliferate, and they are often incommensurate with one another. At least with the Trinity we have a dogmatic framework to work with, provided by post-biblical tradition in the shape of the Nicene-Constantinopolitan symbol of AD 381. We have no such creedal framework for the discussion

---

1. I discuss this further in the context of Christology in the first chapter of Crisp, *God Incarnate*. See also, Crisp, *Deviant Calvinism*, chap. 1.

of atonement. It is not surprising, then, that the biblical building blocks that have been used to make atonement doctrine have been assembled in different ways by different theologians down the centuries, yielding different and sometimes incommensurate ways of thinking about Christ's reconciling work.

1

Methodological Issues

C ontemporary works on the atonement are replete with language
of doctrines, theories, models, metaphors, and motifs. Yet the
consensus among modern theologians is that the New Testament does not offer a *single* explanation of Christ's atoning work. For
instance, in the middle of the twentieth century the Scottish Presbyterian
theologian Donald Baillie remarked, "If we take the Christology of the
New Testament at its highest we can only say that 'God was in Christ' in
that great atoning sacrifice, and even that the Priest and the Victim both
were none other than God. There is in the New Testament no uniformity
of conception as to *how* this sacrifice brings about the reconciliation."[1]
Similarly, T. F. Torrance writes, "No explanation is ever given in the New
Testament, or in the Old Testament, why atonement for sin involves the
blood of sacrifice."[2] Some more recent theologians have argued that the
search for models and theories of atonement is itself a forlorn enterprise.
Instead, we should acknowledge that Scripture offers a number of motifs
or metaphors but no single mechanism for atonement, such as one would

1. Baillie, *God Was in Christ*, 188. For a catena of modern theologians who say something
similar to Baillie about the lack of an explanation for atonement in the New Testament, see
Winter, *Atonement*, 30–37.
2. T. F. Torrance, *Mediation of Christ*, 114.

expect in something more conceptually sophisticated, like a model or theory.[3] Still other contemporary theologians argue that the kaleidoscope of images for Christ's atonement in the New Testament should lead theologians to the conclusion that a plurality of models for atonement is mandated on the basis of Scripture. Thus, Joel Green writes, "The hermeneutical task that occupied Paul and Peter and other New Testament writers, and Christian theologians and preachers subsequently, is located at the interface of this central affirmation of the atoning work of Christ and its contingent interpretation. This continues to be the hermeneutical task today, and this explains not only the presence of but also the mandate for multiple models of understanding and communicating the cross of Christ."[4]

Not only is there no single explanation of the atonement in the Bible, the atonement is not a theological notion whose dogmatic shape is universally agreed upon in historic Christian thought either. It has no canonical definition, no creedal statement that gives it a particular shape beyond the idea that Christ's work reconciles human beings to God. Hence, different accounts of the atonement have proliferated in historic Christianity, and constructive theologians continue that tradition today, bringing forth from their treasure stores things old and new.[5]

This is not to say that there are no symbolic resources in the Christian tradition that might help give dogmatic shape to the atonement. Protestant confessions of the sixteenth and seventeenth centuries and the *Catechism of the Catholic Church* of the twentieth century provide some understanding of the reconciling work of Christ. But, unlike the two-natures doctrine of the ancient Christian church, the views expressed by these documents do not stem from some earlier understanding of the reconciling work of Christ that is universally agreed upon by Christians East and West, on the basis of what is found in the biblical traditions.

3. A good example of this is Colin Gunton's work, *Actuality of Atonement*. In his little book, Michael Winter criticizes modern theologians who agree that the New Testament offers no explanation of the atonement and yet "offer no explanation of it themselves to compensate for that omission" (*Atonement*, 30). While he documents many modern theologians who do appear to omit such explanation, some of the more recent work on atonement does, I think, attempt to address this issue.

4. J. Green, "Kaleidoscopic View," 171. See also Baker and J. Green, *Scandal of the Cross*.

5. In his recent work on divine action, Irish-American philosophical theologian William Abraham even goes as far as to celebrate the fact that this is the case, rather than treating it as a kind of theological embarrassment. See *Divine Agency and Divine Action*, 97.

How should we then understand the views expressed in this symbolic material? For that matter, how should we understand the views expressed in historic theologians on this topic, or the views of contemporary divines as they develop their own ways of understanding the mediatorial work of Christ? Much depends on the status of such accounts. Are they the sober truth of the matter? An approximation to that truth? Merely metaphors or pictures that do not have any necessary connection to the way things actually are? In this opening chapter I will focus in on these methodological questions by attempting to clarify the scope of what might be called the dogmatic ambition of atonement theology. In other words, we shall consider what motifs and metaphors, doctrines, models, and theories of atonement amount to as an important methodological concern in approaching the atonement. This involves some attempt to give an orientation to these different concepts, as well as to offer some account of their interrelationship and of the way in which they function in some of the major views of the atonement.

To that end, this chapter offers one way of understanding motifs and metaphors, doctrines, models, and theories as applied to Christian theology in general, and to the atonement in particular. Having done that, we shall trace out the relationship between these different methodological concepts so as to provide some explanation of how they should function in approaching the atonement. A short concluding section considers the upshot of this discussion for the remainder of this book.[6]

Atonement and Reconciliation

Let us begin with the notion of reconciliation at the heart of traditional notions of the work of Christ. "Atonement" (at-one-ment) is the English word that expresses the concept of reconciliation, and that has passed into

6. Abraham maintains that the classical views of atonement "operate on a simple principle: pick out an image that fits the work of Christ and then upgrade it into a grand theory" (*Divine Agency and Divine Action*, 92). No doubt this reflects Abraham's penchant for pithy turns of phrase, but as the history of these discussions shows, it is surely a caricature. The language of atonement theology may not have received canonical definition, but it has been honed and discussed over centuries of theological reflection. Though particular accounts have developed, as we shall see in part 2 in more detail, and though these depend on particular motifs or images of Christ's reconciliation, it would be grossly unfair (I think) to reduce this to picking an image and beefing it up into a "grand theory."

English-language theological parlance. As the English Reformed theologian Colin Gunton once remarked, "*Atonement* is the portmanteau word used in English to denote the reconciliation between God and the world which is at the heart of Christian teaching."[7] That seems broadly correct, although for present purposes, a narrower working definition of atonement will be more serviceable, one that focuses on human beings and includes an indication of why reconciliation is needed. Thus, *atonement is the act of reconciliation between God and fallen human beings brought about by Christ*. According to Scripture, human beings are estranged from God because of sin. As Romans 3:23 puts it, "All [human beings] have sinned and fall short of the glory of God." Christ's atoning work brings about reconciliation with God by dealing with human sin, which is an obstacle to divine-human relationship. However, the atonement is not merely about the removal of obstacles to relationship with God but also about securing the goods accompanying a right relationship with God.[8] Nevertheless, this is a fundamental concern of atonement theology—in fact, to my way of thinking, the most fundamental concern. For without atonement for sin there can be no reconciliation with God for fallen human beings. Without atonement we are all "dead in our trespasses" (Rom. 5:6; Eph. 2:5; Col. 2:13). We might say that, at a bare minimum, any theologically adequate account of the atonement must assume that the atonement is the act of reconciliation between God and fallen human beings brought about by Christ. In what follows we shall assume this way of thinking about the atonement as a point of departure.[9] With this in mind, let us turn to consider some key terms in atonement theology.

7. Gunton, *Actuality of Atonement*, 2 (emphasis original).

8. Thus, William Lane Craig is right, in my judgment, to say that atonement in the *narrow sense* of being cleansed of sin achieves atonement in the *broader sense* of reconciliation with God (see Craig, *Atonement and the Death of Christ*, 3). But that is not all that the atonement brings about—as the recent work of Eleonore Stump has reminded us (see Stump, *Atonement*). It is not enough for obstacles to reconciliation to be removed; we must be placed in a reconciled state. Craig thinks this conflates atonement and the order of salvation. But that is to make a particular theological judgment about the shape of atonement doctrine. It is not obvious that this is the *only* way, or even the *right* way, to characterize atonement. And, to my mind, Stump is right to suggest that atonement must be about being placed in right relationship with God, not merely about the possibility of such reconciliation. Atonement must be *effectual* if it is really about at-one-ment.

9. A similar point is made by William Abraham. He proposes that "we return to the core, root meaning" of atonement: "the righting of relationship between estranged persons." As he says, "Atonement is fundamentally concerned with the repair of broken relationships" (Abraham,

a. Motifs and Metaphors

Motifs and metaphors play an important—indeed, indispensable—role in atonement theology. Biblical metaphors abound: Christ is the lamb of God who takes away the sins of the world, the shepherd who dies for his sheep, the high priest who enters the holy of holies on our behalf, and so on. Motifs are often metaphors with staying power, for they are recurring. Christ as the lamb of God, as the pascal lamb, as the sacrificial lamb, and so on are examples of such a biblical motif, which is also metaphorical in nature. But in principle motifs may simply be recurring themes or ideas that are not necessarily or fundamentally metaphorical in nature, such as leitmotifs that appear and then recur with variations in a piece of orchestral music. In atonement theology motifs like sacrifice, substitute, satisfaction, ransom, and so on are important features of particular accounts of the reconciling work of Christ. Metaphors often provide important building blocks. Take the notion of the lamb of God being offered up as a sacrifice on our behalf. This is clearly a metaphor and a biblical motif that characterizes Christ's saving work. But it may also become (and has become) a stepping-stone toward more complex ways of thinking about the work of Christ that have at their heart the notion that Christ somehow offers himself up as a vicarious sacrifice for our sins—a theological element that can be found in several different historic and contemporary accounts of the atonement (such as satisfaction and penal substitution).[10] In recent theology there is a tendency to speak of different approaches to the doctrine of atonement as representing different metaphors—as if Christ's reconciling work as a ransom, a satisfaction for sin, a penal substitution, a moral example, or whatever, constitutes a picture or a representation or a symbol that stands in for something else. Of course, these are pictures of the atonement, but (as we shall see) doctrines and models of the atonement are more than just metaphors, though they include metaphors as elements of larger conceptual wholes. Doctrine in Christian theology, as Christine Helmer reminds us, "is said to be concerned with the truth of the eternal

---

Divine Agency and Divine Action, 86). This seems spot-on to me. All other language of atonement depends on this core claim about reconciliation with God.

10. For instance, Richard Swinburne's penetrating account of the atonement as a sacrifice is really an updated version of a satisfaction doctrine, indebted more to Thomas Aquinas than to Anselm. See Swinburne, *Responsibility and Atonement*.

God." It "recognizes God as its source; and like Sacred Scripture, doctrine contains the knowledge that God has revealed about [the] divine nature and about the divine perspective on self and world. . . . Stripped of the accretions that human traditions and interpretations have added to it, doctrine is synonymous with the truth of the gospel."[11] But if that is right, then doctrines, and by extension, models that attempt to offer some explanatory framework for making sense of the atonement, cannot be merely metaphors. For they include, on this way of thinking, irreducibly propositional components.

Getting a clearer idea of the role played by motifs and metaphors in accounts of atonement is important for another reason as well. It helps us to see whether views proposed as particular doctrines or models or theories of atonement actually pass muster. For instance, the ransom view of atonement has recently become a popular option for theologians who are troubled by some of the language and content of other traditional models of Christ's reconciling work, particularly satisfaction and penal substitution. But it is not clear on examination that the ransom view actually amounts to a doctrine or model of atonement. As I will argue in chapter 4, it seems that it is more like a motif or metaphor, for it does not provide a clear mechanism of atonement.

This is only underlined by the fact that, in recent discussion of the ransom view, the notion of *Christus Victor* (Christ the victor), which had previously been regarded as a synonym for ransom, has been decoupled from it. Now there are ransom views and, alternatively, *Christus Victor* views in which Christ's victory is not regarded as part of any act that ransoms fallen human beings. Thus Denny Weaver in *The Nonviolent Atonement* can say, "What this book has called narrative Christus Victor thus finally becomes a reading of the history of God's people, who make God's rule visible in the world by the confrontation of injustice and by making visible in their midst the justice, peace, and freedom of the rule of God. The life, death, and resurrection of Jesus constitute the culmination of that rule of God, and also the particular point in history when God's rule is most fully present and revealed."[12] Later he adds, "Since Jesus' mission was not to die but to make visible the reign of God, it is quite explicit that neither God nor the reign of God needs Jesus' death in the

11. Helmer, *End of Doctrine*, 23.
12. Weaver, *Nonviolent Atonement*, 84–85.

way that his death is irreducibly needed in satisfaction theory."[13] These are significant admissions, and they say something about the way in which one family of metaphors having to do with Christ's work being a ransom can fund distinct approaches to the doctrine of atonement.

b. Doctrines

By the term "doctrine" I mean (minimally) a comprehensive account of a particular teaching about a given theological topic held by some community of Christians or some particular denomination. So, on this way of thinking, a doctrine of the atonement is an account[14] of the atonement that has been taught by a particular group of Christians such as Baptists, Anglicans, Mennonites, Orthodox, and so on. A doctrine is a comprehensive account of a given teaching because it is a complete, theological whole that forms part of what we might call the conceptual fabric of the life of the particular ecclesial community. Doctrines are not normally partial, piecemeal, or ad hoc notions that are thrown together. Rather, a doctrine used in this sense is a conceptual whole that usually develops over time, often in the fires of controversy. This process of doctrinal development is ongoing, even where a doctrine has a stable canonical form. For such doctrines are still the subject of dogmatic scrutiny, revision, and reassessment in light of new insights, new arguments, and, sometimes, new data.

Perhaps the preeminent example of this is the doctrine of the Trinity, which developed from an early devotion to Christ alongside Jewish monotheism into the central and defining theological doctrine of Christianity through the vituperative ecclesiastical struggle that eventually produced the Nicene Creed of AD 381. Unlike the Trinity, the atonement is a doctrine that has no undisputed canonical shape, though it does take on particular forms in certain ecclesiastical contexts, such as the notion of vicarious satisfaction beloved of historic Presbyterians.[15] Doctrines like the Trinity

13. Weaver, *Nonviolent Atonement*, 89. I take these matters up in more detail in chapter 4.
14. Throughout this chapter I use the term "account" as a placeholder that ranges over metaphors and motifs, doctrines, and models of atonement—rather like the term "attribute," in discussions of the divine nature, is a placeholder and can mean "property," "predicate," and so on.
15. See the Westminster Confession (8.5): "The Lord Jesus, by his perfect obedience and sacrifice of himself, which he through the eternal Spirit once offered up unto God, hath fully satisfied the justice of his Father; and purchased not only reconciliation, but an everlasting inheritance in the kingdom of heaven, for all those whom the Father hath given unto him."

that have such a canonical form are typically part of the conceptual core of the faith. For this reason they are sometimes referred to as "dogmas."[16] So dogmas are a particular kind of doctrine that have a definite canonical shape. All dogmas are doctrines, but not all doctrines are dogmas, for some doctrines lack a canonical shape, such as the atonement. It will be helpful for our purposes to observe this distinction. However, even if a doctrine has a canonical form—that is, it is a dogma like the Trinity—which acts as a kind of theological constraint on how it is understood, this does not prevent there from being different ways of making sense of a given dogma consistent with its basic canonical shape. Thus historic Christianity has taken the Nicene Creed as the point of departure for thinking about the Trinity. Yet today there are a number of different accounts of the Trinity consistent with the dogmatic shape of the Nicene position, yielding distinct models that (in some cases at least) are incommensurate in important respects, such as social, psychological or Latin, and constitution models of the Trinity.[17]

It may be objected that the characterization of doctrine as a comprehensive account of a particular teaching about a given theological topic held by some community of Christians, or some particular denomination, is ambiguous in at least two important respects. First, it is ambiguous about the nature of Christian doctrine—that is, about what Christian doctrines like the atonement are supposed to be. Second, it is ambiguous about the dogmatic substance of Christian doctrine—that is, about what Christian doctrines like the atonement are supposed to convey. Let us consider these two sorts of ambiguity in turn.

First, the characterization of doctrine offered here is consistent with one of several ways of thinking about the nature of Christian doctrine. For instance, it is commensurate with the idea that the doctrines of Christian theology are in large measure regulative, providing a grammar for theology that may or may not correspond to some state of affairs beyond

16. Some Protestants may balk at this distinction between dogma and doctrine. But I think it captures an important difference between those doctrines that have canonical form (i.e., some sort of settled shape agreed upon and promulgated in catholic creeds; the incarnation and the Trinity are prime examples) and those that do not (like the atonement). It is possible for a doctrine to be at the heart of the Christian faith and yet lack a clear, canonical form. The atonement is the paradigm of this.

17. For detailed recent essays that deal with each of these trinitarian models, see McCall and Rea, *Philosophical and Theological Essays*. I have discussed them in more detail in Crisp, *Analyzing Doctrine*, chap. 4.

the doctrinal matrix (as postliberal theologians aver). In a similar fashion, the rules of a game such as chess regulate play but do not (necessarily) correspond to a state of affairs beyond the game. Alternatively, it could be that doctrine has more than a merely regulative function. Perhaps (as was intimated earlier in connection with Christine Helmer's work) it also has a propositional function, as much of historic Christianity has presumed. On this way of thinking, doctrines are statements that express concepts that are truth-apt and truth-aimed. A third option is that doctrine has a largely symbolic value. As George Lindbeck puts it, on this view, doctrines are experiential-expressivist in nature; they function "as non-informative and non-discursive symbols of inner feelings, attitudes, or existential orientations."[18] This third option is a much more radically subjective way of thinking about the nature of doctrine, but one that would be consistent with the idea that Christian doctrine is concerned to provide a comprehensive account of a particular teaching about a given theological topic held by some community of Christians, or some particular denomination.

In attempting to give an account of how different approaches to Christ's reconciling work function as Christian doctrine, it is important not to preclude certain live options at the outset. The three live options of Lindbeck's treatment of the nature of doctrine are three ways in which our working definition of doctrine could be construed,[19] though perhaps not the only three ways in which the definition could be construed.[20] My own view is that doctrine is conceptual and propositional in nature, which I take to be the way in which doctrine has been understood in much, though by no means all, of the Christian tradition. But the way I have characterized doctrine here does not require that it be understood in this way.

This brings us to the second ambiguity in the characterization of doctrine, which has to do with the material content, or substance, of doctrine. I have deliberately tried to provide what seems to me to be a *dogmatically minimalist* way of framing Christian doctrine. It seems to me that such

18. Lindbeck, *Nature of Doctrine*, 16.
19. That is, the regulative view, the propositional view, and the subjective and symbolic view mentioned previously. These are the three live options around which Lindbeck structures his discussion of doctrine in *The Nature of Doctrine*.
20. For instance, in *The End of Doctrine*, Helmer suggests a rather different account of doctrine that takes Lindbeck as a point of departure.

dogmatic minimalism is a theological virtue rather than a vice. Think of the Trinity once more. If any central theological concept is dogmatically minimalist in nature, the Trinity is. For in its Nicene form it provides a canonical shape and constraint on what Christians should believe about the divine nature, yet without necessarily committing the believer to a particular way of understanding key notions that comprise fundamental elements of the doctrine, such as "person" and "nature/essence." Something similar is true of the atonement—yet with the vital difference that, unlike the Trinity, the atonement has no definite canonical shape. To use our earlier distinction, it is a doctrine not a dogma.

I have said that the atonement is the act of reconciliation between God and fallen human beings brought about by Christ. I take it that this, or something very much like it, is a kind of dogmatic minimum that all, or almost all, Christians can agree upon. More would need to be said to flesh this out in order to provide a comprehensive account that would constitute a doctrine of atonement. The provision of this additional material can usually be found by appealing to confessions, catechisms, and writings of theologians of particular ecclesiastical persuasions belonging to particular Christian traditions and communions. But even here the results are often dogmatically thin, and (so it seems to me) deliberately so, committing adherents to what seems to be nonnegotiable while leaving certain matters ambiguous or underdeveloped.

For instance, Article 31 of the Anglican *Articles of Religion* states, "The Offering of Christ once made is that perfect redemption, propitiation, and satisfaction, for all the sins of the whole world, both original and actual; and there is none other satisfaction for sin, but that alone." Here is a doctrine of atonement. It certainly expresses the notion that the atonement is the act of reconciliation between God and fallen human beings brought about by Christ. But it construes this in a particular way: as a propitiation (i.e., a way of appeasing God), and a satisfaction. These are two theologically loaded terms. Propitiation focuses our attention upon the manner in which Christ's work brings about reconciliation, and satisfaction provides us with a mechanism by means of which this goal is achieved. But this is also underdeveloped. Much more would need to be said about the role of propitiation and satisfaction, and what is meant by satisfaction in particular, in order for us to have a full-orbed account of the atonement. This requires some model of atonement—most likely some version of the satisfaction view or some version of penal substitution.[21] So, although the *Articles of Religion* appear to commit Anglicans to a particular range or family of views on the reconciling work of Christ (either satisfaction or penal substitution, or something very similar to these views), it is also sufficiently dogmatically thin, so to speak, as to leave open a number of issues that require further development in order to provide a full-orbed understanding of the atonement. And this is usually provided by a model of atonement.

c. Models[22]

At first glance models of atonement have certain apparently paradoxical qualities. On the one hand, such models thicken up the dogmatic minimalism of atonement doctrines, expanding such doctrines, so to speak, so as to provide a fuller explanation of the nature of the atonement and, in particular, the mechanism of atonement. On the other hand, models of atonement do not necessarily attempt to provide a complete or comprehensive view of Christ's reconciling work. Rather, they offer a simplified description of the complex reality that is the work of Christ, which gives particular attention to the nature of that work and its effectiveness in terms of human reconciliation with God.

This apparent tension can be resolved by distinguishing between the conceptual goals of doctrines and models of atonement and their dogmatic function. The conceptual goal of doctrine is to provide a comprehensive account of a particular teaching about a given theological topic held by some community of Christians or some particular denomination. But usually this is dogmatically minimalist in nature. Something can be both conceptually wide-reaching in its scope and yet rather thin in the information it provides, like a map of the world. Such maps function to provide us with general information about the world, such as the shape of its continents

---

21. A number of Reformation and post-Reformation Protestant theologians speak in terms of a vicarious satisfaction although, upon examination, their views are actually species of penal substitution. So it seems that the contemporary popular conflation of satisfaction and penal substitution has some basis in the unfortunate way in which historic accounts of penal substitution are often described, by its defenders, as vicarious satisfaction. A good example of this can be found in Turretin's *Institutes of Elenctic Theology*—one of the most sophisticated products of the period of Protestant Orthodoxy.

22. I have dealt with doctrinal models elsewhere. See *Analyzing Doctrine*; and "The Importance of Model-Building," 9–20.

and seas and the political divisions of different countries. The conceptual goal of a model of atonement is more narrowly focused than that of a doctrine, and a model aims to be conceptually thicker. It is like a road map of the United States, which is limited to one geographical region but gives more information about that region than a map of the world does. What we might call the "dogmatic function" of a road map of the United States is also different from that of a map of the world in that the former provides much more detailed information about how to get about the particular geographical region it represents as well as information about the size of the towns and cities of the region. In a similar way, doctrines of atonement are conceptually broad and thin, whereas models of atonement are narrower and conceptually thicker. Also like the road map, models of atonement do not give comprehensive information but are by their very nature selective in what they convey.

Consider the notion of model utilized in much contemporary scientific literature, which has been appropriated in the science and religion literature as well. A model in this connection offers a coherent simplified description of a more complex reality. It attempts to "save the phenomena," but it does not attempt to give a complete description. As Ian Barbour puts it, "Models and theories are abstract symbol systems, which inadequately and selectively represent particular aspects of the world for specific purposes. This view preserves the scientist's realistic intent while recognizing that models and theories are imaginative human constructs. Models, on this reading, are to be taken seriously but not literally; they are neither literal pictures nor useful fictions but limited and inadequate ways of imagining what is not observable. They make tentative ontological claims that there are entities in the world something like those postulated in the models."[23]

This conception of models can be very helpful when attempting to provide a comprehensive picture of a particular data set that would otherwise be too complex to be rendered into a whole that is easily comprehended. (The diagram of an atom, familiar to any high school student of physics, is a good example of a model in this regard.) Applied to models of atonement, we can say this: such models are pictures of the reconciling work of Christ, its nature, and its effectiveness, which do not necessarily

---

23. Barbour, *Religion and Science*, 115.

claim to offer a complete account of this aspect of Christ's work. Rather, they provide simplified descriptions of a particular data set that would otherwise be too complex to be rendered into a whole that is immediately comprehensible. Although not everyone working on the atonement in recent years would think of atonement models in this way, the language of much of this discussion reflects the intuition that no single approach to the atonement can hope to offer a comprehensive account of it. The attempt to make sense of the atonement in terms of models also reflects the epistemic fallibilism that can be found in much recent work on the atonement. In this context fallibilism is the notion that a particular belief or view—in this case, a belief about or view of the atonement—is partial, and does not (perhaps, cannot) adequately reflect the whole truth of the matter. Such beliefs or views are said to be epistemically fragile and dubitable. For these reasons they should be held tentatively.

Furthermore, Barbour's comments about models in a scientific context also indicate something else that is important to flag in the appropriation of such language for atonement theology. This is whether models of atonement should be understood to be *realist* in nature—that is, reflecting, and expressing in some manner, even if only partially and fallibly, a mind-independent truth of the matter.

Models of atonement could be regarded as instrumentalist rather than realist in nature. Instrumentalism in the philosophy of science is the notion that a particular scientific concept or theory is important because it has some heuristic value—because it is a useful way of organizing certain data, not because it is literally true or false. Applied to theology, we can say that an instrumentalist view of models of atonement (or any other Christian doctrine) conceives of the value of such models as primarily heuristic. The question of truth-aptness, or the extent to which a given atonement model expresses or captures some facet of the truth of the matter, is not salient on this view. However, lest we misunderstand instrumentalism, it is important to see that an instrumentalist view of models of atonement is consistent with there being some truth in the matter. It is just that the instrumentalist is not concerned with questions of truth as such; only with questions of use, function, and application.

Alternatively, models of the atonement could be thought of in terms of theological realism. On this view, although they may only approximate the truth of the matter, atonement models are nevertheless truth-apt and aimed at truth. That is, they are aimed at the explanation or partial explanation of some truth of the matter regarding the atonement—a truth that is mind-independent.[24] The assumption in such models is that there is some truth to be had about the reconciling work of Christ. Accounts of the atonement are not just metaphor all the way down, so to speak, though they may contain metaphorical elements. Nor are they entirely socially constructed, being merely the product of human imagination. Nevertheless, even a theological realist must concede that models as applied to approaches to the atonement can only be approximations to the truth of the matter much as, in a Physics 101 textbook, the depiction of a model atom is only an approximation of the truth of the matter. It is understood that if we were able to see an atom, it would not actually look like the picture in the textbook. There is theological precedent for such reasoning to which we can appeal as well. For in a similar manner, theologians enamored of classical theism often write about the properties of God such as omnipotence or immutability, though, in point of fact, their commitment to a doctrine of divine simplicity entails the denial of any composition in God, including distinct divine properties.

In addition to instrumentalist and realist ways of thinking about models, and atonement models in particular, there are ways of thinking about the atonement, and models of the atonement, that are antirealist in nature. Such accounts decouple the doctrinal content of a given model of atonement from the ambition to give an account of this doctrine that is aimed at truth. A given doctrine or model of atonement may still be a useful fiction on this way of thinking, just as the rising of the sun and its setting are useful fictions from a human point of view. (Strictly speaking, the sun neither "rises" nor "sets," though these metaphors are deeply ingrained in the English language and shape many of the ways in which English speakers relate to our solar neighbor.) According to antirealist accounts of atonement, doctrines and models of the work of Christ are not aimed at truth. They are aimed at something else: eliciting within us a certain disposition or particular response. In a similar fashion, when a narrator begins speaking to an audience with the phrase "Once upon a time," we are habituated to expect what follows to be a fiction of some kind. In the right circumstances, the uttering of such a phrase elicits in us a certain

24. Or, at least, independent of any *creaturely* mind.

disposition and a particular response. It is not the same response as would be had if the narrator had begun with the phrase "This is an update on our breaking news story." In the latter case we expect there to be a connection between what is being said and some truth of the matter, for we expect that the reporting of current affairs at least has the ambition of being truth-aimed. We do not have the same expectation in the case of the telling of a fairy tale.

Although it is possible to approach the atonement and atonement models in an antirealist manner, it seems fairly clear that the vast majority of historic accounts of the atonement have presumed some sort of realism about the atonement. Even if the language of atonement models is not present in much of the historic discussion of this doctrine, it is, I think, fairly safe to assume that theologians attracted to the historic assumption that Christian doctrine is realist in nature will be sympathetic to the idea that some sort of chastened realism applies also to atonement models. By *chastened realism* I mean a realism that makes allowances for things like fallibilism and social context, as well as for the fact that models are, on this way of thinking, only ever approximations to the truth of the matter.[25]

It seems that metaphors are important features of models, as they are important features of doctrine. Yet they are not the whole of a doctrine any more than they are the whole of a model. When the apostle Paul speaks of the church as a body with many parts in 1 Corinthians 12, this is not a model of the church; it is a metaphor. Such metaphors may be used to provide a model of the church as something that is, in many respects, organic and composite, as can be found in the work of a number of historic theologians, which in the Reformed tradition include such luminaries as

25. However, some modern theological treatments of models as applied to theology have argued that they are, in fact, no more than metaphors. For example, Sally McFague writes that "a model is, in essence, a sustained and systematic metaphor" (*Metaphorical Theology*, 67). However, it seems to me doubtful that models are just metaphors writ large. And, upon examination, it is not clear that McFague's position is entirely consistent on this matter. Later in her work she writes that "models are the hypotheses of structure or set of relations we project from an area we know reasonably well in order to give intelligibility to a similar structure we sense in a less-familiar area" (*Metaphorical Theology*, 76). But how are "hypotheses of structure," or "sets of relations," constitutive of metaphors given her claim that models are essentially metaphorical in nature? At the very least, it seems that the reader requires some explanation of how these apparently nonmetaphorical notions feature as parts of models that are supposed to be essentially metaphorical in nature.

John Williamson Nevin.[26] But this involves laying out a conceptual framework for thinking about the nature of the church that a metaphor alone
cannot provide. It is just such a conceptual framework that McFague seems
to be hinting at in her use of terms like hypotheses, structures, and sets
of relations.[27]

d. Theories

What, then, of *theories* of atonement? Here, as with our account of
models, we turn to consider the way in which theories function in scientific work, and we apply that to theology. Like models, theories may
offer generalized accounts of a great deal of complex information, which
may be simplified using concepts independent of the data (e.g., concepts
like incarnation or Trinity, neither of which are to be found in the New
Testament). Unlike models, theories do not necessarily correlate to facts.
Theories can be used to provide an explanation of counterfactual states
of affairs. For instance, one might have a theory about what would hap-
pen to a particular population if it were exposed to a deadly virus: "*If* the
population were exposed to this virus, *then* the following state of affairs
would obtain"; or "*Were* the population exposed to this virus, then the
following state of affairs *would have* obtained." Typically, theories of
atonement are not counterfactual in this sense. They are not deployed in
order to provide explanations of what would have happened had Jesus
done something else. Instead, they are used to offer some explanation of
what we should believe about what did, in fact, obtain in the case of his
incarnation, life, death, and resurrection, as witnessed to by the writers of
the canonical Gospels. Also, a theory can itself be complex. It need not be
a picture that simplifies the data. What is more, it may be used to offer a
complete account of a given data set. In this respect theories may be more
metaphysically ambitious in scope than models—think, for example, of
Einstein's general theory of relativity in physics.

26. See Crisp, "John Williamson Nevin on the Church"; and the overview of W. B. Evans in
A Companion to the Mercersburg Theology.
27. Khaled Anatolios is skeptical of the language of models in atonement theology. He
writes that those who adopt such language "often fail even to consider such basic questions as
what formally constitutes a 'model,' what materially these specific models are, and how many
of them there are" (*Deification through the Cross*, 7). I hope that the remarks given here put
paid to at least some of these concerns.

The language of atonement theories is now commonplace, though this is actually a development that doesn't reflect patristic, medieval, or early modern usage any more than language about models of atonement do.[28] Nevertheless, I suggest that most theologians engaged in the project of providing some doctrinal explanation of the work of Christ as an atonement are attempting to give a model of atonement that they find compelling. They are not actually engaged in providing a theory of atonement. Often the model in question is offered as one, but only one, among several possible models. Some authors do go beyond this to delineate something more like theories of atonement—that is, they attempt to give not just one compelling (and approximate) picture of the work of Christ but also to provide reasons for thinking that the account they set forth is preferable to, or more comprehensive than, competing views. There are also those who have offered what might be called "meta-models," or theories about models of atonement. That is, they hazard a theory that explains why there is a plethora of different, and apparently mutually exclusive, models of the atonement. This is how I understand the kaleidoscopic account of the atonement favored by Mark Baker and Joel Green.[29]

The Relationship between Motifs, Metaphors, Doctrines, Models, and Theories

Having set out the distinction between motifs and metaphors, doctrines, models, and theories of atonement, we may now step back and consider the theological relationship between these different notions. I have argued that the atonement is the act of reconciliation between God and fallen human beings brought about by Christ. Motifs and metaphors of atonement are

---

28. This point has been made elsewhere in the recent literature. See, for example, A. Johnson, *Atonement: A Guide for the Perplexed*, 28. Nineteenth-century theologians like Schleiermacher, Charles Hodge, and John Miley write of "theories" of atonement, not models (see, e.g., Schleiermacher, *Christian Faith*, 460; Hodge, *Systematic Theology*, vol. 2, part 3, chap. 9; and Miley, *Systematic Theology*, vol. 2, chap. 4). But it seems that they mean by theories of atonement what I am calling models of atonement. The classification offered here more closely follows current language of models and theories in the current scientific literature than it does nineteenth-century theological usage. In contemporary atonement theology, Craig is an example of someone who still uses the language of "atonement theory" (see Craig, *Atonement and the Death of Christ*).

29. See Baker and Green, *Scandal of the Cross*. I have discussed this view in more detail in Crisp, *Approaching the Atonement*, chap. 9.

elements that may compose aspects of a doctrine or model of atonement. However, they are not doctrines or models of atonement as such, any more than, say, an illustration is a sermon, or a denouement is a story. It may be that some accounts of atonement that are often thought to be doctrines or models do not, in fact, rise above motifs of metaphors for atonement (e.g., many *Christus Victor*/ransom views).

Doctrines and models of atonement are more than motifs or metaphors. A doctrine of atonement is a comprehensive account of the reconciling work of Christ held by some community of Christians or some particular denomination. Such a comprehensive account will include some mechanism of atonement, unlike motifs and metaphors. Doctrines are also often dogmatically minimalist in nature.

To my way of thinking, models of atonement are in one respect less comprehensive than doctrines of atonement (because of a difference in conceptual goals), though in another respect they usually offer more by way of explanation of the nature of atonement (because of a difference in dogmatic function). By definition they are attempts to give an approximation to the truth of the matter, a simplified picture of more complex data, such as can be found in Scripture, creeds, confessions, and the work of particular theologians. Still, a model, like a doctrine, provides a mechanism for atonement—it does have ambitions to give some explanation of the reconciling work of Christ, even if models do not offer complete explanations as such. It is also the case that models are often the products of individual theologians, whose particular opinions and arguments are offered up as contributions to the furtherance of our understanding of the atonement, as it is understood in particular communities and by particular churches. So, models are narrower in scope than doctrines of atonement. Classic atonement models, on this way of thinking, include satisfaction, penal substitution, the governmental view, the vicarious humanity view of John McLeod Campbell, some versions of the moral exemplar view, and, perhaps, some of the patristic accounts of atonement such as those provided by Athanasius and Irenaeus.[30]

What is more, models in atonement theology often specify more detail by way of explanation of the mechanism of atonement than some doctrines of atonement. Earlier, we saw that this was the case with the

---

30. I give an account of these different views in *Approaching the Atonement*.

dogma of the Trinity, which has a canonical form that is what I have called dogmatically minimalist. Models of the Trinity are attempts to spell out that canonical form more explicitly, offering particular ways of thinking about the doctrine that fill in the metaphysical gaps, so to speak, so as to provide a fuller or richer understanding of the nature of the Trinity. This is true of the atonement as well.

Our earlier example of the Westminster Confession will make the point here. Recall that the Westminster Confession (8.5) says, "The Lord Jesus, by His perfect obedience and sacrifice of himself, which he through the eternal Spirit once offered up unto God, hath fully satisfied the justice of his Father; and purchased not only reconciliation, but an everlasting inheritance in the kingdom of heaven, for all those whom the Father hath given unto him." But here, as with the Anglican *Articles of Religion*, there is a certain dogmatic minimalism at work. It is possible to construct one of several models of the atonement on the basis of what is affirmed in this passage. Taking it as a kind of dogmatic constraint, which provides a theological framework for thinking about the atonement, a model could be provided that explained what divine justice consists in, how Christ satisfies divine justice, and how this act of satisfaction purchases everlasting life for a specific number of fallen humanity. But clearly, there is more than one way to think about each of these constituent parts of the doctrine, which would generate more than one model of atonement. For instance: How is satisfaction related to divine justice? How does Christ's work provide a satisfaction? What about Christ's work is a satisfaction? Does this include all the elements of Christ's life or only his work on the cross? And so on. From this it seems clear that there is an important difference between models and doctrines, and that models are more modest in their explanatory ambitions than doctrines, but often more detailed in the metaphysical stories they provide in order to make sense of the doctrinal claims they seek to explain.

Theories of atonement are more comprehensive than either doctrines or models. Of the current accounts of the atonement, one seems to fit this category particularly well, and that is the kaleidoscopic view of Mark Baker and Joel Green. The idea here is to provide a theory about how we should think about different models of the atonement relative to one another and to the doctrine of atonement. Baker and Green do not put matters in this way. Nevertheless, on the classification offered here it would be appropriate to think of their account in these terms rather than as another model or doctrine of atonement because they claim to be offering a way of understanding all the existing models of atonement as partial metaphorical windows onto some larger whole. This is not so much another model as a meta-model or a theory about how to regard extant models of atonement, one that also takes into consideration other relevant factors like social location and epistemic purview.

The Upshot

What can be learned from this methodological reflection on some of the key terms and concepts that inform a discussion about the atonement? First, such engagement helps to get clearer the theological ambition of different doctrines of atonement. Second, this sort of work raises important questions about the scope of atonement theology—what can such reflection actually achieve, theologically speaking, if there is no universally agreed upon doctrinal core to the reconciling work of Christ? Third, there is a question about how we characterize different accounts of atonement. Since the 1930s and the work of Gustaf Aulén,[31] it has been common to classify atonement doctrines into a threefold typology. If our analysis is on target, this seems far too simplistic as a way of demarcating the differences that exist between different ways of conceiving the saving work of Christ. Not only does this flatten out the differences between particular doctrines; it distorts the nature of the differences that exist between the different historic approaches to this matter. For if some of these approaches are mere motifs or metaphors, and others are doctrines or models that set out a mechanism for atonement, while still others are more like theories about atonement models, then what we have is not a typology of different doctrines of atonement. Instead, we have different levels of theological explanation regarding the atonement. Motifs and metaphors are partial pictures or windows into the doctrine; doctrines are more complex wholes that have motifs and metaphors as constituent elements; models are more narrow but conceptually richer attempts to provide a particular way of understanding the reconciling work of Christ; and theories about atonement models offer a way of thinking

31. Aulén, *Christus Victor*.

about these different doctrines relative to particular cultural and contextual hermeneutical concerns that shape the particular accounts of the work of Christ.

With these general methodological considerations in mind, we may turn next to the question of the value and necessity of the atonement.

---------- 2 ----------

The Value and Necessity
of Atonement

In the previous chapter we looked at some general methodological considerations concerning the doctrine of atonement. In this chapter we turn to the question of the value of Christ's reconciling work. We might frame the chapter with this question: *Does Christ's work have to have a certain intrinsic, objective moral value in order for it to be acceptable to God as an act of atonement?* This question is part and parcel of classical theological discussion of the atonement. Famously, the great Scottish medieval divine, John Duns Scotus, and those who followed him, argued that divine justice does not *require* the death of the God-man as recompense for human sin. On one understanding of Scotus's position, God could have accepted some act of atonement that had less objective moral and forensic value and still have been just in so acting. As Richard Cross puts it, "On Scotus's account, an act is meritorious if and only if God assigns a reward for it."[1] But this doctrine, usually called *acceptatio* or "acceptation," seems to be entirely wrongheaded to me. So does the related idea that the value of any act of atonement is entirely up to God and has nothing to do with any intrinsic merit the action in question possesses.

1. Cross, *Duns Scotus*, 104.

This latter view, called *acceptilatio* or "acceptilation,"[2] is sometimes conflated with acceptation. In this chapter, I shall argue that both the notions
of acceptilation and acceptation are mistaken. God must accept an act that
has an objective moral value at least proportional to the demerit of the
trespass it atones for in order for this act to be morally acceptable as an
act of atonement. This encapsulates what I shall call the *proportionality
understanding of the value of atonement*—or *proportional view* for short.
I shall use this proportional view to draw out reasons for thinking that
(a) the atonement had to be an act of God Incarnate, and (b) this sort of
reasoning about the value of the atonement implies a certain picture of the
divine nature. Thus, the chapter aims to show how considerations about
the value of the atonement have substantive implications for theology
proper (i.e., the doctrine of God).

The argument proceeds in the following manner. First, a brief account
of the theological construals of acceptilation and acceptation is given.
Making sense of exactly what each of these two notions entails clears the
ground for what follows. In the second section I offer some objections to
acceptilation and acceptation. In a third section, I offer an argument in
favor of the proportional view. In a fourth and final section of the chapter, I argue that these considerations have important implications for a
doctrine of God.

Acceptilation and Acceptation

Like a number of other historians of dogma, R. S. Franks begins his discussion of acceptilation by noting its pre-Christian origins as a forensic
concept in Roman law:

> According to its [Roman] derivation, *acceptilatio* means "a reckoning as
> received," *acceptum* being the proper name for the credit side of the led-
> ger. In Roman law, however, the term had a special technical use. It meant
> the discharge of an obligation by the use of a solemn and prescribed form
> of words, in which the debtor asked the creditor whether he had received

2. This could mean that any divine act could be an act of atonement. Or it could mean that
there are only certain divine action types that could be acts of atonement, rather than any divine
act. Acceptilation could be taken either way, although if the latter were adopted, some explanation of why only some divine action types might be acts of atonement would need to be given.

payment, and the creditor replied that he had—no real payment, however, having taken place.[3]

He goes on to say,

In Christian theology, the term "acceptilation" is commonly used in a loose sense to denote the principle of that theory of the Atonement, in which the merit of Christ's work is regarded as depending simply on the Divine acceptance, and not on its own intrinsic worth. This theory was taught by Duns Scotus, who says that "every created offering is worth what God accepts it as, and no more," and further, that Christ's human merit was itself strictly limited, but God in his good pleasure accepted it, as sufficient for our salvation (*Com. In Sent. lib.* iii. Dist. 19).[4]

But there is some confusion about whether Scotus did teach this doctrine. The twentieth-century dogmatician Otto Weber claims Scotus taught the doctrine of "'Acceptance' (*acceptatio*)."[5] By contrast, the nineteenth-century American Presbyterian theologian William Shedd appears to have mistakenly believed that Scotus was a source for the conceptually distinct, though closely related, doctrine of acceptilation.[6] Franks himself concedes in his volume on the work of Christ that "there has been . . . much confusion between acceptation and acceptilation."[7] And in his essay on acceptilation, he observes,

The theory of Duns Scotus is certainly not very suitably spoken of as one of acceptilation. In the solution of an obligation by acceptilation there is no payment at all; whereas, in the theory of Duns there is a payment, though it is accepted beyond its intrinsic value. But the usage of applying the name "acceptilation" to Scotus' theory is probably too confirmed

3. Franks, "Acceptilation," 61. Cf. Berkhof, *History of Christian Doctrines*, 179–81; and Muller, *Dictionary*, s.v. "acceptatio" and "acceptilatio."
4. Franks, "Acceptilation," 62.
5. Weber, *Foundations of Dogmatics,* 289n89. Bavinck expresses similar views in *Reformed Dogmatics*, 401–2.
6. See Shedd, *History of Christian Doctrine*, 348–49. Cf. Shedd, *Dogmatic Theology*, 733.
7. Franks, *Work of Christ*, 393n5. A measure of this confusion can be seen in Berkhof's comment on what is allegedly Scotus's theory, when he says that "a merit that is not at all commensurate with the debt owed is willingly accepted by God. This theory is generally called the *Acceptilation Theory*, but according to Macintosh (*Historic Theories of the Atonement*, 110) it should really be called the *Acceptation Theory* of the atonement" (Berkhof, *History of Christian Doctrines*, 180).

to be done away with. It is to be understood, then, that the term is used only loosely.[8]

I am not concerned with Scotus's exegesis here, although it appears that Scotus advocated acceptation not acceptilation. But it is a mark of the misunderstanding surrounding the distinction between acceptilation and acceptation that noted historians of doctrine do not appear to be able to agree on whether Scotus held to acceptation or acceptilation. Hence, the first task is to get a clearer picture of acceptilation and acceptation, beginning with the former.

As Franks intimates, the theological application of acceptilation goes beyond its denotation in Roman law as some act according to which a debt owed is remitted without payment. But exactly what is added to the notion in theology is moot. I want to suggest that there are in fact two ways in which the theological application of acceptilation could be parsed. Both of these accounts are consistent with Franks's claim that at the heart of the theological version of acceptilation is the notion that *the merit of Christ's work is regarded as depending simply on divine acceptance, and not on its own intrinsic worth.*

According to the first construal of this claim, God treats Christ's work *as if* it had a value sufficient to remit or otherwise satisfy divine justice for the sin committed by fallen humanity, although it does not, strictly speaking. This first construal of acceptilation involves a kind of moral and/or forensic fiction. For this reason, I shall refer to it as "fictionalist acceptilation." "Fictionalist" in this context means that Christ's work *does not have this value although God may impute this value to Christ's work.* That is, God may treat Christ's work as though it has or accrues a merit requisite to atone for sin, although, in fact, it does not possess or does not accrue this merit—indeed, it accrues no merit. We can put this more formally as follows:

Fictionalist Acceptilation (FATL): Christ's work has no particular intrinsic, objective moral value whatsoever, but God imputes a particular value to it.

FATL requires the somewhat implausible assumption that Christ's work has no intrinsic, objective moral value. This seems implausible because

---

8. Franks, "Acceptilation," 62.

Christ's work is usually thought to be a moral work, whatever particular moral value it is assigned or thought to possess. The idea that Christ's work has no moral value—is axiologically neutral, as it were—until and unless God imputes some moral value to it seems very peculiar indeed. Some indication of how odd this is can be had by imagining a tutor who says to her undergraduate student, "Your essay cannot be marked according to the university grading scheme because it has no intrinsic academic qualities whatsoever (whether good or bad). However, I will treat it as if it had the academic qualities requisite to a first-class piece of work and grade it accordingly." Notice that the tutor is not saying that the student's essay is so poor that it cannot score much of anything in terms of scholarly attainment. Rather, the tutor is claiming that the piece of work cannot be graded according to the university's marking scheme because it possesses not a single academic quality that would make it eligible to be marked according to that scheme. This is precisely what is implausible about the claim that Christ's work has no moral value whatsoever, that it is morally neutral unless God imputes some moral quality to it.[9]

But a second way of parsing theological acceptilation can be had, according to which God accepts Christ's work as having a value sufficient to remit or otherwise satisfy divine justice for the sin committed by some number of fallen humanity simply because *God stipulates that it has this value, although without this stipulation it would have no value whatsoever*. This is different from the first, fictionalist account of acceptilation because on this second view the entire moral value of Christ's work is attributable to divine fiat, which is all that is necessary for the work in question to have a certain moral value conferred upon it. In other words, on this way of thinking God *says* Christ's work has a certain moral value, and thereafter *it has* that value. It is not that God treats Christ's work *as if* it had a value that it does not, imputing to Christ's work a moral quality it lacks, which is what the fictionalist view requires. Instead, Christ's

---

9. Undoubtedly, more would need to be said about this particular issue. For instance, something should be said about whether something counts as a moral act only if the person acting is intending to act morally, is aiming at some moral outcome, and so on. Similarly, one would have to say something more about the connection between responsibility and the morality of an action. But such qualifications only serve to strengthen my case: traditionally, theologians have thought Christ's work was intended by him to achieve a certain moral outcome and that he was responsible for placing himself in circumstances where he could bring about such an act of atonement.

work does have the requisite moral value necessary for it to be acceptable to God as an act of atonement because, and only because, God makes it so. But, crucially, if God did not stipulate that Christ's work has this value, it would not have this value, which is why this is a version of acceptilation not acceptation. However, God does stipulate that it has this value. So it has this value.

This is rather like the difference between a prince treating a traitor as if he has not committed treason even though, in fact, he has committed treason (the fictionalist construal of acceptilation) and a prince pronouncing a traitor nonculpable in such a way that the speech-act of pronouncing judgment upon him somehow brings about his having a new legal status, by virtue of the powers invested in the sovereign (the nonfictionalist construal of acceptilation). This second, nonfictionalist account of theological acceptilation we shall dub "stipulative acceptilation," since it depends on God stipulating by divine fiat that a given act has a particular moral quality. We can put this more formally:

> **Stipulative Acceptilation (SATL):** Christ's work has no particular intrinsic, objective moral value whatsoever until and unless God assigns a particular value to it, whereupon it acquires the moral value assigned by divine fiat.

There is a deeper theological issue upon which SATL relies. It presumes that the value or merit of a particular act depends upon the value or merit assigned to that act by God, which is, of course, the stipulative element of this version of acceptilation. But this requires a version of theological voluntarism—specifically, the idea that the moral value of a particular action depends entirely upon the divine "will," or *voluntas*.[10] In fact, SATL implies that Christ's work has a moral value if, and only if, God assigns some moral value to it, which entails a rather strong version of theological voluntarism.

What, then, distinguishes acceptation from acceptilation? Historical theologian Richard Muller maintains that acceptation refers to "an act of grace and mercy according to which God freely accepts a partial satisfaction as fully meritorious."[11] In which case, the difference between the

10. Does theological voluntarism obtain in the case of fictionalist acceptilation too? Not in the same way precisely because, according to the fictionalist, God is imputing to Christ's work a quality it does not have, rather than stipulating that it has this quality through an act of divine will.

11. Muller, *Dictionary*, s.v. "acceptatio."

theological versions of acceptilation and acceptance is that, according to acceptance, God is in some sense willing to accept an act worth less than the value required to atone for human sin as sufficient to atone for human sin. The key difference is that acceptance presumes the act in question has some moral value, just not enough moral value to make it sufficient in and of itself to warrant atonement without the interposition of divine grace.[12]

But as with acceptilation, acceptance could be taken in one of two ways. The first of these involves a version of fictionalism. We might frame it thus:

> **Fictionalist Acceptance (FATT):** Christ's work has a particular intrinsic, objective moral value, but it does not have a moral value sufficient to atone for the sin of some number of fallen humanity, unless God imputes that value in addition to the intrinsic value such an act already possesses.

The fictionalist version of acceptance is somewhat different and rather more plausible than its fictionalist acceptilation counterpart. On this way of thinking, Christ's work does have an intrinsic, objective moral value. It is just that the value it possesses is not sufficient to atone for human sin.[13] God has to supply what is lacking in the moral quality of Christ's work in order to bridge what we might call the "moral gap" between the actual moral value of Christ's work and the moral value required to atone for human sin. And, according to this fictionalist acceptance, this occurs via God imputing a certain moral value to Christ's work over and above the actual intrinsic value it possesses. This is rather like a college tutor saying to her undergraduate student, "Your essay is worth less than a first-class mark, but I will treat it as if it were a first-class piece of work and grade it accordingly." The essay is worth something, but it is not of sufficient worth to merit a top mark. The same is true, the relevant changes having been made, with respect to the work of Christ. Its intrinsic worth is not doing the moral work in making Christ's act of atonement acceptable as an act of atonement. Rather, God's willingness to accept it as such despite its not being of sufficient value is doing that work.

---

12. For this reason, we might think of acceptilation as a rather extreme version of acceptation: the value of the work of Christ is less than it needs to be in order to be of strictly inverse proportionality to the demerit of sin. The two differ on the question of whether the work of Christ has some value or no value (unless God ascribes or imputes some value to it).

13. This appears to be something like the view Franks imputes to Duns Scotus.

The second version of acceptation, like the second version of acceptilation, is stipulative:

> **Stipulative Acceptation (SATT):** Christ's work has a particular intrinsic,
> objective moral value, but it does not have a moral value sufficient to atone
> for the sin of some number of fallen humanity, unless God stipulates it has
> that value in addition to the intrinsic value such an act already possesses.

Here, as with the stipulative construal of acceptilation, theological voluntarism is implied, although a weaker version thereof.[14] Like FATL, SATT
means that there is a lacuna between the intrinsic value Christ's work has
and the value necessary for a particular act of atonement to be a satisfaction for human sin. It is this "moral gap" that God makes up for by
assigning the work of Christ a moral value greater than its intrinsic moral
value. To return to our undergraduate essay example, this is rather like a
tutor commenting, "Your essay is worth less than a first-class mark, but I
will correct the text of your essay, providing the missing components that
are required in order to make it into a first-class piece of work." Whatever
the morality of such an arrangement, it is certainly not merely a matter
of imputing certain academic qualities to a piece of work that does not
have those qualities.

But this raises an important theological question about how Christ's
work can have an intrinsic moral and/or forensic value that God then may
supplement by stipulating that its actual salvific value is greater than its
intrinsic moral and/or forensic value. Why would God bring about some
act of atonement that has this moral and/or forensic deficit that God then
has to make good? One possible answer to this is that in creating the world,
God ordains that certain creaturely actions have a particular intrinsic
value. An example of this might be acts of human kindness or courage.
Christ has a human nature. So certain sorts of acts performed by Christ
have an intrinsic moral value corresponding to the fact that these actions
are the actions of a divine person that has assumed a created "part," in
the sense of being acts performed by the Son of God through his human

---

14. In fact, SATT includes only a partial theological voluntarism because it allows that
certain moral actions have an intrinsic, or inherent, moral value independent of any divine as-
signment of moral value—though for Christ's work to be counted as of sufficient moral worth
to atone for sin, God must assign it a moral value greater than its intrinsic, or inherent, moral
worth. In that case, we would need some explanation of how an act comes to have some (but
not enough) objective moral value in the first place.

nature. The acts of Christ *qua* human have a certain intrinsic moral value as the actions of something created, in addition to the value they have in virtue of being acts performed by God the Son through his human nature. But even the most exalted human moral act does not have a moral value sufficient to atone for the sin of fallen human beings because created beings, being finite, can only perform acts that have a finite moral value, and (by hypothesis) the disvalue of human sin as a whole outweighs the moral value of any single human act. Hence, the work of Christ's human nature in salvation, taken in abstraction, as it were, from the hypostatic union, cannot have the requisite value to atone for human sin.

Accordingly, the only reason Christ's work does have the value sufficient to atone for human sin is because it is an act of the God-man, not an act of a mere man; his divine nature makes up the moral deficit left by the value of the act *qua* human, ensuring salvation. This means that the moral gap between the value of the human act of Christ (in atonement) and the value required for that act to be able to offset the demerit generated by human sin *is* supplied by God, as the advocates of acceptation claim, in the person of the Son. It is the work of God the Son that bridges the moral gap that exists between the intrinsic worth of the moral act of Christ *qua* human and the worth necessary for Christ's work to be salvific.

In which case, acceptation has gotten something right about the morally insufficient value of the human aspect of Christ's work, viz. salvation. But whereas the defender of acceptation will claim that the atonement as a whole work of the God-man is of less value than that requisite to atone for human sin, on this alternative view the atonement taken as a whole has the requisite value to atone for human sin, because it is the work of God Incarnate. So this reasoning actually supports the proportional view, not acceptation. To see this, we will need to flesh out the proportional view. Before doing so, let us consider some problems with acceptilation and acceptation.

Problems with Acceptilation and Acceptation

If at least some creaturely acts have a moral value (perhaps an intrinsic moral value), FATL cannot get off the ground. I know of no theologian who would seriously entertain the idea that no creaturely acts have any moral value. So I shall discount FATL.

Superficially similar problems beset SATL. Here Christ's work only has a moral value if God assigns a moral value to it. But if God does assign it a particular moral value, it has that value thereafter. This is superficially similar to FATL because SATL still requires that the work of Christ possesses no moral value in and of itself, until and unless God stipulates it has a moral value. Notice that this is not the same as saying that Christ's work has the merit it does purely because, in the mercy of God, Christ has been appointed the mediator of salvation. This latter position is entirely consistent with the idea that Christ's work has an intrinsic value requisite for the atonement of human sin, whereas the former is not.[15] The real problem with SATL is its implied voluntarism: God could simply stipulate that a given work has a particular moral value, and it would thereafter have that value. But then, why should the work of Christ, which is so costly to the divine Trinity, be the work singled out as the atonement for human sin? Without further qualification, Christ's work seems an arbitrary and unnecessarily costly choice of action upon which to bestow the moral value requisite for atonement. Surely God could have chosen to bestow this moral quality upon any number of other acts with the same result. Take, for instance, the pricking of Abraham's finger with a pin or the breaking of Mephibosheth's legs. Perhaps, even the killing of a scapegoat would be an appropriate subject for SATL. For it is not clear why, according to SATL, the creaturely act of atonement must be the action of a human being if the core idea here is that God *stipulates* that a given act may have the worth requisite to atone for human sin.

So it seems that these actions and many, many others (perhaps any old action by any given creature) could be made an act of atonement for human sin given the species of theological voluntarism informing SATL. But this is to trivialize the atonement of Christ in a manner that is surely unacceptable.[16] Although the defender of acceptilation can say some act of atonement is necessary for salvation (provided God cannot merely forgive sin without punishment), it remains true that according to acceptilation, the choice of one particular creaturely action to constitute the act of atone-

15. John Calvin adopts this latter view when he says, "Apart from God's good pleasure Christ could not merit anything; but he did so because he had been appointed to appease God's wrath with his sacrifice. . . . Christ's merit depends upon God's grace alone, which has ordained this manner of salvation for us" (*Institutes* 2.17.1).

16. A similar point is raised by Hodge in *Systematic Theology*, 2:487–88.

ment for human sin is entirely arbitrary.[17] So, in sum, the claim common to the different versions of acceptilation—namely, that the merit of Christ's work is regarded as depending simply on divine acceptance and not on its own intrinsic worth—requires the theologian to make sacrifices most will find deeply implausible.

What of acceptation? Does it fare any better? The simple answer is that it does not. We have seen that both versions of the doctrine share in common the idea that theological acceptation is an act of grace and mercy according to which God freely accepts a partial satisfaction as fully meritorious. But this is morally dubious at best. It is true that there are analogues to this sort of arrangement in human transactions. I may accept an offer of twenty dollars as compensation for the destruction of a book although, strictly speaking, the book was worth more than that. There may be good reason for doing so. Perhaps the person who destroyed the book is a poor student who does not have financial resources to replace the book in question. But this is a sort of informal relaxation of the demands of strict justice that cannot apply in situations where serious felonies have been committed, like murder. The judge cannot let the culprit go free having been convicted of the murder because he is a poor student, or because he is truly sorry for what he has done. Justice must be served. And, in common with many classical theologians, it seems to me that divine justice *must* be satisfied in this way. God cannot simply waive away our sin, forgiving it without penalty. That would be to act unjustly, according to the strict letter of the moral law. Nor, for the same reason, can God accept some act as atonement for human sin that has less moral value than the deficit it is provided to offset. This applies to both FATT and SATT, respectively. God cannot treat Christ's work as if it has the requisite moral value, although its actual value falls short of what strict justice requires. Neither can God stipulate that Christ's work has the requisite moral value, making it such that Christ's work has a value that it does not, in the absence of divine fiat. Each of these acts is inconsistent with strict justice, where this notion of strict justice includes a notion of retribution—at least one central

17. Objection: God could require that the action be (a) the act of a human (to atone for human sin) and (b) a moral action. Response: Without some principled means by which to circumscribe the voluntarism at work in SATT, it is difficult to see why we should grant the advocate of SATT either of these qualifications, which appear to be entirely ad hoc. But, even if they are granted, it only reduces the size of the problem. It does not eliminate it.

strand of which is that there must be a fit between punishment and sin.[18]
If human sin requires a certain punishment according to the divine moral
law, then God must ensure that the punishment in question is met to the
full either in the person of the sinner or perhaps in the person of some
suitable substitute. Otherwise, the punishment does not fit the sin and
strict justice (in conformity with the divine nature) is abrogated.[19]

The Proportional View

This brings us to the proportional view, which argues for the conclusion
that Christ's work as a whole must have an intrinsic, objective moral value
at least sufficient to atone for human sin in order for it to be acceptable
to God. That is, an act of atonement must have a moral value at least
proportional to the sin it atones for. We might put it like this:

1. Some actions have an objective moral value.
2. God cannot justly impute or otherwise attribute (by divine fiat, say)
   a moral value or property to a particular action that the given action
   lacks.
3. Atonement for the sin of some number of fallen humanity must be
   an act that as a whole has a certain objective moral value in order
   to be acceptable to God.
4. That objective moral value must be at least proportional to the sin
   for which it atones in order to be acceptable to God as atonement
   for that sin.
5. Christ's work is an act that, as a whole, has the requisite objective
   moral value at least proportional to human sin in order to atone for
   human sin.
6. So, Christ's work is acceptable as an act of atonement.

Although this reasoning forms a logically consistent whole, it raises
several theologically controversial issues. The first proposition is contro-

18. Retribution may stand on its own as a justification for punishment, but it might also
be a part of a more complex whole. Such mixed or hybrid views have been much discussed in
modern legal theory. For an overview of this literature, see Brooks, *Punishment*.
19. I have discussed this issue of divine retribution in more detail in Crisp, "Divine Retribution."

versial if, like the advocate of acceptilation, one thinks that no creaturely actions have an objective moral value, and/or that the only moral value any action has is a value assigned it by divine fiat. But not every theologian who is a voluntarist will want to deny that at least some actions have an objective moral value, provided *objective moral value* is equivalent to *the moral value assigned this sort of act by divine fiat*.[20] But I suppose few theologians will be tempted by acceptilation because, as was suggested in the previous section, there is little theological support for the idea that no creaturely actions (or even no human actions) have intrinsic moral value. For one thing, it is very difficult to make sense of a biblical conception of sin if no human action has an intrinsic moral value. For then no human act can possess or generate a demerit for which salvation would be necessary.[21]

In the context of this work, the second proposition is probably the most contentious, since it effectively blocks acceptilation and acceptation. Those theologians sympathetic to some version of fictionalism with respect to the value of the work of Christ will object that God can impute a moral property to a particular action, and that this is just what God does in the case of the value of the atonement. There are other theological applications of fictionalism, including other ways in which fictionalism is applied to the atonement.[22] One need not embrace all these theological applications of fictionalism to find the general principle that God might impute certain qualities or properties to a given thing, or a given act, credible. However, I do not find the application of fictionalism to acceptilation plausible, for reasons I have already rehearsed in the previous section of this chapter; such an application of fictionalism requires that strict retributive justice be set aside, which is, it seems to me, impossible if God is essentially just and if retributive justice is one aspect of divine distributive justice. For an essentially just God must act justly, and a retributively just judge must

20. The problem here should be obvious: if the moral value of a particular act is determined by divine fiat alone, then it does not appear that such acts have an *objective* moral value. The value is, in one theologically relevant sense, entirely *subjective*, being the value assigned to that act by the will of one (admittedly divine) entity.

21. Even the concept of *hamartia* (ἁμαρτία) or "missing the mark," used in the New Testament to denote human sin (e.g., Matt. 1:21), carries a moral payload. Any human act that has the property of *hamartia* will *ipso facto* be an immoral act. We return to the question of sin in chapter 7.

22. I outline some of these in *Word Enfleshed*, chap. 7. Craig is critical of this in *Atonement and the Death of Christ*, 191–93.

ensure that punishment fits sin. (We shall return to this matter in the last section of the chapter.)

The fourth proposition contains the phrase, distinctive of the proportional view, that the value of the atonement must be at least morally proportional to the demerit of the sin committed in order to be acceptable to God. This gains some plausibility from its application elsewhere in fairly uncontroversial circumstances. For instance, if someone owes a debt to his bank and his friend agrees to pay that debt, the friend must pay the full amount owed. It would not be sufficient if he were to pay part of the debt. The bank would not be willing to waive the particular amount owed as long as some lesser token amount was paid off; the full amount must be remitted. The fact that in other human transactions we might be disposed to waive the entire debt (if the money is owed to another friend, say, rather than a bank) does not necessarily undermine the point being made here. I suggest that in the case of a friend waiving all but a token repayment of a debt, the friend is forgiving the debt by forgoing payment. The debt is not paid. The debt is still owed, but the friend freely forgoes full payment of what is owed. This makes sense in human transactions of this informal variety (like the example of the damaged book, used earlier) because we are sometimes willing to relax the legal requirements of a debt for the sake of friendship. The fact that we would not be willing to do this in a more formal, forensic context only underlines the fact that there are circumstances in which such legal relaxation is usually considered inappropriate. We may be in two minds about paying our debts, depending on the circumstances involved. But strictly speaking, where a debt is owed, it ought to be paid. That much is surely a tenet of natural justice that the vast majority of reasonable people would agree upon.[23]

Lastly on this point, the third and fifth propositions make it clear that the moral value requisite to atonement must apply to the work of atonement taken as a whole, not the value of Christ's work *qua* human or *qua* divine, in keeping with what was said about the value of Christ's whole work at the end of the first section of the essay.

But, even if we grant these controversial propositions, is the proportional view theologically adequate? Is it sufficient for Christ's work to be *merely* proportional to the sin for which it is offered as atonement? The

---

23. Compare the argument of Lewis, "Do We Believe in Penal Substitution?," 203–9.

great medieval divine Thomas Aquinas suggests it is not. In the *Summa Theologica* he says, "He properly atones for an offence who offers something which the offended one loves equally, or even more than he detested the offence. But by suffering out of love and obedience, Christ gave more to God than was required to compensate for the offence of the whole human race. . . . Christ's passion was not only a sufficient but a superabundant atonement for the sins of the human race."[24]

Here Aquinas, like a number of classical theologians, presumes that the work of Christ was an act of sheer unmerited grace, something he was not obliged to carry out, an act of supererogation the merit of which he could use in a vicarious act of satisfaction, to atone for human sin. Similarly, in *Cur Deus Homo* Anselm of Canterbury reasons that atonement for human sin, being the work of the God-man, must have a value greater than the disvalue of sin—indeed, an infinite value.

> [*Anselm*]. Consider also that sins are as hateful as they are bad and that the life which you have in mind [i.e., the life of the God-man] is as loveable as it is good. Hence it follows that this life is more loveable than sins are hateful.
>
> [*Boso*]. This is something which I cannot fail to appreciate.
>
> A. Do you think that something which is so great a good and so loveable can suffice to pay the debt which is owed for the sins of the whole world?
>
> B. Indeed, it is capable of paying infinitely more.
>
> A. You see, therefore, how, if this life is given for all sins, it outweighs them all.[25]

Anselm's case requires the following logical steps:

a. An act must outweigh the sin for which it is offered as atonement: "You do not therefore give recompense if you do not give something greater than the entity on account of which you ought not to have committed the sin" (*Cur Deus Homo* I.21).

b. The gravity of human sin is such that fallen human beings owe God everything they are and are capable of doing: "If, in order that I may not sin, I owed him my whole being and all that I am capable of, even when I do not sin, I have nothing to give him in recompense for sin" (*Cur Deus Homo* I.20).

24. Aquinas, *Summa Theologica* III.48.2.
25. Anselm, *Cur Deus Homo* II.14, in Davies and Evans, *Major Works*, 335.

   c. The work of the God-man, being the work of a person of infinite value and honor, generates a merit that has infinite worth (*Cur Deus Homo* II.14, quoted above).

   d. This merit may be used by the God-man to satisfy divine justice on behalf of fallen human beings, since he does not require this merit for his own salvation, being perfect: "But Christ of his own accord gave to his Father what he was never going to lose as a matter of necessity, and he paid, on behalf of sinners, a debt which he did not owe" (*Cur Deus Homo* II.18).

What is important to note here is that, on the proportional argument and the reasoning of Thomas and Anselm, the demerit of sin is more than balanced out by the merit of Christ's work. In none of these arguments is there a moral shortfall in the value of the work of Christ as an atonement that God must make up. Clearly, the proportional view is metaphysically weaker than those of Anselm and Thomas. But importantly, the concept of proportionality acts as a kind of theological threshold here. If the atonement must be more than proportional in value to the sin it atones for (infinitely valuable, even), then its value is *at least* proportional to that sin. To see this, consider the following triumvirate of propositions:

   i. Christ's work is an act that as a whole has the requisite objective moral value at least proportional to human sin in order to atone for human sin.

   ii. Christ's work is an act that as a whole has an infinite objective moral value because it is the work of the God-man.

   iii. Christ's work is an act that as a whole *necessarily* has an infinite objective moral value because it is the work of the God-man.

The first of the three—that is, (i) above—reproduces proposition (5) of the proportional view; (ii) and (iii) follow Anselm's supposition that the God-man is a person of infinite value and honor, able to perform a vicarious act that generates a merit of infinite worth sufficient to atone for human sin. But whereas (ii) presumes only that Christ's work has this moral value, (iii) affirms that the work of Christ is necessarily a work of infinite objective moral value because it is a work of God

Incarnate.[26] There is an ascending order of modal strength here, where each succeeding proposition entails, but is not entailed by, the previous one. Each of (i)–(iii) effectively blocks acceptation and acceptilation. But of the three, the last Anselmian proposition is surely the one on target: the atonement of Christ is not just proportional in value to the demerit of human sin. It is necessarily an act of infinite value outweighing the disvalue of all human sin because of the intrinsic dignity, honor, and value of the person who performs it.

Acceptation, Salvation, and Theology Proper

But why must Christ's work have an objective moral value at least proportional to the demerit of human sin? Here we come to considerations touching on the divine nature. Some theologians, including the advocates of acceptation, presume that divine justice may permit forgiveness, although God may have good reason to punish some sinners for their sin.[27] In which case, God may forgive sin without punishment, though he may not. Others, like Anselm, claim that divine justice does not permit forgiveness. Sin must be punished either in the person of the sinner or in the person of some substitute.

Although there are eminent theologians on both sides of this debate, I favor the Anselmian position. One could consistently maintain that God might have forgiven sin without punishment, although he chose not to, and that the work of Christ necessarily has an infinite value because it is the work of the God-man. Then, God chooses whether to forgive or punish sin, opts to punish, and sets in place the work of Christ as a means

26. This is consistent with the idea, mooted earlier, that Christ's human nature *qua* human nature has only a finite value. The reason why Christ's work has an infinite value, unlike the work of any other human being, is that it is the work of God Incarnate. His work *qua* human is the work of a divine person. It has a value corresponding to the honor and dignity of the person performing it.

27. See Aquinas, *Summa Theologica* III.46.2 ad 3. Richard Swinburne claims that "there would have been nothing wrong in God forgiving us without demanding reparation" (*Responsibility and Atonement*, 149). But this is surely to fall foul of the Socinian objection that if God could forgive sin without reparation, he ought to do so. Otherwise, the atonement becomes a wholly unnecessary, morally repugnant act that God could have forgone with impunity. Moreover, Swinburne's language may lead the unwary to confuse forgiveness, where a wrong is remitted without payment of any kind, with punishment. The two concepts are, strictly speaking, antithetical. One can punish or forgive, but one cannot forgive by punishing, or by punishing, forgive.

of atonement in the knowledge that this work necessarily has an infinite value. But, following Anselm, I think the following is closer to the truth: God could not refrain from punishing sin, all things considered, because it would be unjust for God to forgive sin without punishment, and God is essentially just. Divine retribution is one aspect of divine distributive justice, whereby God distributes deserts for particular creaturely actions. In which case, not only is it true that God must punish sin; God is not free not to punish sin because it is in God's nature to be just, and a requirement of justice is that sin be punished. But God must ensure there is a fit between punishment and sin. Human sin is punished either in the person of the sinner or in the person of a substitute. God elects that the God-man perform an act of atonement on behalf of human sinners, knowing that necessarily such an act would have an infinite value, and would therefore qualify as a recompense for human sin of at least sufficient value to atone for that sin. And Christ freely takes up this role as the mediator of the means of salvation for human sin.

The atonement, on this view, is, in some important sense, necessary for the salvation of fallen humanity. But necessary how? Surely in the sense of a *necessitas ex suppositione*, or "necessity on account of supposition." In this case, the supposition in question is that, though God is free to create or refrain from creating this particular world, if God creates, then the created world must be consistent with the divine character. It might be thought that the atonement has a consequential but not absolute metaphysical necessity, due to the fact that God elects to bring about the salvation of some number of humanity, though God might have elected to punish the whole mass of fallen humanity. In which case, there are possible worlds in which God creates but does not redeem humanity. But such a state of affairs could obtain only if we deny that God must display mercy in order for the character of God as a whole to be displayed in the work of creation. For then God could bring about a world in which the divine mercy is not displayed, contrary to what has been assumed thus far.

But, like Anselm, I deny this. God cannot act in a way inconsistent with the character of God. Among other things, this means that if God does create a world of creatures that fall, God must ensure that grace and mercy are displayed in that world in the salvation of some number of fallen creatures, in order that the name of God is vindicated. In which case, some act of atonement consistent with God's divine mercy is required in order for God to display his attributes and vindicate his name. This means God is, we might say, "constrained" by the divine character to create a certain kind of world, one where the grace and mercy of God are displayed in the salvation of some number of fallen creatures. But this is not to deny the consequential necessity of the atonement; it is only to circumscribe what we mean by such consequential necessity. The atonement is necessary consequent on God choosing to create the particular world God does. God could not have created a world in which all fallen humans are damned, given the character God has. But God could have created other worlds than the one actualized. In fact, in good Thomistic style, we can affirm that God could have created an infinite number of feasible worlds (i.e., worlds consistent with the theological "constraint" imposed by his own character), or (perhaps) with God not creating any world.

Conclusion

On the theological account sketched in this chapter, the atonement as a whole has to have a value at least proportional to the sin it atones for, on pain of God acting unjustly. I have offered some reason for thinking that the Anselmian account of divine justice, according to which God must punish sin in a retributive manner, is right. And I have tried to point out some of the most important implications this has for theology proper. It means God's essential justice has a certain character. It also has implications for what we say concerning God's reason for creating—and here I have opted for the view that God must, not merely may, display the divine justice and mercy in creation, thereby vindicating God's name before all creatures. Finally, these considerations have implications for what we can say about the theologically vexed notion of divine freedom. It turns out that the God of salvation is a God of a certain character, who acts in accordance with that character, and cannot act any other way. This is perfectly consistent with a certain construal of divine freedom. It still means God exists *a se,* such that none of his actions are externally constrained. But the most theologically interesting upshot of the foregoing is this: If God must create a world where this character is displayed in justice and mercy, then it appears that, although God may withhold mercy from any given individual in accordance with Scriptures like Romans 9:18, God cannot withhold mercy *tout court*. And this entails that the God of salvation must act not only justly but also graciously and mercifully.[28]

This is an important conclusion for our larger project of giving a constructive account of atonement. For on the one hand, it says something about the divine nature, and especially about divine justice. On the other hand, it says something about the value and importance of the atonement as a work of divine reconciling grace. An adequate understanding of the atonement must be one in which both of these things are taken into consideration—or so I shall argue in subsequent chapters.

28. Of course, this conclusion is independent of claims about the scope of atonement. That is, it is consistent with a range of views about the number of those for whom Christ's atonement is effectual. It is also consistent with the claim that Christ dies for the sins of the whole world, in accordance with biblical passages like John 3:16. For a discussion of this latter point, see Crisp, "Anglican Hypothetical Universalism."

Models of Atonement

Having given some account of preliminaries in part 1, we turn in part 2 to consider some of the most important historic accounts of atonement in Christian theology. This will serve as a conceptual backdrop to the constructive work of part 3. The idea in part 2 is not to give an exhaustive account of all the various ways of thinking about the atonement in the Christian tradition. Such a project has been attempted by others elsewhere.[1] Rather, the focus in this work is upon central and influential ways of thinking about the nature of the atonement that are relevant for the constructive third part of the book. In each case, I have attempted to make as clear as possible what the core claims of a given view amount to, and then provide a charitable but critical assessment of the view. It transpires that not all of these accounts of the atonement are on an equal footing. Upon analysis, some (like the ransom view) do not appear to amount to a complete doctrine of atonement. Others, like the moral exemplar view, are common coin in atonement theology, though they are often misunderstood. So, part of the project of this section of the work is also to clear up mistakes about particular views of the atonement, setting the record straight so that we do not end up tilting at windmills like that venerable knight, Don Quixote. The hope is that this ground-clearing exercise

1. The most exhaustive treatment is still that of Franks, *Work of Christ*.

will also have its own value as a series of chapters devoted to clarifying and explicating, as well as criticizing, some of the most important ways of thinking about the atonement that can be found in Christian theology.

Chapter 3 concerns moral exemplarism. In it I argue that moral exemplarism is often misunderstood. There are in fact two ways to construe the doctrine. The first is an account that does not amount to a doctrine of atonement; the second does. Despite this fact, as it stands the doctrine has serious drawbacks and is probably better understood as a component of a richer account of atonement rather than as a stand-alone understanding of the nature of Christ's reconciling work.

Chapter 4 turns to the consideration of the notion of ransom, which has been particularly influential in much recent theological work on atonement. I argue that this is not, in fact, a complete doctrine of atonement but more like a motif that may feature in a more expansive understanding of Christ's work.

Chapter 5 considers the doctrine of satisfaction, with particular reference to the version of the doctrine pioneered by the great medieval divine Anselm of Canterbury. This is one of the most controversial doctrines in contemporary atonement theology. It is also arguably the most influential atonement doctrine in the history of Christian thought, for it influenced subsequent work in medieval theology as well as Reformation and post-Reformation theology—especially with respect to penal substitution. (Although, as I have already indicated, satisfaction is distinct from penal substitution, which is a matter that is often misunderstood in the literature.) After giving an account of Anselm's version of the doctrine and contrasting it with a more Thomistic version, I turn to the recent critique of the Anselmian view by Eleonore Stump, arguing that Stump's presentation of Anselm's position is mistaken in important respects. Although Anselm's doctrine is not without its shortcomings, it is a much more promising way of thinking about the reconciling work of Christ than Stump's argument suggests.

Chapter 6 rounds out this part with a look at penal substitution and the problems it raises. In the recent literature, no doctrine of atonement has come under more criticism than this one. Nevertheless, it is not without its defenders (e.g., William Lane Craig, Stephen Holmes, and Garry Williams). This chapter sets out what are historically the most important objections to the doctrine, as a prelude to the constructive section that follows this one. Although I am critical of penal substitution, my own constructive account owes much to this doctrine and may be thought of as an answer to some of the traditional and contemporary worries about the doctrine that have been raised in the literature.

3

Moral Exemplarism and Transformation

We have already seen that in much historic Christian theology the atonement is the doctrine according to which Christ somehow reconciles fallen human beings to Godself by means of some saving act—usually focused in important respects upon his life and ministry, and culminating in his death on the cross and his resurrection.[1] One important issue for those seeking to understand this Christian doctrine is *the mechanism of atonement*. Recall that this is the means by which Christ brings about the reconciliation of fallen humanity with God. A central question for atonement theorists is this: *How is it that Christ brings about the reconciliation of fallen humanity with God? What is the mechanism by means of which this obtains?* It is this question about the nature of atonement that frames the present study.[2]

1. Not everyone sees it this way, however. For a discussion of different ways of conceiving the nature of atonement, see J. Johnson, *Patristic and Medieval Atonement Theory*.
2. This is not uncontroversial. For instance, Michael Gorman is skeptical of attempts to provide what he calls "the mechanics of atonement." (We might dub this *atonement mechanism skepticism*—a matter to which we shall return at the end of the chapter.) Gorman writes, "New Testament writers are far less interested in the *mechanics* of atonement than they are in the *results* of atonement. In fact, I would suggest that the mechanics are largely a mystery and will always be precisely that" (*Death of the Messiah*, 210, emphasis original). But, *pace* Gorman and

There are many different accounts of the atonement in the Christian tradition, with many different views on the mechanism of atonement. There are also accounts of Christ's work that do not amount to doctrines of atonement as such. This is often because the views in question deny that Christ's work and ministry are salvific. The theological importance of Christ's work for fallen human beings is thought to lie elsewhere.[3] I will focus on a family of atonement views at least some members of which do not amount to doctrines of the atonement in this sense—namely, moral exemplarist views. Put very roughly, *moral exemplarism* is the view according to which Christ's work is primarily an example that should elicit a particular transformative response in individuals who encounter it, rather like a single act of courage in the midst of a pitched battle may have the effect of transforming terrified members of an army corps into a fighting unit, thereby turning the tide of the conflict. It is often said that moral exemplarist views are somehow theologically deficient, though where the deficiency lies is rather more difficult to say.[4] However, there are far fewer attempts to defend moral exemplarism, let alone argue that at least some versions of moral exemplarism do, in fact, constitute atonement doctrines.

This chapter does just that. I will outline two distinct strands of moral exemplarism. The first, which I shall call *mere exemplarism*, does not yield a doctrine of atonement though it does provide a way of thinking about Christ's life and ministry that is theologically salient. According to mere exemplarism, Christ's work is *merely* an example that should elicit a particular response in individuals who encounter it. Although a moral example can be a powerful thing—think of modern examples like Saint Theresa of Calcutta, Martin Luther King Jr., or Dietrich Bonhoeffer—someone who is merely a moral example is not a person whose work is salvific in the sense I am after here. For, by my lights, mere moral examples do not (and, given

---

others, many historic Christian theologians working on this topic have been interested in the "mechanics of atonement" as much as the results of the atonement, as any standard textbook on the subject would quickly demonstrate.

3. However, some accounts of the work of Christ do not amount to a doctrine of atonement because they do not provide a clear view of the mechanism of atonement, not because they deny that the work of Christ is salvific. I think that some versions of the ransom view are like this, as I will argue in the next chapter.

4. See, e.g., McGrath, "Moral Theory of the Atonement," 205–20. The idea that imitating Christ's example is integral to the Christian life—and especially for Christian sanctification—is, however, much less controversial. For an intriguing recent treatment of this issue, see Cockayne, "Imitation Game," 3–24.

our fallen state, cannot) bring about reconciliation with God. So their role as moral exemplars is not (and, given our fallen state, cannot) be salvific.

I will contrast this mere exemplarism view with a richer account, which I shall call *extended exemplarism*. This extended account includes almost all that the mere exemplarist view entails, aside from the restriction that the exemplarism in question is a "mere" exemplarism. It goes beyond mere exemplarism to suggest a conceptually thin way in which Christ's work is, in fact, atoning. So, on this richer account, in addition to being a moral example that should elicit a particular response in individuals who encounter it, Christ's action is also salvific. Having outlined the two versions of exemplarism, I will defend them against several standard objections. Although I do not endorse a version of exemplarism as a stand-alone account of Christ's work, like almost all atonement theorists, I think that this way of conceiving Christ's work represents an important feature of any adequate understanding of the atonement, even if it needs to be augmented in important respects in order to yield an acceptable account of the atonement. In this way, we might characterize at least some version of exemplarism as a necessary but not sufficient feature of a complete account of the atonement. But if that is right, then it is worth trying to get a clearer picture of the conceptual shape of different versions of moral exemplarism as contributing factors to a doctrine of atonement. It is also worthwhile asking why moral exemplarism may not be sufficient as a way of conceiving Christ's saving work.

We shall proceed as follows. In the first section, I give some distinctions that set up the discussion. Then, in the second section, I outline the mere exemplarist view and distinguish it from the extended exemplarist view. The third section raises some problems for moral exemplarist approaches to the work of Christ. Finally, the conclusion draws together the strands of the foregoing, offering some reflections on how this discussion fits into a broader atonement theology.

Some Introductory Remarks

Before setting out the two versions of moral exemplarism, some introductory remarks are in order.

First of all, I shall refer to the work, ministry, and teaching of Christ, including his death and resurrection, as *the work of Christ*. This elides the question of what it is about Christ's life and ministry, including his death and resurrection, that is salvific—a matter that is contested in the Christian tradition. For some theologians, Christ's incarnation, life, and ministry are a kind of prerequisite for his crucifixion, which is what is salvific (thus, Anselm and Calvin, among others). For others, however, his incarnation and ministry are just as much a part of his reconciling work (thus, Athanasius and Irenaeus, among others). We do not need to take a view on this matter here.[5] In any case, the exemplarist tradition tends to treat Christ's life and ministry and his death and resurrection as all, in some sense, works (or aspects of one work) that are exemplary. This is true even though the cross is usually the focus of discussion, as with most other historic accounts of the work of Christ. Note that I do not say that for the exemplarist these different aspects of Christ's life, work, and ministry are *salvific* either individually or taken together. For (as we shall see) that is one of the central matters at issue in the exemplarist tradition.

Next, I shall not spend much time discussing theologians who represent the exemplarist tradition. There is some dispute about whether particular thinkers should be included in this way of thinking about the work of Christ, perhaps the most famous of which is the medieval Parisian theologian Peter Abelard.[6] But for our purposes, it is sufficient that (a) this way of thinking about the work of Christ has a long history, and (b) there are clear and undisputed representatives of this way of approaching Christ's work in the Christian tradition.[7] These two things are not at issue in the atonement literature.

Two Versions of Moral Exemplarism

In a recent reference work on the topic, Adam Kotsko writes, "Exemplarism, sometimes also called the 'moral influence theory' of the atonement, refers to the view that the primary goal of Christ's saving work is to pro-

5. Though I have taken a view in *Word Enfleshed*.
6. For an essay that denies Abelard was a mere exemplarist, see Quinn, "Abelard on the Atonement," 335–53. Also worthy of mention in this connection is T. Williams, "Sin, Grace, and Redemption," 258–78. The *locus classicus* is now translated as Peter Abelard, *Commentary on the Epistle to the Romans*, the editorial introduction to which sets out the issues—namely, the interpretation of Abelard's position on the atonement. I have discussed this in *Approaching the Atonement*.
7. Paradigmatic exemplarists include the Italian-Polish Reformation-era theologian Faustus Socinus; Immanuel Kant; the "father of modern theology," Friedrich Schleiermacher; the twentieth-century Anglican philosopher and theologian Hastings Rashdall; and, in more recent times, John Hick.

duce positive moral change in human individuals and communities."[8] This is a fairly common characterization of the view. The idea is that moral exemplarists make positive moral change the primary goal of the atonement, and that this privileging of moral change over other potential outcomes distinguishes it from alternative accounts. The problem is that this leaves unexplained how the moral exemplarist view amounts to an account of Christ's work as an atonement—that is, how this conception of the work of Christ is supposed to be a salvific as opposed to a non-salvific account of Christ's work. For, on the face of it, the claim that the exemplarist regards Christ's atonement as primarily a matter of producing moral change in human persons seems ambiguous. It is not clear whether what is in view is a claim about moral change/transformation, or, alternatively, a claim about salvation.[9]

Kotsko seems to think that matters may be clarified by appealing to the oft-repeated theological distinction between so-called "subjective" and "objective" accounts of the atonement. According to subjective views, the importance of Christ's reconciling work has to do with its appropriation by a particular individual and the subjective change the person undergoes as a consequence. By contrast, objective views of the atonement are those according to which the most salient feature of Christ's reconciling work is his action on behalf of the believer in salvation independent of the change this brings about in the individual believer. But since all accounts of the atonement include both subjective and objective elements (in the sense that these terms are being used here), this is not very illuminating. If moral exemplarism does, in fact, provide us with a doctrine of the atonement, then what is the mechanism of atonement? How is Christ's moral example or moral influence supposed to be salvific? This is never explained.

It is precisely this explanatory lacuna that I want to address. As far as I am aware, there is no other treatment of exemplarism that distinguishes something like mere exemplarism from something like extended exemplarism. When the exemplarist tradition is discussed, it is usually as a form of (what I am calling) *mere exemplarism* (what Kotsko, following the older atonement literature, calls "moral influence theory"). This is a pity. As we shall see, there is an important distinction to be made here,

8. Kotsko, "Exemplarism," 485.
9. We shall see that in the case of extended exemplarism, it is both. But these two things (viz. moral change and salvation) are not synonymous.

one that has potentially significant implications for our understanding of
the doctrine of atonement.

a. Mere Exemplarism

According to mere exemplarism, Christ's work is a moral example to
us of how we ought to live—a life of self-sacrificial love culminating in the
giving up of his own life in order to vindicate his message. But it is not in
addition to this a means by which we are reconciled to God. Comparisons
with other great moral teachers would yield a similar picture. Thus, if we
were to consider the moral example of Dr. Martin Luther King Jr. or of
Saint Theresa of Calcutta or even of philosophers like Socrates or other
religious figures like Gautama Buddha, much the same could be said of
them as is said of Christ in mere exemplarism. They are moral examples.
Their lives provide a pattern of moral living, perhaps even a kind of loose
framework to which one might want to conform. (This may be easier in
some cases than in others. For instance, I am not sure all the recorded aspects of Socrates's life are exemplary or provide a clear moral framework
that might be imitated. However, the legends of Gautama Buddha's life
are—for some people—exemplary, and his teachings on the Four Noble
Truths and the Eightfold Path have provided the basis for the various traditions of Buddhism.)

Saying that Christ's work may be a mere moral example does not trivialize or disparage the significance of Christ's work for those who take
this view. (The qualification "mere" in mere exemplarism should be read
like the "mere" of Lewis's *Mere Christianity*, not the "mere" of a "mere
trifle.") It is perfectly consistent with mere exemplarism that the sort of
change this brings about in the person who takes to heart the moral task
of conforming her life to that of Christ is, in fact, transformative in the
way in which Laurie Paul speaks of transformative experience.[10] Such experiences can certainly be momentous and lasting. To see this, consider
the following example:

10. Paul, *Transformative Experience*. In this connection, Cockayne writes, "Copying certain
examples of behaviour from historical individuals might change our own thinking and behaviour
in certain ways. However, if imitating Christ is essential for the redemption of human agents
through the process of sanctification, and eventually, deification, then it will be important that
our account of imitation captures the transformative nature of this process. It is not obvious
that mere behaviour replication can do this" ("Imitation Game," 7). That seems right to me.

Smith is a professor of ethics with no clear religious affiliation. In her search for the good life, she reads the works of many different moral thinkers, and she eventually alights upon the teaching of Christ as reported in the Sermon on the Mount in Matthew 5–7. Intrigued, she begins to read all four of the canonical Gospels, beginning with Matthew, and progressing through Mark to Luke and John. She finds herself deeply moved by the person of Christ as he appears in these narratives. His moral teaching on simplicity of life, his self-sacrificial love, and his devotion to God and to the community—especially to the poor and disadvantaged—is something that resonates deeply with her desire to find a comprehensive moral vision that may shape her own interior life. Upon reading about Christ's passion, she is struck by how he is portrayed as living out a consistent ethic, even though it ultimately costs him everything, rather like Socrates. Yet here, in Christ, is an example of someone who sought not merely to teach the youth to be critical of authority, or to question everything, but who sought to provide a deep and consistent moral foundation upon which a person may grow and flourish. Nowhere is this more evident than in the manner in which Christ forgives his executioners from the cross upon which he was crucified.

The effect upon Smith is profound. She reads and re-reads the Gospels, Mark being her favorite because of its immediacy. The person of Christ jumps off the page, arresting her with each new reading. Through this engagement with the text of Scripture, and deep reflection upon what she has been reading, Smith comes to see that Christ's work, teaching, and, ultimately, his self-sacrifice on the cross for the principles that guided his life present an irresistible picture. He is a model of the good life, an exemplar like no other she has encountered in her research. For in the person of Christ, there is a combination of piety, devotion to duty, purpose, clear moral teaching of the highest order, and a ministry suffused with a desire to love others and address their physical and spiritual needs, especially with respect to the poor and marginalized. Transfixed by the moral example of Christ and his self-sacrificial act of crucifixion, Smith undergoes a significant moral and spiritual reorientation. She vows to amend her life in order that she may align herself and her religious convictions with the example of Christ as a model for the good life that is predicated upon the need to love other people in her community, and especially the poor and disadvantaged, in practical ways in order to bring about moral and political change.

In her work on transformative experiences, Laurie Paul distinguishes between *epistemic* transformation and *personal* transformation. An experience is epistemically transformative if you can only know what it is like by undergoing the transformation yourself. For instance, seeing a particular color for the first time. A personal transformation is one in which your view on an issue that is fundamental to who you are is changed. For example, reading *The Communist Manifesto* and having one's political views changed forever as a consequence. When a transformative experience includes both an epistemic and a personal aspect, it is truly transformative. A good example of this is becoming a parent. Those who have become parents often say that it is a transformative experience that they could not have prepared themselves for, and (often) did not fully understand prior to actually having a child. Something about undergoing the experience of becoming a parent for oneself changes a person in a way that no textbook could explain adequately.

Religious conversion is another paradigm of truly transformative experience because it too has both epistemic and personal aspects. In the example of Smith, we have an instance of an experience that is arguably transformative. It may even be a kind of religiously transformative experience—that is, truly transformative, including epistemic and personal aspects. There are certainly secular followers of Christ whose encounters with his life and teaching could be characterized in terms of nontheistic religious experiences that are transformative in this sense.[11] I say "nontheistic religious experiences that are transformative" advisedly. For it seems to me that one could have a religious experience that is transformative on the basis of an encounter with the Christian understanding of the work of Christ as found in the canonical Gospels and yet not become a theist as a consequence, let alone a Christian.[12] Alternatively, it seems feasible for a person to encounter the biblical portrayal of Christ and undergo a theistic religious transformative experience (either from a prior state of atheism or agnosticism, or just plain old religious apathy) yet without becoming a Christian as a consequence.

Such transformative religious experiences do not yield the sort of moral and spiritual reorientation that includes reconciliation with God, as one would expect if the transformation were salvific—that is, part of an ac-

---

11. One recent popular example borne out of work being done in conversation with Miroslav Volf at Yale's Center for Faith and Culture is Krattenmaker's *Confessions of a Secular Jesus Follower*.

12. Krattenmaker is an example of a nontheistic Jesus follower. Hindu devotion to Christ as an avatar of Vishnu is an example of what we might term "henotheistic Jesus devotion."

count of Christ's work understood in terms of atonement. For, as we have characterized Smith, her engagement with the work of Christ lacks certain markers that one would expect for the exemplarism in question to be recognizably Christian in nature. There is no indication that she has an awareness of sin, or an understanding of the need for Christ to reconcile her to God, for example. In fact, there is no reason to think that Smith's engagement with Christ's work as an instance of mere exemplarism has anything about it that marks it out as distinctively *Christian*. Smith could do all she is reported as doing in the story and also be changed significantly in the process and yet not become a member of a believing community, hold to any distinctively Christian doctrines, or engage in any particular Christian practices. Even if we have a very minimal account of what change an agent must undergo in order to become a Christian or a member of a Christian faith community,[13] it looks like Smith's experience could be significant and transformative in some important respects without her becoming a Christian.

Now, Christ's work may be atoning even if Smith is not aware that it is atoning. I am not denying that. In other words, she may be saved by the atonement without knowing it, and while committed to a mistaken account of the work of Christ. There is nothing particularly implausible in that suggestion. But then, Christ's work would be an atonement for sin and mere exemplarism would be false. Given that Smith holds views consistent with mere exemplarism even after her transformative engagement with the work of Christ, she would (on this way of thinking) remain committed to a false picture of Christ's work. God may still include her within the scope of salvation by means of Christ's atonement as an act of divine grace. But that is a different matter.

As I have characterized mere exemplarism, it is not sufficient for Smith to undergo the religious transformative experience she does for it to count as a transformative experience of the atonement. Something is still missing, some quality that would make the work of Christ into an atonement as far as Smith is concerned. This is true whether the transformation she undergoes leaves her religious but not a theist, or a theist but not Christian.

---

13. I avoid the term "church" here because there are some Christian faith communities that do not appear to be churches in the classical sense of the term—e.g., the Society of Friends (Quakers) or the Salvation Army. I will return to the place of the church in the doctrine of atonement in chapter 9.

The point is that the transformation does not make of Smith a believer in what is sometimes called the "great things of the gospel." It falls short of that, though it may be the catalyst for a profound and lasting change in Smith's moral and spiritual orientation. Hence, the mere exemplarist view of Christ's work does not amount to an account of atonement (as I am understanding the term here—namely, as the doctrine according to which Christ somehow reconciles fallen human beings to God by means of some saving act). It may be that she has only a partial grasp of Christ's work and fails to see that it is, in fact, an atonement. And, as I have indicated, it may be that Christ's work is, in point of fact, an atonement for Smith, even though Smith has failed to perceive that. Be that as it may, it looks like mere exemplarism does not amount to a doctrine of atonement.

b. Extended Exemplarism

Let us turn to extended exemplarism. As I indicated at the beginning of this chapter, extended exemplarism includes almost all the conceptual content of mere exemplarism. Like the mere exemplarist, the extended exemplarist thinks of Christ's work as a moral example of how we ought to live—a life of self-sacrifice culminating in the giving up of his own life in order to vindicate his message. But in addition to this, the extended exemplarist thinks that this very way of conceiving of the work of Christ provides her with a (thin) notion of reconciliation—that is, with an account of Christ's work as an atonement. To see this, let us consider a second example:

> Jones is an ordinand in seminary and a close friend of Professor Smith. Jones has long held that Christ is a moral example whose life and work should form the moral foundation of a person's life. In fact, it was she who first suggested this to Smith, which set Smith off on her reading of the Gospels in her own quest for the good life. However, in her own theological formation, Jones has come to see that regarding Christ merely as a moral example is theologically insufficient. Only if Christ's example of love in his crucifixion is able to transform a person—changing them from someone alienated from God's love to someone living a life of self-sacrifice and practical ministry, especially ministry to the poor and disadvantaged, as a follower of Christ and a member of the church—is his example sufficient. For, Jones thinks, the transformative work of Christ's loving example must bring us back into

relationship with God. It must bring about not just a moral transformation but a spiritual reorientation and reconciliation with God.

It is more explicit in this example than in the case of Professor Smith that Jones has undergone what Laurie Paul calls an "extended transformative experience,"[14] that is, a transformative experience that takes time, that may have different phases, and that may lead the person undergoing the experience to a very different way of life that she could not have anticipated prior to undergoing the experience in question. Through engagement with Christ's saving work, and especially his crucifixion, Jones comes to see that the love Christ displays is a divine love that should elicit a response of love from her. It should transform her, so that she comes to see something new about God's love in Christ reconciling the world to Godself, as well as a personal transformation through such an encounter. This total transformation (in the sense given by Laurie Paul) is at its core about bringing Jones back into alignment with the God from whom she has become estranged by means of the love of Christ exemplified in his work on the cross. Such a religious experience may be construed as an instance of joint-attention with God, as Eleonore Stump and Adam Green (among others) have recently suggested. As Joshua Cockayne puts it in glossing Green's work on the topic,

> According to Green's model, the individual who experiences God through joint-attention does not have to perform an inference to establish that she is experiencing God, but there is a kind of intersubjective relation that occurs between God and her. The individual experiences something of God's emotions or intentions whether that be God's loving, or God's forgiving, or God's imparting mercy.[15]

Perhaps Jones's transformative experience as a consequence of encountering and engaging the work of Christ as an atonement involves joint-attention in this way. Perhaps through engaging with the work of Christ Jones comes to see something of God's grace and love, comes to understand that Christ has shown her divine grace, and comes to think that she is experiencing that love through the report of the atonement in the

14. Paul, *Transformative Experience*, 97.
15. Cockayne, "Imitation Game," 16. He is commenting on A. Green, "Reading the Mind of God."

canonical Gospels that is applied directly and experientially to her through the secret working of the Holy Spirit. Perhaps it is this concatenation of different elements that together brings about her regeneration.[16]

Clearly, Jones's transformation includes a (conceptually thin) doctrine of atonement, which is something missing from the case of Professor Smith. Yet Jones's account is still recognizably a version of moral exemplarism: Christ's moral example, and his display of divine love, motivate Jones to undergo the religious transformative experience that leads through various stages to regeneration and salvation.[17] It is important to note here that in the example of Jones there is no additional mechanism of atonement aside from Christ's moral example that factors into Jones's story. (Neither the notion of joint attention nor the internal work of the Spirit constitute mechanisms of *atonement* as such. They have to do with the application of the benefits of Christ's atonement to the believer.) It is a matter of Jones coming to understand Christ's moral example as a means by which she may be reconciled to God that yields the religious transformative experience that constitutes a thin understanding of atonement.

Some Objections to Moral Exemplarism

As I have already suggested, moral exemplarism has often been the subject of criticism. In this section, we will focus on some of the standard objections to moral exemplarism found in the theological literature.

The first objection we shall designate *the subjectivist-moralist worry*. This relates to the discussion of subjective views of the atonement that was raised in connection with Adam Kotsko's essay. The worry is this: The exemplarist tradition is thoroughly subjective in its understanding of the work of Christ. The focus is on inward, moral transformation rather than on the objective work of Christ for us on the cross. Consequently, it presents an inadequate understanding of Christ's saving work. Hastings Rashdall is sometimes thought to provide an example of this alleged inadequacy. He writes,

16. We will consider the ontology of regeneration in chapter 9.
17. For an interesting treatment of religious conversion as a transformative experience that draws on the work of L. A. Paul in dialogue with Søren Kierkegaard, see Torrance, "Can a Person Prepare to Become a Christian?"

The Church's early creed "There is none other name given among men by which we may be saved" will be translated so as to be something of this kind: "There is none other ideal given among men by which we may be saved except the moral ideal which Christ taught by his words, and illustrated by his life and death of love; and there is none other help so great in the attainment of that ideal as the belief in God as he had been supremely revealed in him who so taught and lived and died." So understood, the self-sacrificing life which was consummated by the death upon the Cross has, indeed, power to take away the sins of the whole world.[18]

But, it is not clear to me that the moral exemplarist must conclude that the importance of Christ's work is merely subjective and purely moralistic. One of the takeaways from Laurie Paul's work is surely that transformative experiences can produce momentous change in the person who undergoes them, change that reshapes a person's life. That appears to be true of the mere exemplarist example of Professor Smith. It is even more the case for the extended exemplarist, Jones. It seems that the way this concern is often raised mischaracterizes the moral exemplarist tradition. The idea is not to recommend a kind of moral formalism as reflected in the teaching of Christ—a sort of Kantianism in a clerical collar. Rather, I take it that the idea is about how Christ's example can be morally and spiritually transformative. The subjectivist-moralist worry is even less applicable to the extended exemplarist because it is clear that on this way of thinking Christ's work does much more than bring about subjective change or moral reorientation. It is truly transformative (in the sense used earlier in connection with the discussion of Laurie Paul's work) and does encompass a notion of atonement.

A second and related objection is *the problem of salvation by meritorious works*. Alister McGrath puts it bluntly in his assessment of Rashdall's version of mere exemplarism: "It amounts to nothing less than a doctrine of salvation by merit."[19] Such concerns are often raised with respect to

18. Rashdall, *Idea of the Atonement*, 463. McGrath regards this excerpt from Rashdall as evidence for the view that "man must find his own way to salvation by his good works executed in the imitation of the example of Christ" ("Moral Theory of the Atonement," 212). It is not quite as clear to me that this is the only way to read Rashdall's views here.

19. McGrath, "Moral Theory of the Atonement," 219. McGrath is scathing in his assessment of Rashdall's version of exemplarism, but he is more sympathetic to what he takes to be the more sophisticated version of the view found in Immanuel Kant's *Religion within the Limits of Reason Alone*.

the exemplarist tradition. But it is not clear that this must be the case of either the mere moral exemplarist or the extended moral exemplarist. Take the mere exemplarist. The transformation undergone by Professor Smith is not a case of salvation by merit because it is not clearly an example of salvation at all. Her engagement with the work of Christ results in a transformative experience. But on neither the religious-but-not-a-theist interpretation of Smith's experience nor the theist-but-not-Christian interpretation would it be true to say that Smith conceives of her engagement with the work of Christ in terms of salvation by merit or by works. This is just a misunderstanding of what is at issue.

This objection also misses the mark with respect to the case of Jones, the extended exemplarist. Her engagement with the work of Christ does not yield an idea that by performing certain actions she will place herself in the right state to merit salvation or to gain access to divine salvific grace. Rather, through the transformative process of engaging the work of Christ she comes to see that his loving work reconciles her with God. She understands that by engaging with Christ's work in a deep, spiritually reorienting manner, her alienation from God can be healed. There is no reason why this must be thought of as the work of Jones making herself right with God in some manner. A more charitable way to think of what is going on here is in terms of a work of divine grace through a kind of joint attention. God working through the example of Christ's loving action draws Jones to Godself.

The third concern is *the problem of sin*. Neither Smith nor Jones seems to have a particularly robust understanding of sin, let alone the doctrine of original sin. For many theologians, this is the most serious problem facing advocates of the exemplarist tradition. However, much of the force of this objection depends on one's broader theological commitments. Not all Christians hold to a doctrine of original sin or think that sin is a deep and debilitating problem for fallen human beings (e.g., the Orthodox, with their notion of the ancestral sin[20]). Given that mere exemplarists do not regard Christ's work as salvific, and therefore do not think of it as an atonement, strictly speaking, the problem of sin does not arise in quite the same way. (One could object that the mere exemplarist has too sunny an estimation of human beings, but, though not unrelated, that is

20. See Romanides, *Ancestral Sin*.

a rather different sort of worry.) Admittedly, as I have characterized the view here, the extended exemplarist doesn't think of sin as the obstacle to reconciliation with God. Rather, alienation is the problem at issue; a broken relationship that needs to be healed. That may be thought an inadequate account of human fallenness. But it is not clear to me that it is inconsistent with all branches of Christianity (e.g., Orthodoxy), and it is not clear to me that this presents a view of human nature that is objectionably optimistic in a theological sense. For instance, it is not obviously Pelagian or semi-Pelagian.[21]

The fourth objection is the *problem of the missing mechanism*. This does not apply to mere exemplarism, since in that case there is no mechanism of atonement in view, just a significant trigger for a transformative experience. In the case of extended exemplarism there is what I have termed *a conceptually thin mechanism of atonement*. It is still not all that clear *how* Christ's work is an atonement on the extended exemplarist view. Somehow Christ's loving work generates an appropriate response by means of divine grace that illuminates and changes Jones, bringing her reconciliation with God and the kind of regeneration requisite to full participation in the life of the believing community. It might be desirable to have a clearer picture of the mechanism of atonement than this. But the extended exemplarist may resist that claim. Like Michael Gorman, she may be an atonement mechanism skeptic. That is, she may think that the New Testament authors don't give us a clear mechanism of atonement and are not interested in doing so. Rather, their focus is on the practical consequences of Christ's saving work. Perhaps, the extended exemplarist might say, this should inform how we think about the nature of the atonement today. Perhaps we should be less concerned with clarifying the mechanism of atonement (which does not seem to have been a preoccupation of the New Testament authors) and more concerned about the practical (and measurable?) difference our atonement theology makes—a kind of pragmatic approach to atonement theology.[22]

21. Pelagianism is (very roughly) the heresy which says that human beings are capable of bringing about their own salvation through meritorious action. Semi-Pelagianism is the unorthodox view that human merit coupled with divine grace may bring about human salvation. In other words, it is the view that human beings can really and truly contribute to their own salvation.

22. Here I have in mind something like an analogue to Richard Swinburne's notion of pragmatic faith, where a person acts in a certain manner in the hope that belief will follow practice. See Swinburne, *Faith and Reason*, chap. 4.

But even if one is persuaded by the sort of atonement mechanism skepticism of biblical scholars like Gorman, there do seem to be important ways in which even the extended exemplarism of Jones is deficient from a New Testament point of view. We cannot give a complete account of this here. It will have to suffice to indicate three important biblical-theological motifs that seem to be lacking on the extended exemplarist way of thinking about the atonement—motifs to which we shall return in giving a constructive account of the mechanism of atonement in part 3. These are that Christ's work is *vicarious, representational,* and *expiatory*. I will briefly touch on each of these issues in turn.

Christ's atonement is *vicarious* in nature. This seems to me indisputable on the basis of the New Testament texts and in the history of reflection upon them in atonement theology. Christ acts on behalf of fallen human beings, so to speak (e.g., Rom. 5:12–19; 2 Cor. 5:21; Gal. 3:10–13; 1 Pet. 2:24; 3:18). There are different ways in which one can act vicariously. The sort of vicarious act I have in mind here is one that is consistent with the notion of representation.

A *representative* is a part of a particular body or group. As biblical scholar Simon Gathercole points out, "Substitution entails the concept of replacement, X taking the place of Y and thereby ousting Y: the place that Y previously occupied is now filled by X. In representation, X in one sense occupies the position of Y, as in substitution. There are differences, however. In representation, X does not thereby oust Y but rather embodies Y. Indeed, it is usually a presupposition of representation that X belongs to group Y, and so the representative is part of the body represented."[23] Not all substitutes are also representatives in this sense. (Think of a body double who may act as a substitute for a democratic political leader, though the body double is not in fact the duly elected representative.) It seems to me that in the case of the atonement, Christ acts vicariously as a representative (see Rom. 5:12–19 and 1 Cor. 15). He acts on behalf of fallen human beings, and he represents those human beings as someone who is himself a human being.[24]

To this we may add the notion of *expiation*. That is, Christ's atonement blots out human sin; he makes amends so that human beings may be reconciled with God. (The language of "sin offering" in Pauline theology,

23. Gathercole, *Defending Substitution*, 20.
24. See Gathercole, introduction to *Defending Substitution*.

including the notion of Christ being "made sin for us" is salient in this respect. See Rom. 3:25; 5:9; 1 Cor. 5:21; Eph. 1:7; 2:13; Col. 1:20.)[25] If Christ's atonement is a sin offering provided in order to expiate human sin (on analogy with the scapegoat of the Old Testament), then this may also turn away wrath even if it is not a propitiation, strictly speaking. Compare a situation in which someone breaks an expensive vase, and then makes amends by purchasing a replacement as a substitute for the one that was broken. This act of expiation or making amends might also please the person whose vase was broken, thereby preventing unhappiness or anger even if the happiness this generates is merely a foreseen but unintended outcome (the intention being to make amends rather than to placate the person whose vase was smashed).

It is difficult to see how the exemplarist can address these three New Testament atonement motifs. Even if one is a mechanism skeptic, some account needs to be given regarding the biblical material that points in the direction of Christ's work being an atonement that is vicarious, representational, and expiatory. The onus is on the exemplarist to provide some account of these matters.

Conclusion

Despite the resurgence of interest in the doctrine of atonement in recent biblical studies, systematic theology, and analytic theology, the exemplarist tradition has remained largely under-explored (with one or two notable exceptions[26]). Even when it is introduced into the discussion, it is largely in order to dismiss it as an inadequate account of Christ's work. Sometimes, it is mentioned alongside other "theories" or models of atonement, as with Gustaf Aulén's influential threefold typology of satisfaction, exemplarist, and ransom or *Christus Victor* views of the atonement.[27] None of these ways of thinking about the exemplarist tradition do it justice. I have argued

25. I think there is also a *prima facie* case for thinking that God may be propitiated by Christ's atonement, though this is a much more controversial theological claim, which I won't defend here. The difference is that propitiation turns away wrath, whereas expiation removes sin-guilt.

26. John Hick is the most notable recent proponent of some kind of moral exemplarism. But his account is derivative. It is not really in any sense an improvement upon, or development of, his predecessors such as Kant, Schleiermacher, or Rashdall. Nevertheless, his account is accessible. See Hick, *Metaphor of God Incarnate*.

27. See Aulén, *Christus Victor*.

that some versions of exemplarism—namely, mere exemplarism—are not in fact doctrines of atonement at all, although engagement with Christ's work understood in these terms may yield significant moral and transformational change in a person. Nevertheless, there is a second version of exemplarism, the extended account, that does amount to a doctrine of atonement. I have also argued that a number of standard objections to moral exemplarist views of Christ's work fall short of rebutting exemplarism. Nevertheless, moral exemplarism does seem to have deficiencies. Its doctrine of sin may be insufficient (depending on one's views on this matter). A not unrelated concern is the fact that the exemplarist tradition doesn't sufficiently engage three concepts in atonement theology rooted in Scripture. These are the notions of vicarious action, representation, and expiation—matters to which we shall return in subsequent chapters. It is difficult to see how exemplarism alone, without theological augmentation, can adequately address these issues. For this reason, it seems to me to present an incomplete account of the work of Christ understood as a doctrine of atonement.

4

The Ransom Motif

Ｗe come to the second account of the atonement which we shall consider in detail in this part of the book. Gustaf Aulén closes his famous study of the atonement with these remarks about what he calls the "classic" account of the doctrine—what I take to be a version of the ransom model of atonement:

> I have tried to be consistent in speaking of the classic *idea* of the Atonement, never of the, or a, classic *theory*; I have reserved the word *theory*, and usually the word *doctrine*, for the Latin and "subjective" types [of doctrines of atonement]. For the classic idea of the Atonement has never been put forward, like the other two, as a rounded and finished theological *doctrine*; it has always been an idea, a *motif*, a theme, expressed in many different variations. It is not, indeed, that it has lacked clearness of outline; on the contrary, it has been fully definite and unambiguous. But it has never been shaped into a rational theory.[1]

Recalling the discussion of terminology from the first chapter, it would seem that Aulén has in mind something like the following rough-and-ready distinction. An idea of atonement is a concept or notion that captures some central thought about a particular way of thinking about Christ's

---

1. Aulén, *Christus Victor*, 174–75.

reconciling work that has not been developed into a model. Such atonement ideas are motifs or pictures—that is, conceptual windows that offer
a partial view onto some larger whole. As I indicated in the first chapter,
a model of atonement is a simplified description of the complex data of
Scripture and the Christian tradition that bear upon this topic, on analogy with scientific models. Such models approximate to the truth of the
matter and offer a more expansive view of the larger whole. Something
similar could be said about atonement models, *mutatis mutandis*. But I
would want to add this caveat (in keeping with chapter 1): A theory is
potentially more comprehensive than a model, being a system of ideas
or a conceptual framework that makes sense of a lot of data in some
overarching account of an area of intellectual endeavor. For this reason,
theories are often thought to be more generalized than models, with the
latter informing theories but being insufficient to generate a theory, while
theories may have particular applications in models of certain data sets.

Often in the theological literature on soteriology one reads of *theories*
of atonement, but (as I argued in the first chapter) on this way of thinking it may be that "model" is the more accurate term. For we are trying
to give a simplified description of complex data, and it may be that more
than one model is required to do so. (Of course, one might have a theory
about models of atonement, and there are such theories in the literature
as well.[2]) Moreover, if, as is often claimed in contemporary work on the
atonement, no one account of the atonement exhausts what can be said
about the doctrine, it may be that the attempt to find an overarching theory
of atonement by means of which to understand all the different data on
the topic is a forlorn one. The search for a particular model that may approximate to the truth of the matter is, on this way of thinking, a more
modest quest and, perhaps because of this, one more likely to succeed.

What then of *doctrines* of atonement? As we have already seen, in
Christian theology a doctrine is (minimally) a comprehensive account
of a particular theological topic held by a particular communion. In his
discussion of the nature of doctrine George Lindbeck adds to this the
notion that church doctrines are also essential to the identity or welfare
of a particular community.[3] But I think that is too stringent in the case of

2. For instance, Mark Baker and Joel Green's kaleidoscope theory about atonement models.
See Baker and Green, *Scandal of the Cross*; and J. Green, "Kaleidoscope View."
3. Lindbeck, *Nature of Doctrine*, 74.

atonement. Although some account of atonement certainly is essential to the Christian faith, it is not clear to me that particular doctrines of atonement—particular construals of that central notion, as it were—are *essential* to particular communities. For the atonement does not have a dogmatic definition in most Christian traditions.

In my view, doctrines provide propositional content to Christian claims about particular theological topics—claims that are truth-apt. That is, doctrines are aimed at truth; they presume there is a truth of the matter and attempt to express that in propositional form.[4] Normally speaking, a doctrine of atonement implies a particular model for understanding this aspect of Christian teaching. Hence, we might say that Anselm's understanding of the doctrine of atonement implies a particular way of conceiving atonement, which can be expressed in a model for understanding the work of Christ—namely, satisfaction.

Aulén doesn't go into great detail about the difference between his use of "idea" and "doctrine" and so forth, but I think that what I have said here is consistent with the views he does state, and it captures his worry that an idea of atonement is much more provisional, and incomplete, than a doctrine of atonement. For an idea of atonement may provide a motif or picture of Christ's work without giving a worked-out mechanism by means of which atonement takes place—which is just to say that an idea of atonement is not a doctrine of atonement, not a comprehensive account of Christian teaching on the topic, and not a complete model of atonement either, though it may be an aspect of a particular presentation of Christian teaching on the matter or of a model.

In recent years, and in large measure because of the influence of Aulén's work, there have been a number of attempts to provide a "rational theory" of the ransom atonement motif. Indeed, one might talk of it as the doctrine of choice for a range of contemporary theologians approaching the work of Christ.[5] Yet alongside this burgeoning work on the ransom view

4. Thus my account of doctrine roughly corresponds to the first cognitive-propositional account in Lindbeck's typology of theories of Christian doctrine in *The Nature of Doctrine*, 16.

5. This includes thinkers from a range of different ecclesial traditions. For example: Aulén was Lutheran; J. Denny Weaver, author of *The Nonviolent Atonement*, is Anabaptist; Gregory A. Boyd, contributor to Beilby and Eddy, *The Nature of Atonement*, is (broadly) Baptist; Jeremy Treat, author of *The Crucified King*, is a free evangelical who is broadly Reformed in his sensibilities; N. T. Wright is an Anglican bishop and author of *The Day the Revolution Began*; John Macquarrie was a Presbyterian-turned-Anglican who wrote *Principles of Christian Theology*, which commends a version of *Christus Victor*.

there has not been a corresponding clarity about what we might call the mechanism by means of which atonement is supposed to obtain. To put it another way, often in reading accounts that purport to offer a ransom doctrine, rather than merely a ransom motif, one is left wondering how it is that Christ's work achieves the reconciliation of human beings with God.

In this chapter I attempt to do several things to address this issue, which I take to be the most important issue facing those wishing to articulate a ransom doctrine of atonement (as opposed to utilizing a ransom motif as part of some larger, more comprehensive account of atonement). First, I shall set out four versions of the doctrine that can be found in the work of several modern theologians. These are particular examples of what I shall call *interpretive strategies* for understanding the ransom view. They comprise: (1) the denial of ransom in order to make room for an alternative understanding of Christ's victory; (2) the attempt to expand the ransom motif into a complete doctrine of atonement; (3) the attempt to assimilate the ransom account into some other understanding of atonement; and (4) the attempt to relegate ransom to some less fundamental component of a rather different understanding of atonement. The first of these strategies is not a ransom view, strictly speaking, though it is clothed in the language and conceptual trappings of the ransom view. The second is unsuccessful because (as we shall see) it is unable to move beyond a motif to a model of atonement. The third and fourth may provide ways in which to use ransom in constructive accounts of atonement as a part of a larger doctrinal whole, and I shall indicate how this might be achieved. In a closing section, I offer some reflections on why this conclusion is important for contemporary constructive accounts of Christ's work.

Variations on Ransom and *Christus Victor* Views of Christ's Work

Let us turn to the matter of the theological form of the doctrine. Although Aulén and others, in imitation of him, speak of the ransom view (also called the *Christus Victor* view or the dramatic view) as the classic idea of atonement (which rather begs the question),[6] I take it that the central claim of this view has to do with the notion of ransom rather than

6. Aulén, *Christus Victor*, 20.

atonement. Often it is expressed like this: *Christ's work of redemption is fundamentally about him buying back human beings from the powers of sin, death, and the devil. His work is a ransom price that is paid to these powers in order that some number of fallen humanity may be redeemed from destruction and brought to salvation.* As with contemporary hostage scenarios, in this model of atonement humanity can only be released from bondage by the payment of a ransom price. In this case, the ransom price is the redeeming work of Christ.

Call this notion—that atonement is about a ransom being paid to bring about human liberation from bondage to sin, death, and the devil—*the core claim* of the ransom model. In much historic discussion of this model, the core claim is embedded in a larger story about the aims and purposes of the work of Christ. Aulén places the core claim in the broader context of a story about the victory of Christ over the powers of sin, death, and the devil. The central theme of this "dramatic" view is "the idea of the Atonement as a Divine conflict and victory; Christ—*Christus Victor*—fights against and triumphs over the evil powers of the world, the 'tyrants' under which mankind is in bondage and suffering, and in Him God reconciles the world to Himself."[7] He goes on to say, "This salvation is at the same time an atonement in the full sense of that word, for it is a work wherein God reconciles the world to Himself, and is at the same time reconciled."[8] J. Denny Weaver, elaborating on Aulén's *Christus Victor* idea, writes, "This atonement image used the image of cosmic battle between good and evil, between the forces of God and those of Satan. In that fray God's son Jesus Christ was killed, an apparent defeat of God and victory by Satan. However, Jesus' resurrection turned the seeming defeat into a great victory, which forever revealed God's control of the universe and freed sinful humans from the power of sin and Satan."[9]

The most infamous of these redemption narratives in which the core claim is embedded is the bait-and-hook story of Gregory of Nyssa. In his *Great Catechism*, he says this:

For since, as has been said before, it was not in the nature of the opposing power to come in contact with the undiluted presence of God, and to

7. Aulén, *Christus Victor*, 20.
8. Aulén, *Christus Victor*, 20.
9. Weaver, *Nonviolent Atonement*, 15.

undergo His unclouded manifestation, therefore, in order to secure that the ransom in our behalf might be easily accepted by him who required it, the Deity was hidden under the veil of our nature, that so, as with ravenous fish, the hook of the Deity might be gulped down along with the bait of flesh, and thus, life being introduced into the house of death, and light shining in darkness, that which is diametrically opposed to light and life might vanish.[10]

Similar accounts can be found in a number of other patristic authors, including Irenaeus, Origen, John Chrysostom, John of Damascus, and even Augustine of Hippo, who writes, "As our price He held out His Cross to him like a mouse-trap, and as bait set upon it His own blood."[11] But clearly the defender of a ransom model of atonement need not hold to these rather lurid stories about divine deception of the devil in the incarnation. The core claim is independent of the particular stories in which it has often been embedded. This is important because some of the more superficial criticisms of the ransom view depend on the stories in which the core claim is embedded—for example, the objection that, on Nyssa's bait-and-hook story, God appears to deceive the devil. The fact that the ransom account doesn't depend on any of these narratives means that such objections are beside the point in assessing its merits, for they are not part of its conceptual core.

But is ransom truly the core claim, or is it Christ's victory over sin, death, and the devil? Denny Weaver's view has been widely canvassed and discussed in the recent atonement literature. One of the key claims he makes is that his own brand of *Christus Victor*, which he calls "narrative *Christus Victor*," does not imply that God is involved in a violent act in bringing about the death of Christ. This is a controversial claim, offered as a contribution to the contemporary debate about violence and atonement. It is not clear to me how the crucifixion can be regarded as anything other

10. Gregory of Nyssa, *Great Catechism*, chap. 24. Chapter 26 of the *Great Catechism* makes it clear that Gregory thinks God deceives the devil in proceeding as he does. Cf. John of Damascus, who says, "Therefore Death will advance, and, gulping down the bait of the Body, be transfixed with the hook of the Divinity: tasting that sinless and life-giving Body, he is undone, and disgorges all whom he has ever engulphed: for as darkness vanishes at the letting in of light, so corruption is chased away by the onset of life, and while there is life given to all else, there is corruption only for the Corrupter" (*On the Orthodox Faith* 3.27).

11. Grensted, *Short History*, 44. Grensted cites all these representatives of the ransom view in his helpful digest of the doctrine.

than an act of violence, and one that, in some sense, God permits for the purposes of reconciliation. But, in fact, it seems to me that Weaver's position does not depend in any fundamental way on claims about violence in the cross, despite his own views to the contrary. The reason for this is that he maintains that his own brand of *Christus Victor* is not about the death of Christ at all, but about the reign of God, the unveiling of which can be seen in Christ's work in his life, death, and resurrection. Thus Weaver says, "What this book has called narrative Christus Victor thus finally becomes a reading of the history of God's people, who make God's rule visible in the world by the confrontation of injustice and by making visible in their midst the justice, peace, and freedom of the rule of God. The life, death, and resurrection of Jesus constitute the culmination of that rule of God, and also the particular point in history when God's rule is most fully present and revealed."[12] Later, he goes on to say, "Since Jesus' mission was not to die but to make visible the reign of God, it is quite explicit that neither God nor the reign of God *needs* Jesus' death in the way that his death is irreducibly *needed* in satisfaction theory."[13] This represents "one of the most profound differences between narrative Christus Victor and satisfaction atonement."[14]

According to Weaver, Christ's death was a consequence of his dedication to living out the reign of God. By accepting this mission, he acceded to death, which was a function of that mission, not its goal.[15] But if narrative *Christus Victor* is actually about the reign of God in history exemplified in a particular manner by the life and work of Christ, where his death is not a goal of that work, not something necessary for that work, but merely a function of his faithfulness to his mission, then it is difficult to see how Weaver's narrative *Christus Victor* amounts to a ransom view of *atonement* at all. For Christ's work is not about reconciling fallen humans to God, according to Weaver, but about the culmination of God's reign on earth. In one respect, Christ is the victor on this view—the one whose work is the culmination of the victory of God's reign. But not because he offers himself as a ransom to pay for human sin. We might say that

12. Weaver, *Nonviolent Atonement*, 84–85. For a recent symposium on the matter of violence and atonement where many of the contributors (including Weaver) draw on the *Christus Victor* view, see Jersak and Hardin, *Stricken by God?*
13. Weaver, *Nonviolent Atonement*, 89.
14. Weaver, *Nonviolent Atonement*, 89.
15. Weaver, *Nonviolent Atonement*, 91–92.

Weaver's position is a *Christus Victor* motif without the core claim, and therefore, without being a ransom view at all.

There are those, however, for whom the victory motif is more fundamental than ransom, though ransom still has a role to play. This is N. T. Wright's view. He says,

> The cross is for Paul the symbol, as it was the means, of the liberating victory of the one true God . . . over all the enslaving powers that have usurped his authority. . . . For this reason I suggest that we give priority—a priority among equals, perhaps, but still a priority—to those Pauline expressions of the crucifixion of Jesus which describe it as the decisive victory over the "principalities and powers." Nothing in the many other expressions of the meaning of the cross is lost if we put this in the centre.[16]

Divine victory over the powers of sin, death, and the devil is indeed an important biblical and theological component of the ransom view, which is why this view is often called *Christus Victor*. But it is the upshot of that view, its consequence, not the view itself. In other words, it is because Christ's work is a ransom that he is victorious over these powers; ransom is not merely one way of construing Christ's victory, it is the reason why his work is characterized as a victory over sin, death, and the devil. So, *pace* Weaver and Wright, to make victory a more fundamental component than ransom is to turn this account of Christ's work on its head. Ransom is the core claim; victory is the result.

Kathryn Tanner has also recently argued that ransom is not, in fact, the fundamental motif at the heart of this account of the atonement, but for different reasons. First, she demotes Aulén's argument. "*Christus Victor* is not a model at all," she remarks, "in that it fails, per se, to address the mechanism of the atonement. Christ is battling the forces of evil and sin on the cross but how is the battle won?"[17] The question is rhetorical, of course. But the expected response is clear: we don't know because we are not told.

16. Wright, *What Saint Paul Really Said*, 47. For an insightful critique of Wright's account of atonement, see Spence, *Promise of Peace*, chap. 1.

17. Tanner, *Christ the Key*, 253. Compare Khaled Anatolios, who writes that *Christus Victor* "does not exist as a pervasive and mainstream current in either the New Testament or the early church but is most accurately designated as an extremely idiosyncratic christological and soteriological transposition of the Lutheran principle of *sola gratia*" (*Deification through the Cross*, 13).

Tanner then provides an alternative: "Aulén does not see, however, that the incarnation is the very means by which the fight is waged and won. This claim is fundamental nonetheless to the early church theologians to whom he appeals. All of them view the incarnation . . . as the key to the salvation of humanity."[18] This is in fact the underlying mechanism of atonement in Gregory of Nyssa's bait and hook story, on Tanner's way of thinking.[19] A particularly vivid example of this can be found in St. Cyril of Alexandria's analogy of the iron in the fire. He writes,

> There was no other way for the flesh to become life-giving, even though by its own nature it was subject to the necessity of corruption, except that it became the very flesh of the Word who gives life to all things. This is exactly how it accomplishes his own ends, working by his own life-giving power. There is nothing astonishing here, for if it is true that fire has converse with materials which in their own natures are not hot, and yet renders them hot since it so abundantly introduces them to the inherent energy of its own power, then surely in an even greater degree the Word who is God can introduce the life-giving power and energy of his own self into his very own flesh.[20]

Adopting St. Cyril's view, Tanner says that Christ's atoning work comprises the whole of his life from the first moment of incarnation to his resurrection. It is not restricted to his work on the cross, as if that can be abstracted from his incarnate life as the particular event by means of which human salvation obtains. What is more, in the very assumption of human nature there is a salvific communication of idioms in Christ (like St. Cyril's analog of the iron in the fire), whereby the attributes of human life become the properties of the Word and (some of) the properties of the Word become properties of humanity.[21]

Although she does not spell out exactly how this communication of idioms does the work of atonement, the idea seems to be this: In the very

18. Tanner, *Christ the Key*, 254. Earlier she says that "the cross saves, not as a vicarious punishment or an atoning sacrifice or satisfaction of God's honor or as a perfectly obedient act. . . . The cross saves because in it sin and death have been assumed by the one, the Word, who cannot be conquered by them. Christ is the victor here, following Gustaf Aulén's famous typology, but the underlying model is that of the incarnation itself" (29).

19. Tanner, *Christ the Key*, 255.

20. Cyril of Alexandria, *On the Unity of Christ*, 132–33. Tanner cites much of the same passage in *Christ the Key*, 256.

21. Tanner, *Christ the Key*, 254.

act of incarnation God the Son purifies the particular human nature he assumes in such a manner that the properties of the resulting sanctified nature may be ascribed to other instances of human nature by his divine power. What is more, only by recapitulating each stage of human life in a sinless manner, and by dying and rising again, is Christ in a position to offer the salvific benefits of his perfect incarnate life and death to fallen human beings via the communication of idioms. For only by recapitulating human life, and death, and by defeating death by resurrection, can he be said to have sanctified the whole of a human life, the benefits of which may then be ascribed to other, fallen human beings. It cannot be just in virtue of the assumption of a particular human nature that Christ brings about human salvation, even if the assumed nature is purified in its hypostatic union with a divine person. Such a physical account of the atonement (as it is sometimes called) would leave opaque the mechanism by means of which the assumption of one human nature brings about salvation for other entities possessing a human nature in need of salvation. Tanner's account is more than a physical account of the atonement because she includes a notion of recapitulation, affirming the need for the life, death, and resurrection of Christ as aspects of the one work of atonement.[22] Nevertheless, Tanner's patristic-inspired doctrine of atonement, which relocates the heart of the mechanism from ransom to the vicarious humanity of Christ, doesn't explain how it is that the assumption of human nature, or the communication of idioms in the person of Christ, or the recapitulation of the stages of human life in the life of Christ brings about human salvation.

Elsewhere, I have suggested that one way to repair Tanner's reasoning at this juncture is to introduce a clearer notion of *representation*.[23] Then, the communication of idioms (what she calls "the wonderful exchange") that obtains in the incarnation may provide a basis for atonement because Christ acts as our representative in assuming a human nature. The saving benefits of the work of Christ could then be imputed to other human beings by the power of the Holy Spirit in salvation. Following T. F. Torrance

22. Compare Khaled Anatolios on St. Athanasius's soteriology: "Through his incarnation, the Son repairs our human participation in his imaging of the Father from within the human constitution; anything short of a full incarnation would leave humans disconnected from both Father and Son" (*Retrieving Nicaea*, 107). Anatolios is commenting on St. Athanasius's work, *On the Incarnation*.

23. See Crisp, *Revisioning Christology*, chap. 6.

(whose view is similar to that of Tanner in some important respects), we might dub this the *vicarious humanity doctrine of atonement*.[24] It is not entirely clear how Tanner thinks this story goes. But perhaps it is analogous to this one:

> Vikram, a leading figure in Indian society, wishes to overthrow the caste system of India. In order to do so, he chooses as his bride a woman of the lowest caste, an Untouchable named Indira. In marrying Indira, he marries one particular woman. Nonetheless, his action resonates beyond the change that marrying Vikram makes to Indira's life, across the lives of all or many women of the lowest caste. His action begins the process that will lead to their emancipation. It has whole-caste consequences.

Something like this story could be applied via Tanner's incarnation as atonement doctrine to the work of Christ. Like Vikram, God the Son unites himself to something "untouchable" from a divine perspective—namely, a particular human nature that suffers from the effects of the fall—sanctifying it in the very act of assumption. But this particular action has much wider consequences. Through the assumption of the particular human nature of Christ, God the Son emancipates, or begins the emancipation of all fallen human beings. His work has *whole-caste consequences*.[25]

Admittedly, much more would need to be said if we were attempting to offer a complete defense of Tanner's account. For present purposes, however, it is sufficient to see that she construes *Christus Victor* as a species of the ransom view, which (a) fails to apprehend what is most fundamental about the atonement—namely, the very act of incarnation itself, coupled with the communication of idioms and a doctrine of recapitulation—and (b) is an incomplete account of atonement without this.

24. The historian of doctrine J. N. D. Kelly dubs this view the "physical" or "mystical" account of atonement, "which linked the redemption with the incarnation. According to this, human nature was sanctified, transformed and elevated by the very act of Christ's becoming man. Often, though not quite correctly, described as the characteristically Greek theory, it cohered well with the Greek tendency to regard corruption and death as the chief effects of the Fall" (*Early Christian Doctrines*, 375). But I distinguish the physical model from the vicarious humanity model in this way: the physical model presumes that the assumption of human nature is sufficient for atonement; the vicarious humanity model presumes that the assumption of human nature is necessary but not sufficient for atonement.

25. See Crisp, *Revisioning Christology*, 128, where the substance of this paragraph appears. I have adapted the text slightly.

Her own view is, I think, suggestive and interesting and really does capture something important about many of the patristic accounts of atonement that Aulén and his epigone have overlooked.[26] And, like Tanner, I agree that the *Christus Victor* account does not provide a mechanism of atonement and that for this reason it is incomplete as a model of atonement. But it is not clear to me that her alternative plugs that conceptual gap, for it is not clear to me how God the Son's act of assuming human nature plus recapitulation plus the communication of idioms actually amounts to salvation. This combination of notions may provide the raw materials for a mechanism for atonement. Nevertheless, it is still far from clear *given what she actually says* exactly how atonement is achieved.

Hans Boersma's work represents another recent attempt to rehabilitate Aulén's position. Although he thinks it represents "the most significant model of the atonement," he also maintains, like Tanner, that "it does not explain *how* Christ gains the victory."[27] It is a strange model of atonement that does not provide a clear account of the mechanism by means of which Christ is said to bring about human reconciliation with God. So it is puzzling that Boersma thinks this is true of the "most significant" model of atonement, since, one would think that a significant model of atonement would offer a complete, developed understanding of Christ's work, including some story about the mechanism of atonement. However, on Boersma's reckoning this is not the case with the ransom view. It requires supplementation by St. Irenaeus's doctrine of recapitulation in order to provide a complete account of the means by which atonement obtains.[28] "Christ's victory over the powers of darkness is the telos and climax of his work of recapitulation," says Boersma. "In other words," he continues, "the victory is the *result* of the entire process of recapitulation."[29] Like

---

26. This is one reason why Tanner's argument makes much better sense of a wider range of data. Whereas Aulén simply elides discussion of potential counterexamples to his *Christus Victor* in the Fathers—e.g., Athanasius, *On the Incarnation* and the views of Gregory Nazianzus— Tanner's view can incorporate them, along with the views of Gregory of Nyssa and others, as different ways of expressing her incarnation-as-atonement model.

27. Boersma, *Violence, Hospitality, and the Cross*, 181.

28. In fact, he later points out that Irenaeus's doctrine includes elements of ransom, mediation, and moral example—which, according to Aulén's typology, represent the three historic models of atonement. See Boersma, *Violence, Hospitality, and the Cross*, 200; and Aulén, *Christus Victor*, chap. 8. Irenaeus's position is set forth in his *Against Heresies*.

29. Boersma, *Violence, Hospitality, and the Cross*, 181.

Tanner, the Irenaean view Boersma has in mind involves Christ recapitulating each stage of our human development, providing a sinless template of human life, death, and resurrection, the benefits of which can then be transferred or imputed to fallen human beings. But as with Tanner, it is not clear how the addition of claims about the vicarious humanity of Christ, or about his recapitulation of each stage of human life, provides a work that atones for the sin of other human beings. Vicarious humanity or Irenaean recapitulation do not do this work without some further explanation about how it is that the benefits of Christ's work may be transferred from Christ to other, fallen human beings in need of salvation. Unfortunately, Boersma doesn't appear to go beyond this in his provision of a better way of construing *Christus Victor*.

Four Interpretive Strategies

Let us take stock. From these cameos of different treatments of the ransom view we may derive four interpretive strategies. The first of these distinguishes ransom and victory motifs in Christ's work, removes ransom, and provides a different account of the way in which Christ's work is a victory, one in which ransom plays no significant part—in fact, one in which Christ's death is no longer a necessary component. This is Weaver's position. The second interpretive strategy treats the ransom view as a distinct account of atonement with its own integrity, though it may be incomplete in important respects, or in need of further development (e.g., Aulén).[30] This usually involves placing the core claim within the context of a particular narrative about how salvation is brought about by Christ, such as that provided by Gregory of Nyssa's bait and hook story. The third strategy augments ransom with additional notions which are supposed to fill in the conceptual gap in the ransom account, providing a clearer mechanism of atonement (thus, the assimilation of ransom to recapitulation in Boersma and recapitulation plus the communication of idioms in Tanner). Depending on how we construe matters, there may also be a fourth strategy here, which, to all intents and purposes eviscerates the doctrine, removing the core claim and replacing it with a different mechanism of

---

30. John Macquarrie presents a version of the ransom view that he takes to be a complete model of atonement in *Principles of Christian Theology*, 318–21.

atonement, or relegating the core claim to some secondary status, sub-stituting some more fundamental notion that performs the explanatory heavy lifting with regard to the mechanism of atonement. This, I think, is one way of understanding Tanner's approach in her vicarious human-ity account. It is different from the first strategy in that it does not drive a wedge between ransom and victory but makes ransom and victory two motifs that belong to some more fundamental understanding of Christ's work.

The question is, are any of these strategies successful? As to the first, it should already be clear this is not a ransom view at all, but a distinct account of Christ's work that retains some of the trappings of the ransom account, but where victory is the dominant motif. For this reason, it can be discounted. The second strategy does not yield a distinct ransom model of atonement.[31] The instances of the third and fourth strategies we have considered are also incomplete, though for different reasons. Although they assimilate ransom to some larger model, or relegate it to some sec-ondary status in a model that has a more fundamental core claim about the mechanism of atonement, these larger wholes are still insufficient as complete accounts of atonement. For neither Boersma nor Tanner pro-vide their readers with a clear mechanism of atonement even when they augment ransom with additional notions (as in the case of Boersma), or displace it, making some other, related understanding of atonement more conceptually fundamental (as with Tanner). Nevertheless, the direction in which the strategies of Boersma and Tanner point is, I suggest, the right one. The way to understand ransom is not as an atonement model as such, let alone an atonement doctrine, but as an atonement motif. To this I would add the following: Ransom is a motif that pertains to one *consequence* of atonement—namely, the victory of Christ over sin. It is not a motif about the nature of the atonement per se, but about its upshot. In the next section we shall set out one way of understanding ransom in this manner.

---

31. One recent attempt to provide a ransom model can be seen in the work of open theist and evangelical theologian Gregory Boyd. He says that "the Christus Victor model was, in various forms, the dominant model for the first millennium of church history" ("Christus Victor View," 46). We have seen that there is good reason to doubt this claim about the his-tory of the doctrine. In any case, Boyd is no clearer on the mechanism of atonement than other defenders of his view, as his fellow contributor Thomas Schreiner points out. See Boyd, "Christus Victor View," 52.

Ransom as Victory Motif

Recall that the core claim of the ransom view is something like the following:

> Christ's work of redemption is fundamentally about him buying back human beings from the powers of sin, death, and the devil. His work is a ransom price that is paid to these powers in order that some number of fallen humanity may be redeemed from destruction and brought to salvation.

There is a significant problem with the core claim as it stands, having to do with *the reification of powers to whom Christ's ransom is paid*. It is not clear to me how sin and death are powers to which a ransom should be paid for the release of human beings. Nor is it clear to me why the devil should be paid a ransom for the release of human beings. True, Scripture speaks of human bondage to sin, of death as the wages of sin, and of the devil as the tempter. All three are spoken of (as we saw N. T. Wright affirming earlier) in semi-personal terms in the biblical record, as "powers and principalities." Whatever one makes of this (and, to be frank, I do not know what to make of it), what seems to me to be the most fundamental problem with the core claim is that it says ransom is paid to these powers in Christ's work of redemption. It is not at all clear to me how Christ's work could be a ransom that is paid to such powers, or even how such powers might be said to be "paid off" by means of Christ's work, beyond some sort of poetic or rhetorical claim similar to the idea that religion is the opiate of the masses.

More problematic, perhaps: How does paying a ransom to sin, death, and the devil produce reconciliation with God? I don't think sin and death *are* entities with whom one can enter into a transaction. Sin is a "want of conformity unto, or transgression of, the law of God" (thus the Westminster Shorter Catechism, answer to question 14). This is not a power in the sense of some semi-personal principality but, rather, a moral state; and one can hardly enter into transactions with moral states, because moral states aren't agents. Similar considerations apply to death, which is just the cessation of the life of an organism, or body. One cannot enter into transactions with the absence of bodily life. That is meaningless. As to the devil, a very foolish person might enter into transactions with him, but why would God do so? And what sound theological reason is there for thinking that human beings sold themselves into slavery to the devil upon commission of original sin, so that they must be bought back from him at such a terrible price? This, it seems to me, is pure sophistry.[32] God does not transact with the devil for human salvation. For as Anselm made plain in *Cur Deus Homo* I.7, both fallen humans and the devil belong to God:

> But since in fact neither the devil nor human beings belong to anyone other than God or stand outside God's power, on what grounds was God obligated to do anything with his own, about his own, or in his own, other than to punish his own slave who had persuaded a fellow slave to abandon their common master and transfer allegiance to him, a traitor harboring a fugitive, a thief who received a thief along with what he had stolen from his master? For both of them were thieves, since at one thief's persuasion the other thief stole himself from his master.[33]

But perhaps we can demythologize the core claim, denuding it of reference to powers to whom Christ pays a ransom.[34] Call this *the demythologized core claim*:

> Christ's work of redemption can be pictured as him buying back human beings subject to sin and death. It is like a ransom price that is paid out in order that some number of fallen humanity may be redeemed from destruction and brought to salvation.

But once we exchange the core claim for the demythologized core claim, it becomes clear why ransom is no more than an atonement motif. It provides no mechanism for atonement; its language is metaphorical, comparative, unfitted to giving us a clear basis for a doctrine of atonement. However, it may be regarded as an auxiliary claim about the outcome of atonement. The upshot of Christ's work is indeed the release of human beings subject

---

32. Objection: 1 John 3:8 says, "Everyone who commits sin is a child of the devil; for the devil has been sinning from the beginning. The Son of God was revealed for this purpose, to destroy the works of the devil." Response: This does not mean literally that human sinners belong to the devil but, rather, that human sinners are associated with the devil, who is a habitual sinner, whose works of sin Christ has come to destroy. But this is consistent with what is stated above.

33. Anselm, *Cur Deus Homo* I.7, in *Anselm: Basic Writings*, 251.

34. Macquarrie also attempts a demythologized version of the ransom account, but his involves importing elements of sacrifice and Christ's prophetic office into what I am calling the "core claim," thus making ransom one element in a larger whole. See *Principles of Christian Theology*, 318–21.

to sin and death. When viewed in these terms his work is a ransom price of sorts: it is the price requisite to bring about human reconciliation, paid by Christ. He is our substitute; he represents us in atonement. But it is not a ransom in the sense that it really is a work equivalent in value to the price fixed for the ransom of some number of fallen humanity from another power, whether sin, death, the devil, or God. Hence, when we read in Mark 10:45 that "the Son of Man came not to be served but to serve, and to give his life a ransom for many," or in Colossians that "he has rescued us from the power of darkness and transferred us into the kingdom of his beloved Son " (1:13) and that "he disarmed the rulers and authorities and made a public example of them, triumphing over them in [the cross]" (2:15), I presume we should understand such passages as conveying a picture of Christ's work. The picture is this: in his life, death, and resurrection Christ somehow brings about human reconciliation with God, buying us back, as it were, at the great price of his own life in an act of vicarious supererogation.[35]

The Dogmatic Limitations of Ransom

In this chapter I have argued that ransom is an atonement motif, not a model or doctrine of atonement. Thus, Aulén was right to say it was not a historic *doctrine* of atonement, but wrong to think that more work on the motif would produce a complete model in due course. The main reason for this is that ransom does not provide a distinct mechanism for atonement. It is merely a motif. What is more, it is a motif about the upshot of Christ's work, not about its nature. Finally, I am in agreement with critics of ransom who argue that it is not, as is often claimed, *the* patristic doctrine, or *the most common* patristic view of Christ's work. It is an ancillary motif in a number of patristic accounts. These writers did not have carefully worked out accounts of the atonement. What is more, there are several other atonement themes in patristic theology, including

---

35. Objection: What of Heb. 2:14–15? It states, "Since, therefore, the children share flesh and blood, he himself [i.e., Christ] likewise shared the same things, so that through death he might destroy the one who has the power of death, that is, the devil, and free those who all their lives were held in slavery by the fear of death." Response: I take this to be a reference to the devil's role as the agent through whom sin is supposed to have entered the creation in the primeval prologue of Genesis 1–3. It would be odd to think he has some sort of devolved responsibility for death when Christ declares that he has the keys to Death and Hades in Rev. 1:18.

the Irenaean recapitulation view beloved of Boersma and the notion of vicarious humanity that has recently been developed by theologians like T. F. Torrance and Kathryn Tanner. It may be that these themes do provide the elements of a distinct doctrine of atonement. But if they do, it is not the ransom view, which was only ever an idea in search of a model of atonement.

5

Satisfaction Guaranteed

In this chapter we will consider the doctrine of satisfaction. It is arguably one of the most important and influential treatments of atonement. The version of the doctrine made famous by Anselm of Canterbury (AD 1033–1109) in his treatise *Cur Deus Homo*[1] (Why the God-Man)
represents the first truly systematic account of the atonement in the history
of theology. In subsequent medieval theology it was taken up by Thomas
Aquinas, among others, who amended the doctrine in important respects,
as we shall see. In time, it also became arguably the most important influence on the Reformation doctrine of the atonement that developed into
penal substitution.

It is tempting, in giving an account of satisfaction, to reiterate the structure of Anselm's argument before considering how Aquinas amended it.[2]
But there are good reasons for resisting this temptation. For one thing, I

---

1. All citations to Anselm's works in English given in this chapter are from *Anselm: Basic
Writings*. Where relevant, I have also supplied references to *S. Anselmi Cantuariensis Archi-
episcopi Opera Omnia*, henceforth given as *Opera Omnia*, followed by volume number and
page reference.
2. I have offered a short account of Anselm's doctrine in *Approaching the Atonement*, chap. 4.
A classic work on Anselm's account of atonement is McIntyre, *St. Anselm and His Critics*.
More recent treatments can be found in Brown, "Anselm on Atonement," and Sonderegger,
"Anselmian Atonement."

am interested primarily in the *theological form* or shape of the doctrine, and in providing as strong a version of it as I can, rather than in Anselm exegesis. Although Anselm's account is a remarkable and ingenious piece of theology, rich in detail and argument, it has some well-known drawbacks. It is also structured in a way that might helpfully be changed in order to get at the central claims of the doctrine without his conceit of writing as if Christ had never become incarnate, and then attempting to provide conditions for atonement that (unsurprisingly) yield the claim that only one who is both fully human and fully divine would be able to provide reconciliation between God and fallen humanity.[3]

So, in this chapter, rather than rehearsing Anselm and Aquinas, we shall provide *Anselmian* and *Thomistic* versions of satisfaction that draw on these historic discussions, though they are distinct from them.[4] With these versions of the doctrine in place we will then turn to criticisms of the Anselmian doctrine, paying particular attention to the recent objections raised by Eleonore Stump in her magisterial study, *Atonement*. I shall argue that the Anselmian can meet the objections raised by Stump. In fact, it seems to me that, with certain important qualifications, the doctrine of satisfaction provides us with a defensible doctrine of atonement. Even if we think that the mechanism of atonement at its heart needs some augmentation or finessing (as I will argue), its central claim about the nature of atonement as satisfaction is, it seems to me, a compelling theological insight that should be taken very seriously by contemporary theologians in search of a theology of atonement.[5]

3. I refer to Anselm's famous claim at the outset of *Cur Deus Homo* to approach the topic "*remoto Christo*" (leaving Christ out of the picture, as if nothing concerning him had ever taken place). *Cur Deus Homo*, preface, 238. Cf. *Opera Omnia* 2:42.

4. I adopt these two terms of art with a nod to Eleonore Stump, who does something similar in the first three chapters of *Atonement*. Similarly, Katherine Sonderegger distinguishes between the "historical" Anselm and the "theological" Anselm as a means of distancing her account from that of Anselm himself. See Sonderegger, "Anselmian Atonement."

5. This may come as a surprise to some readers given that satisfaction is the whipping boy of much contemporary atonement theology. But it seems to me that this is a mistake, as I hope will become clear as we go on. I rehearse standard objections to Anselm's doctrine, which are often not very good, in *Approaching the Atonement*, chap. 4. I will not be repeating those objections here. Stump's worries are much more sophisticated than the standard ones. For a recent constructive attempt to restate and develop an Anselmian account of atonement that raises some important conceptual issues, see Farris and Hamilton, "Logic of Reparative Substitution."

Anselmian Satisfaction

The Anselmian and Thomistic versions of the doctrine have a similar conceptual shape, though with some important differences. In order to get as clear a picture of these similarities and differences as possible, I shall set out the theological form of each version of the doctrine in numbered sentences and then comment on these sentences as a means of explaining their importance in the structure of the argument for each of the two views.

The central claim of any doctrine of satisfaction is that Christ's act of atonement is a supererogatory act that is voluntarily offered as a gift to God instead of the punishment of the sinner. In other words, fundamentally, satisfaction is an act of *compensation* or *reparation*. Just as one might compensate someone who has had something precious stolen by a close relative with some appropriate act of reparation, so in the satisfaction account of atonement Christ provides an act of compensation to God the Father in place of the punishment due for human sin and dereliction.

With this in mind, here is an outline of the Anselmian version of the argument:

1. God is essentially just.
2. Divine distributive justice is retributive in nature.
3. Sin is heinous; it derogates from God's honor.
4. The penalty for sin must be sufficient requital for human sin.
5. The penalty for sin may be met in one of two ways: either the punishment of sin or some appropriate supererogatory act of sufficient value that it may be accepted as a satisfaction for human sin.
6. The atonement is hypothetically necessary for satisfaction. God cannot forgive sin independent of satisfaction.
7. The atonement "restores" divine honor; it is sufficient requital for human sin.
8. The benefits of atonement are appropriated by means of the sacramental life of the church.

Let me now offer some remarks on each of these sentences. The first two of these are that God is essentially just and that divine distributive justice is retributive in nature. The claim that God is essentially just is a commonplace in the Christian tradition, so I shall simply assume it, without argument, in what follows. Essential justice means that God is just in his very nature. Indeed, for Anselm, God is Justice itself—the very form of justice, if you will—since Anselm thinks God does not merely exemplify justice but, being metaphysically simple, is identical with Justice (see *Monologion* 17; *Proslogion* 9–12, 18–19). The particularities of divine simplicity need not concern us here, however. It is sufficient for our purposes to claim simply that God is essentially just without offering further explanation of the manner in which God is said to be essentially just. The Anselmian, like the historical Anselm, presumes that the aspect of divine justice that is distributive (having to do with punishments and rewards) is retributive in nature (*Cur Deus Homo* I.12). In fact, Anselm thinks that there is a right ordering of justice to punishment that depends on the notion of recompense. He writes, "Forgiving sin . . . is the same as not punishing it. But to order sin in the right way when no recompense [satisfaction] is made *just is* to punish sin [lit. is nothing but to punish sin]. So if sin is not punished, it is left unordered."[6] And God cannot tolerate disorder in the creation. In legal theory there are different ways one can construe retributivism, including versions that mash together aspects of retribution with other justifications for punishment.[7] One thoroughgoing version of this doctrine is what we might call *pure retributivism*. It can be characterized as follows:

> **Pure Retributivism:** A nonconsequentialist approach to the justification of punishment that is backward-looking—that is, concerned with the sinful act and its history. At the heart of this view is the notion of *desert*. Usually such views include a principle of responsibility (calibrating *mens rea* to *actus reus*), a principle of proportionality (that ensures the relative gravity of punishment is proportionate to the moral gravity of the offense), and

6. "Sic dimittere peccatum non est aliud quam non punire. Et quoniam recte ordinare peccatum sine satisfactione non est nisi punire: si non punitur, inordinatum dimittitur" (Anselm, *Cur Deus Homo* I.12, in *Opera Omnia* 2:69). Stump thinks that Anselm's view is that God forgives sin once satisfaction is offered, or even that satisfaction is the means by which sin may be forgiven. But that does not seem to be Anselm's view. Anselm thinks that satisfaction provides the requisite compensation for humans to be reconciled with God but not that this is a means to forgiveness, since forgiveness involves foregoing punishment or satisfaction. See, e.g., Stump, *Atonement*, 56, 64.

7. For a helpful recent overview of the literature in legal theory, see Brooks, *Punishment: A Critical Introduction*. The literature in punishment theory is large and complex. My remarks here distill some of the salient aspects of this literature, which I tackled in more detail in "Just Desert?"

a principle of just requital (that ensures that the intentional harsh treatment endured for a criminal act voluntarily undertaken by the offender is morally good).

Of course, Anselm himself does not explicitly endorse this sophisticated version of retributivism in his work. But it is this sort of view that we shall presume in the Anselmian account—which is not, I think, inconsistent with the retributivist outlook of Anselm himself. Thus, the Anselmian maintains that God is just by nature and that the aspect of this justice that pertains to the distribution of rewards and punishments is calibrated to something like pure retributivism. It is the past sinful action of the individual that is the focus of attention, and it is presumed that the individual is a moral agent who is responsible, and therefore culpable, for the sinful acts she or he commits, and as such *deserving* of punishment. This leads us to consider in more detail the problem to which atonement is the solution. For Anselm and the Anselmian, the problem is human sin.

The third statement of the Anselmian doctrine of satisfaction addresses this matter. It states that sin is heinous and derogates from God's honor. Much ink has been spilt in attempting to describe and excoriate the historical Anselm's idea that it is divine honor that is at the heart of the doctrine of satisfaction. Anselm remarks, "If someone violates another's honor, it is not enough for him to pay back that honor if he does not also offer something satisfactory to the one he has dishonored, as compensation for the harm he caused by dishonoring him." Moreover, "all those who sin ought to repay God the honor they have stolen from him; and this is the recompense that every sinner ought to make to God."[8] The objection to this is that if God's honor is infringed by human actions so that it is derogated or denigrated by human sin, this suggests that human action can affect God. Yet God is impassible. Even if we do not think God is impassible, the idea that human sin could affect God, causing some sort of affront, paints God in the colors of a medieval feudal tyrant, which is hardly the God of Abraham, Isaac, and Jacob.

8. "Sicut enim qui laedit salutem alterius, non sufficit si salutem restituit, nisi pro illata doloris iniuria recompenset aliquid: ita qui honorem alicuius violat non sufficit honorem reddere, si non secundum exhonorationis factam molestiam aliquid, quod placeat illi quem exhonoravit, restituit. . . . Sic ergo debet omnis qui peccat, honorem deo quem rapuit solvere; et haec est satisfactio, quam omnis peccator deo debet facere" (Anselm *Cur Deus Homo* I.11, in *Opera Omnia* 2:68).

But Anselm is clear that "nothing can be added to God's honor or taken away from it, as far as God is concerned. For God himself is his own incorruptible and utterly immutable honor" (*Cur Deus Homo* I.15). The dishonor to God brought about through sin is, in fact, a way of speaking about a derogation *in what the human agent wills*. It is a dishonor to God in the sense that it fails to measure up to the sort of act of obedience that we owe to God. But it does no damage to God, or change God in any way. This is a common trope in Anselm's thought. He thinks that any failure of will is a failure to measure up to the *ratio* or standard that God has ordained.[9] Hence, derogation is the right way to think about the kind of act in view here: it fails to meet a standard, and in that sense it "dishonors" God. But it does not damage or affect God in any way.

Anselm seems to think that the gravity of sin is calibrated to the kind of being against whom the sin is committed. This amounts to a kind of *status principle* that informs his account of sin.[10] But this way of thinking presumes a chain of being that has fallen out of favor in modern philosophy and theology. We don't usually think that a human has greater worth than, say, a dog just by virtue of the fact that the human is an instance of a particular biological kind. However, all the Anselmian needs to motivate the claim that sin is heinous is the idea that sin committed against the Creator has a certain seriousness distinct from sin against other creatures because we owe all that we are to our Creator. Thus, a sin against the Creator is a sin that is truly wicked; it is heinous. Yet, on the face of it, not all sin is committed against God in the sense that it is *directed toward God*. Sinning against another creature is not always obviously a sin against God in this way. If I slap my grandmother, my sin is directed against her. She is the one I intend to harm, not God. It may be that in sinning against my grandmother I also sin against God indirectly by virtue of sinning against one of God's creatures, the bearer of the divine image. Nevertheless, this is not to sin against God, strictly speaking, but to sin in such a way that it

9. As is well known, Anselm defines freedom of choice as "the power to preserve rectitude of will for the sake of rectitude itself" (*On Freedom of Choice*, chap. 3, 151). Cf. "Ergo quoniam omnis libertas est potestas, illa libertas arbitrii est potestas servandi rectitudinem voluntatis propter ipsam rectitudinem" (*Opera Omnia* 1:212). In other words, it is the power to measure up to rectitude or a standard of right choice for the sake of acting in a manner consistent with this divinely ordained standard. Thus, on Anselm's way of thinking, the truly free person is the one who always acts in a manner consistent with the divine will.

10. A point made by Kvanvig, *Problem of Hell*, chap. 1.

is also indirectly an affront to God—a "dishonoring" of God. There are sins that are directed at God, such as blasphemy, where God is the direct object. But, plausibly, most sins are not directed against God in this way and are not intended to harm God but, rather, other creatures.[11] In which case, the idea that all sin against God generates a demerit that is heinous pertains to a delimited number of sins, like blasphemy—the sort of sins that Roman Catholic theology deems *mortal* because they are said to endanger one's soul.

Now, it is not clear to me that *all* sin is directed against God, and it is not clear to me that the heinousness of sin should be calibrated to the worth, dignity, or honor of the person against whom one sins. Slapping one's grandmother is a terrible thing to do, and not less terrible than slapping the Queen just because one's grandmother is a private citizen rather than the monarch of the realm. Normally, we would think that slapping one's grandmother and slapping the Queen are both wicked because it is wrong to act in such an unprovoked and violent manner to another person, whatever their station in life. Nevertheless, it is also true to say that sinning against the monarch has legal consequences that may be more serious than those accompanying the slapping of one's grandmother because of the political implications of acting violently toward a prince to whom one owes fealty. But clearly that is not the same as claiming that, merely by virtue of her legal and constitutional status, slapping the Queen is more serious than slapping one's grandmother. Rather, it is to say that, by virtue of her status, slapping the Queen has more serious legal and political consequences than slapping one's grandmother. But clearly, the legal implications of an act are not the same as its moral status.[12]

Nevertheless, unlike Anselm himself, the Anselmian need not wade into these troubled waters. Instead, the Anselmian may decouple the claim

11. It may be worth underlining the point made earlier that sin directed at God with the intention of harming God does not imply commitment to the claim that creaturely acts *can* harm God. But one can aim at harming a person without actually being capable of causing harm to the person in question—e.g., a small, angry child attempting to make physical contact with an Olympian wrestler.

12. At least, they are conceptually distinct. But often they are in fact distinct as well. Some legal theorists in the positivist tradition, such as H. L. A. Hart, have argued that normative moral questions should be kept distinct from legal questions, which are descriptive not normative in nature. In which case, there is yet another sense in which the moral and legal dimensions of an act are distinct, provided one subscribes to the version of positivism in view. See Hart, "Positivism and the Separation of Law and Morals."

about heinousness from the question of the status principle and calibrate it instead to the moral law of God. This is tantamount to making heinousness primarily a matter of contravening divine law rather than impugning the status of Godself. Then, the heinousness of sin may simply be a function of the fact that it is an act that is in want of conformity unto, or transgresses, the law of God (to adapt the language of the answer to question 14 of the Westminster Shorter Catechism).[13] Just as when someone breaks the law of a particular human jurisdiction they may become liable to some penalty or punishment (depending on the nature of the crime committed), so also it may be that transgressing the law of God makes a person liable for a penalty or punishment. The problem is, in cases of mundane crimes, penalties or punishments are calibrated to the sort of crime committed, for not all crimes are heinous. The same is not true of sins on Anselm's view because it seems that for him all sin, however apparently trivial, generates an infinite demerit on the basis that they are committed against a being of infinite worth and dignity. In other words, he has particular reasons for calibrating the heinousness of sin to the status principle, reasons to do with his claims about derogating from divine honor. But this way of thinking has strange and counterintuitive consequences. For instance, Anselm seems to think that all sin, whatever its nature, generates an infinite demerit because it is committed against a being of infinite worth and honor. But if all sin generates an infinite demerit, then it seems that all sin is on par with respect to moral consequences (for all sin is infinitely demeritorious). That seems odd. The person who bears false testimony in a case by fabricating an alibi and the person who commits murder are not, we think, guilty of committing crimes or sins that are equally morally serious. For this reason penalties for bearing false witness are different from the punishment applied for murder.

Perhaps the Anselmian can prescind from judgment about this matter, allowing merely that the heinousness of sin represents a kind of *moral threshold* beyond which any moral act generates the kind of demerit that

---

13. Anselm himself speaks of sin rather differently as "nothing other than failing to pay back what one owes to God" (*Cur Deus Homo* I.11). Elsewhere, in his work *On the Virginal Conception and Original Sin*, he makes it clear that he locates sin in the will, which sins as a consequence of the privation of original justice. His idea in *Cur Deus Homo* is that sin is a debt owed to God and recompensed through punishment or satisfaction. I am suggesting that the Anselmian takes the view that sin is a particular kind of debt, one generated by transgressing God's moral law.

places the individual in a state of moral deficit that requires some act of atonement. The thought is that the moral seriousness of *any* sin, however apparently trivial or serious, is sufficient that it crosses the threshold of heinousness. And the reason for this is that any sin is a want of conformity unto, or transgression of, the moral law of God. In other words, just in virtue of committing some act that is in want of conformity to or transgresses the law of God, the sinner has committed an act that is heinous in the relevant sense. It may be that, in addition to this, some sins are more morally serious than others, requiring more serious penalties or punishments. But this is consistent with the idea that all sin crosses this threshold of seriousness or heinousness because all sin is wicked. To illustrate the point, compare the idea that two people are both at least six feet tall, though one is six and a half feet, and the other is just over six feet. They both cross the six-foot threshold, though one is still much taller than the other. Call this *the threshold account of the heinousness of sin.*

Some will balk at the idea that any sin, however apparently trivial, turns out to be heinous on this threshold account. But it is built into the Anselmian view that all sin is heinous. As we have seen, Anselm himself thinks that all sin is against a being of infinite worth and honor and as a consequence generates an infinite demerit. So Anselm's view is even stronger than this Anselmian claim about heinousness. Yet, behind this claim about the seriousness of sin in Anselm's work is the intuition that any act that falls under the description of sin is an act that is morally serious—indeed, we might say, of *mortal* seriousness. This is all that the Anselmian argument I have been outlining here requires. Setting to one side the status principle and the idea that all sin is directed against God, the Anselmian may still borrow the central insight of Anselm himself, which is that all sin is heinous—not necessarily because it is directly committed against a being of infinite worth and honor, but because it transgresses a divine command.

Now, this threshold account of heinousness is attractive in part because it doesn't require the Anselmian to be drawn into complex and potentially fraught moral discussion about the calibration of the heinousness of sin to some sort of status principle. But it does have a further implication that is potentially problematic and must be addressed. This is that all sin in crossing the heinousness threshold warrants an everlasting punishment (in hell). Why would, say, the person bearing false witness be liable to a penalty or punishment that is, like that of the murderer, everlasting in nature because their sin generates an infinite demerit? Even if the two individuals endure a different kind of punishment in any given moment at which they are receiving punishment for their sin, it is difficult to see how the disvalue or harsh treatment of a given punishment is really different from the disvalue or harsh treatment of another punishment if, in the final analysis, both suffer everlastingly. It is true to say at a given moment they may suffer differently. But that difference is effaced once the duration of punishment is without end—being, in effect, infinite.[14]

Here too, the Anselmian might simply avoid these complications about the difference between infinite and equal punishments by claiming the following two things. First, that all sin, however apparently trivial, is sufficiently serious to meet the threshold of heinousness because it is a want of conformity unto, or transgression of, the law of God. And second, that whatever penalty or punishment is warranted for a given sin (and penalties or punishments may differ in particular cases[15]), its heinousness is what is theologically salient for the purposes of atonement. In other words, because all sin is heinous, all sin places the sinner in a state such that some further significant act is required in order to deal with its moral consequences. Specifically, morally heinous acts (i.e., sins) require punishment in the person of the agent or else some act of satisfaction to atone for them.[16] Note that on this way of construing the threshold account of sin's heinousness, no specific period of punishment is stipulated. It may be that all sin is worthy of an everlasting punishment by virtue of meeting the threshold of heinousness. But it may be that it is merely that all sin places the sinner in the morally serious condition of being liable for

14. This point is argued for by Kvanvig in *Problem of Hell*, chap. 1. The idea is that if punishment in hell is *infinite*, then any difference of punishment at a given moment is ultimately effaced. Compare a situation in which there are two people suffering different punishments at a given moment, enduring different levels of suffering as a consequence. If the punishment were of finite duration, then punishments would entail different levels of suffering. But once the punishment is infinite, this difference disappears. In short, an infinite punishment entails an equal punishment overall.

15. Compare the historic theological distinction between *poena sensus* and *poena damna*. The first of these is the punishment of the senses—that is, the particular form a given punishment takes in hell. The second is the damnable aspect of punishment—that is, that the person being punished in hell is punished everlastingly.

16. A further possibility is that God forgives human sin, setting punishment or satisfaction to one side. But this is no part of the Anselmian doctrine. We will return to this presently when considering the Thomistic account of satisfaction.

punishment by God, who has commanded that the punishment of sin is death and exclusion from the divine presence. This leaves open-ended the question of the duration as well as the nature of the punishment served, on analogy with the way in which felonies may be subject to significant punishment even though the precise terms of that punishment (its nature and duration) may differ depending on variables like the circumstances and nature of the crime committed.

Let us take stock. In contrast to the view of Anselm, the Anselmian account provides the following justification for the claim that sin is heinous (with due thanks to the framers of the Westminster Shorter Catechism): all sin is a want of conformity unto, or transgression of, the moral law of God. Because all sin is transgressive in this sense—that is, in the sense that it transgresses *the moral law of God*—all sin meets a threshold of heinousness. And for such action human beings are normally liable for punishment because they are culpable.[17] God has commanded that the punishment of sin is death and exclusion from the divine presence (e.g., Rom. 5:8–10; 6:23). So all sinners are liable to death and exclusion from God's presence unless some suitable satisfaction is offered. In this Anselmian version of the argument and in keeping with Anselm's view, it is presumed that given God's essentially just nature sin *must* be punished, not merely that it *may* be punished. God cannot set to one side the demands of justice in retribution in order to forgive sin because—so the thought goes—this would be tantamount to God acting contrary to the character or nature of God, which is metaphysically impossible. This is an important difference between the Anselmian and Thomistic variations of the argument for satisfaction, as we shall see.

We come to the fourth statement. This is that the penalty for sin must be sufficient requital for sin. There must be a proportionality between the moral seriousness of the offence itself and the punishment or penalty it incurs. Such proportionality is what brings about appropriate requital. Not all acts that bear the marks of a retributive justification have this notion of requital baked into them. For instance, acts of revenge are not

17. The use of "normally" in this sentence does the work of a *ceteris paribus* clause. That is, *other things being equal*, human transgressions are normally acts for which we are culpable. Obviously, there are limit cases that represent potential exceptions to this, such as those who may act transgressively when they are mentally impaired or disturbed and therefore do not have the theological equivalent to *mens rea*.

necessarily proportionate. Though they may bring about requital of a certain kind, it is not (or not necessarily) appropriate or proportionate. This is why acts of revenge are usually extra-judicial acts. They fail to meet the proportionality requirement of the sort of retributivism we encountered in pure retributivism. However, this is a constituent of the Anselmian view.

According to the fifth statement, the penalty for sin may be met in one of two ways: either the punishment of sin or some act of supererogation of sufficient value that it may be accepted as a satisfaction for sin. Punishment is what we might call the default option. That is, because of the heinousness of human sin, fallen human beings are liable for punishment. They are culpable, and they deserve to be punished as a consequence.[18] Punishment takes the form of exclusion from God's presence everlastingly (Rom. 6:23). However, some suitable act of supererogation may be offered instead of punishment as a satisfaction. By an act of supererogation, I mean an act that is above and beyond the call of duty. The idea is something like this: Fallen human beings are not in a position to offer satisfaction for their own sin because they are already sinners in need of redemption. They owe all they have and all they are to God, as Anselm puts it (*Cur Deus Homo* I.11). So Christ's atonement is a means by which appropriate compensation can be offered to God (by God) on behalf of fallen humanity. Because Christ is a divine person with a sinless human nature, he is able to act vicariously on behalf of other human beings as a human being. And because he is a *divine* person with a human nature, he is able to provide an atonement of sufficient value that it can meet the demerit of human sin and dereliction. Anselm goes further than this, arguing that the atonement of the God-human is of infinite value because the action of a divine person has infinite value (*Cur Deus Homo* II.14). The Anselmian only requires the more modest axiological claim that Christ's work is of sufficient value to meet and balance out the disvalue of human sin, without necessarily spelling out the nature of this dis-

18. Objection: If all fallen human beings are punishable, then what of our limit cases mentioned earlier? What of those fallen human beings who are not (obviously) moral agents—e.g., children before the age of reason or those who are incapable of moral action (such as the severely mentally impaired)? Are they also punishable, even though they lack the theological analog to *mens rea*? Response: They may be excluded from God's presence because they bear original sin even if they are not moral agents or not culpable for actual sins. This is analogous to someone who bears a communicable disease and who is quarantined as a consequence. I discuss this in more detail in chapter 7, "Sin and Salvation."

value.[19] Because Christ's act is not required of him, being a voluntary act of atonement (*Cur Deus Homo* II.10), and because it is not done out of duty or obligation, being an act of grace and mercy, he may use the merit it generates to compensate for human sin. This is satisfaction.

The sixth statement maintains that atonement is hypothetically necessary for satisfaction. God cannot forgive sin independent of satisfaction. Now, we have already noted that on the Anselmian view, God cannot forgive sin independent of satisfaction. But we must be careful to circumscribe the manner in which it is said that God *cannot* forgive sin independent of satisfaction. In chapter 2 I argued that the necessity in question is not metaphysical necessity but a kind of consequential necessity—specifically, a kind of *necessitas ex suppositione* ("necessity on account of the supposition"). The supposition here is that for any world God chooses to create, that world must be one that is consistent with the divine nature. God cannot act against Godself, so to speak. But that is not much of a constraint; we all must act in a manner consistent with the nature we possess. Given that God is essentially just, any world God creates will be one in which the justice of God is exercised and displayed appropriately, though there may be different ways in which that may be done that are world-indexed—that is, particular to a given world. Suppose we grant this supposition. Then, the world God actually creates—that is, *this* world—must be one that reflects God's justice. This means that when it comes to the matter of the heinousness of human sin, it must be that God either punishes sin or accepts some satisfaction for sin. God cannot forgive sin if by *forgive* we mean setting the debt of sin to one side. So, given that any world God creates will be a world in which God's justice is exercised, and given that God creates this world, this world is one in which God's justice must be exercised. We have already seen that on the Anselmian view, divine distributive justice is essentially retributive. Thus, in creating this world God's justice must be exercised, and in the case of the heinousness of sin, God's retributive justice must be exercised in punishment or its requirements met by means of some suitable act of satisfaction. In this way, the atonement is said to be hypothetically necessary—that is, necessary assuming certain conditions about the divine nature and divine justice and its exercise in any world God creates.

19. Although, as I explained in chapter 1, there are good reasons for thinking that Christ's work is indeed of infinite value. My point here is just that such a claim is not required for the Anselmian view to go through.

The seventh statement is that atonement "restores" divine honor; it is sufficient requital for human sin. Since God is immutable and impassible, no creaturely act may in fact damage or otherwise affect God on the Anselmian view. Nevertheless, atonement may restore divine honor in as much as it may restore what is derogated from God in the dereliction of human sin. This is the compensatory aspect of satisfaction at work: Christ's death generates a supererogatory merit that may be used as compensation for the dishonor to God brought about by human dereliction. God does not *need* this compensation. But because God is essentially just, there must be some act of compensation of sufficient value to meet the demerit of human sin in order to balance off the demerit of sin. This is what Christ's atonement provides.[20] And it is the mechanism at the heart of the satisfaction doctrine.

The eighth and final statement in this Anselmian version of satisfaction is that the benefits of Christ's atonement are appropriated by means of the sacramental life of the church. One of the puzzles of Anselm's doctrine of atonement is that he does not really connect the atoning act of satisfaction to the appropriation of the benefits of that act in the person of the sinner. He leaves his readers with a kind of explanatory gap, or lacuna, regarding the appropriation of Christ's benefits. The reader who finishes reading *Cur Deus Homo* is left wanting to know, "How may I appropriate the benefits provided by Christ's satisfaction?" Filling in this lacuna in Anselm's doctrine is not terribly difficult. Presumably, for a Benedictine monk like Anselm, the answer is obvious: One avails oneself of the benefits of Christ's passion by means of the seven sacraments of the church, and especially, baptism (whereupon the child is regenerated), penance (where a person is shriven of the guilt associated with actual sin), and the Eucharist (where the believer may encounter and be nourished by the body of Christ, which is corporeally and sacrificially present). For many, indeed, the majority of Christians who are either Roman Catholic or Eastern Orthodox, this *sacramental response* will suffice as an answer to the existential question about appropriation. For Protestants, the sacramental response is rather more problematic. But a Protestant variation of the Anselmian doctrine can be had fairly easily, the relevant changes having been made. Like Roman Catholic and Eastern Orthodox Christians, Protestants will

---

20. The reader will recall the discussion about the value of the atonement in chapter 2. I am presuming the results of that discussion here.

want to say that the benefits of Christ's reconciling work in atonement are appropriated by faith through the secret work of the Spirit (a matter to which we shall return in chapter 9). But unlike their Roman Catholic and Eastern Orthodox confreres, Protestants normally conceive of this as an action that obtains independent of particular sacramental means. It is simply an occasional spiritual work brought about immediately in the life of the believer by means of the secret work of the Holy Spirit uniting the believer to Christ. This may be fructified sacramentally in baptism and Eucharist. But it is not (or at least, is not *normally* thought to be) dependent on them. Rather, it is principally an immediate work of God associated with the Third Person of the Trinity within the life of the believer—what we might call *the pneumatic response* to the lacuna in Anselm's argument.

Whichever variation on an Anselmian theme one takes with respect to the eighth sentence of the Anselmian view, whether sacramental or pneumatic, the requirement that Christ's work is appropriated by the believer can be met, and can include the sacramental life of the church, or some analog to this, as a component part.

Some may worry that the pneumatic response is not really a version of our eighth statement above—which was that "the benefits of atonement are appropriated by means of the sacramental life of the church"—but an alternative to it. In response to that sort of worry it is worth emphasizing that I have said the outward sacramental appropriation of Christ's benefits may form *part* of the answer to Anselm's appropriation lacuna for many Protestants. This is especially true of Protestants in the tradition of the Magisterial Reformation (such as Lutherans, the Reformed, and Anglicans). But the point is that the sacramental means of the church is not the primary site of the appropriation of Christ's saving benefits on this way of thinking. Instead, it is in the secret transformative work of the Spirit in the life of the believer that this work is done. For Protestants who eschew the traditions of the Magisterial Reformation and who are enamored of an Anselmian account of atonement (e.g., Anselmian Mennonites or Anselmian Pentecostals, supposing there are such persons), some revision to our eighth sentence will be in order. Even if that is so, I judge that this is not a serious theological difficulty because whatever we make of the eighth sentence and Anselm's appropriation lacuna, it is not a part of Anselm's doctrine, but a gap in explanation on his account that needs to be addressed.

Thomistic Satisfaction

Let us now turn to the Thomistic variation on the Anselmian version of satisfaction. This depends on the claim that God *may* (not *must*) punish sin. Rather than thinking that the exercise of divine retributive justice is inexorable, like the Anselmian, the Thomist thinks that it is *discretionary*, dependent on God's willing to act in a retributive manner. Here is an outline of the Thomistic version of the argument:

1. God is essentially just.
2. Divine distributive justice is retributive in nature.
3. Sin against God is heinous; it derogates from God's honor.
4. The penalty for sin must be sufficient requital for human sin.
5. *The penalty for sin may be met in one of three ways: the punishment of sin; some appropriate supererogatory act of sufficient value that it may be accepted as a satisfaction for sin; or the forgiveness of sin.*
6. *The atonement is conditionally sufficient for satisfaction. God may forgive sin independent of satisfaction, but God has independent moral reasons for providing satisfaction in Christ.*
7. The atonement "restores" divine honor; it is sufficient requital for human sin.
8. The benefits of atonement are appropriated by means of the sacramental life of the church.

I have set in italics the two sentences in this Thomistic version of satisfaction that differ from the Anselmian doctrine: sentences 5 and 6. Sentence 5 adds a third way in which the penalty for sin may be met—namely, forgiveness. We have seen that this is explicitly denied on the Anselmian version of the doctrine. The Thomistic version presumes that God may set aside the exercise of justice in favor of forgiveness without satisfaction. Rather like the parent who forgives the penitent child without punishment, God may in principle forgive the penitent sinner without satisfaction. However, God may have good moral reasons for serving punishment upon the sinner or for requiring satisfaction—reasons having to do with the moral seriousness of human sin. Thus, this third option of forgiveness may in fact be only a conceptual difference from the Anselmian position inasmuch as the Thomist grants that God does *in fact* punish sin or provide satisfaction.

It is just that *in principle* God may forgive sin without punishment or satisfaction. It is this distinction that is provided for in sentence 6.

This completes our treatment of the two versions of satisfaction. We may now turn to the recent critique of this sort of view in the work of Eleonore Stump.

Stump on Anselm on Satisfaction

As I said at the beginning of this chapter, there are a number of traditional objections to satisfaction, particularly in the version articulated by Anselm. I have tackled these elsewhere, and I will not rehearse these objections here.[21] Rather, I will focus on the recent treatment of the sort of doctrine espoused by Anselm in the magisterial work of Eleonore Stump. There are two reasons for this strategy. The first is that Stump's treatment of atonement is by far the most sophisticated account of the doctrine in a generation. Thus, it behooves us to engage it in a work like this one. Second, one of the important strategies of her book is to distance herself from what she thinks of as traditional Anselmian doctrines of atonement, shifting to a novel account of atonement that draws on (though it is not identical with) Thomistic themes. Thus, it is appropriate to engage her work at this juncture.[22]

We have seen that a central claim of Anselm's argument is that either sin must be punished in the person of the sinner or some satisfaction must be made on behalf of the sinner by someone else in order for God not to be dishonored by human sin. This is the Anselmian *mechanism* of atonement. By contrast, penal substitution is the doctrine according to which the atonement is brought about by means of the vicarious punishment of Christ—or at least, by means of Christ suffering the penal consequences of human sin. There is a clear difference in the mechanism envisaged in satisfaction and penal substitution, though both accounts trade on views about the satisfaction of divine justice. We have seen that in the former, Christ satisfies the debt owed to God by fallen human beings by generating

---

21. See Crisp, *Approaching the Atonement*, chap. 4.

22. Recent critical engagements with Stump's work that take issue with her reading of traditional atonement doctrines include Breiner, "Punishment and Satisfaction"; Craig, "Eleonore Stump's Critique"; Farrow, "Anselm and the Art of Theology"; and Thurow and Strabbing, "Entwining Thomistic and Anselmian Interpretations."

a merit of sufficient worth that may balance out the demerit of human sin. By contrast, in penal substitution Christ is actually *punished* in place of human beings, or he at least suffers the *penal consequences* for human sin that would be punishment if suffered by the sinner. In the punishment versions of penal substitution, Christ actually takes on human sin and guilt, unlike the Anselmian view. And in the penal consequences versions of penal substitution, Christ takes on what would constitute the harsh treatment of punishment were it meted out to deserving fallen human beings. In her introduction to *Atonement*, Stump says, "It is not hard to see the interpretations of the *at onement* given by Anselm, Luther, and Calvin as falling largely or entirely into the same kind of interpretation,"[23] a point that is reiterated later in the book where penal substitution is explicitly identified as a variant of the Anselmian doctrine.[24] But that can't be right. The mechanism of atonement envisaged in the Anselmian view and the one envisaged in the penal substitutionary views espoused by Luther and Calvin are incommensurate. Clearly, saying that Christ performs some act of supererogation that generates a merit that may be applied to human sin is not the same as saying Christ is punished in the place of sinners. Indeed, it would be odd to think that an act of supererogatory merit and an act of punishment are merely variants of the same mechanism of atonement, or that they represent the same kind of interpretation of the reconciling work of Christ. They do not.

In the first few chapters of her book Stump outlines what she takes to be some of the most significant drawbacks to the Anselmian view of atonement. The first is that God must punish sin; God cannot forgive it or set it to one side. It is true that Anselm thinks God must punish sin or receive satisfaction for sin: God may not forgive sin if that means setting punishment aside. But Anselm thinks this is because God's nature is so constituted that it is impossible for God to ignore or forgive sin without failing to be true to Godself in some fundamental sense.

Related to this, Stump claims that the Anselmian view implies that an innocent (Christ) pays the penalty or punishment due the guilty (fallen human beings). She writes,

23. Stump, *Atonement*, 21.
24. Stump writes, "In my view, the most disadvantaged of the variants on the Anselmian interpretation is the penal substitution theory of the atonement" (*Atonement*, 76).

> According to interpretations of the Anselmian kind, what God does to act compatibly with his goodness or justice is in fact to fail to punish the guilty or to exact the payment of the debt or the penance from those who owe it since sinful human beings do not get the punishment they deserve or pay the debt or penance they owe. Worse yet, instead of punishing the guilty or exacting payment or penance from the sinful who owe it, God visits their merited punishment on the innocent or exacts the payment of their moral debt or penance from someone who does not owe it. . . . How is justice or goodness served by punishing a completely innocent person or exacting from him what he does not owe?[25]

But this is to conflate the mechanism of satisfaction with the mechanism of penal substitution, and we have already seen that these represent two distinct accounts of atonement. More than that, Anselm is clear that Christ's satisfaction cannot be a punishment if it is to be an atonement. Punishment and atonement are two different and incompatible ways in which God's honor can be restored, according to Anselm. But Christ's work is not a vicarious penalty or punishment; it is a meritorious satisfaction. The worry about the punishment of the innocent Christ in place of guilty sinners is an important objection to traditional accounts of penal substitution. But since Anselm's doctrine is not a version of penal substitution and does not require that Christ's atonement is a vicarious punishment of any kind, it does no damage to Anselm's doctrine.

The point is important because in chapter 3 of her book Stump says that the objections she raised "earlier to all versions of the Anselmian interpretation apply to the penal substitution theory also."[26] But that is not the case precisely because the means by which atonement obtains in Anselm's thought is different from how it obtains in penal substitution. If Christ's work is a satisfaction, then he is not punished; and worries that depend on the claim that Christ is punished, as with penal substitution, have no purchase in Anselm's doctrine. But that means that at least some objections raised by Stump against Anselm's view don't apply to Anselm's doctrine; they apply only to penal substitution, contrary to her claim here.

Stump is on surer ground when she argues that Anselm's doctrine does not deal with what she calls the "forward-looking" aspect of atonement—that

---

25. Stump, *Atonement*, 24.
26. Stump, *Atonement*, 77.

is, human proneness to sin.[27] But here, too, it seems to me that she mistakes the nature of the problem that Anselm's defenders have to address. For surely the Anselmian can say that Christ's atonement on the cross is sufficient to deal with all human sin across time. It deals with my sin prior to coming to understand Christ's work as an atonement, and after that as well. We might put it like this: The efficacy of Christ's atonement is not restricted to my knowledge of its efficacy, and it is not nullified by the fact that I come to understand its efficacy at a certain point in time. It is efficacious for all my sin. So the Anselmian is able to address Stump's worry about human proneness to sin by saying that although Christ's atonement does not in and of itself prevent humans from continuing to sin, it provides an atonement for that sin. It is not until the eschaton that human beings will be without sin. Until that time we must rely upon divine grace in order to deal with sin in the process of sanctification. It is true that Anselm's doctrine does not offer a complete account of how the Holy Spirit enables the believer to act in a way that pleases God once the benefits of Christ have been applied to her. That is a lacuna in his argument, but to be fair to Anselm, it is not clear that he is trying to address the question of regeneration or union with Christ. He is focused more narrowly on the matter of the mechanism of atonement.

Stump worries that Anselm's view cannot account for the fact that a person may have her sins atoned for and yet warrant punishment. She gives the example of Franz Stangl, the Nazi commandant of Treblinka.[28] Imagine he were to have become a Christian prior to being apprehended by the Allies after the end of World War II. Then, according to the Anselmian way of thinking, Christ would have provided satisfaction for his sin. Yet if that were the case, wonders Stump, then why would Stangl still receive punishment for his crimes against humanity? But surely this is to conflate Stangl's putative faith, and the atonement for his sin accomplished by Christ, with the harsh treatment required for human justice to be served. What is more, this is not a problem peculiar to Anselm's doctrine. Any account of atonement that presumes Christ's work is an act by means of which fallen humans are reconciled to God, and that it is sufficient to atone for all human sin, has the consequence that when it is applied to a particular individual, that individual's sins are remitted. But that doesn't

27. Stump, *Atonement*, 25.
28. Stump, *Atonement*, 26–27.

necessarily mean that such individuals may not suffer the legal consequences of infringing human law. Otherwise, that would mean releasing every criminal who professes Christian faith while in jail.

Stump also worries that Anselm's view does not adequately address the question of shame. She writes, "Having an innocent person suffer the penalty or pay the debt incurred by one's own sin does not take away that shame. If anything, it seems to add to it. There is something painfully shaming about being responsible for the serious suffering of an innocent person, even if that suffering was voluntarily undertaken on one's behalf."[29] That seems right. There is something about having an innocent pay a debt incurred by the guilty that is shaming. However, strictly speaking, Christ does not pay a debt on Anselm's view. He offers up a meritorious action in order to satisfy divine honor. It is accepted in place of human punishment. Yet it does not pay for my sin, strictly speaking. Nevertheless, I may still feel shame because my sin has resulted in Christ performing this meritorious act of satisfaction. But, the Anselmian might wonder, isn't that a good thing? Isn't it a good thing that a person feels shame for her wrongdoing? And isn't that something that the apostle Paul enjoins upon us while rejoicing in his salvation? "O Wretched man that I am!" he says. "Who will rescue me from this body of death?" And his answer: "Thanks be to God through Jesus Christ our Lord!" (Rom. 7:24–25 NRSV, adapted).

The Anselmian doctrine is not without shortcomings, however, and Stump rightly points to some of these as well. In a section in which she considers further shortcomings of the atonement doctrines of Anselm and Thomas Aquinas, she says that Anselm's position principally addresses the need for human moral debt to be met by satisfaction or punishment.[30] But given that this good is available to all human beings in principle, "it is hard to see what connection there could be between the good for human beings provided by Christ's passion and death, on the Anselmian kind of interpretation, and the good (whatever it might be) that comes to a particular person from her suffering."[31] But I don't see what the worry amounts to here. Christ's atonement brings about human reconciliation in principle, so that all may be saved by means of the application of its benefits to the individual. But this has nothing to do with the suffering of

29. Stump, *Atonement*, 25–26.
30. Stump, *Atonement*, 21.
31. Stump, *Atonement*, 32.

mere humans (as opposed to the suffering of the God-man). We all suffer in different ways from natural and moral evils. But I suppose Anselm's doctrine is not concerned with my suffering because of some natural evil. Jane is a Christian, and yet suffers from cancer. Why? We cannot know. But presumably, the Anselmian can say something like this: God reconciles Jane to Godself by means of Christ's atonement. Her salvation is secure in Christ. The cancer she suffers is a consequence of the natural evil introduced into the world via the fall. But the atonement does not address such natural evil directly; it deals with human sin. Natural evil must be met by some other action—perhaps God's work of recreation, which awaits the eschaton.

Anselm and Divine Love

Perhaps the most serious objection Stump raises for Anselm's doctrine (in chapter 3 of *Atonement*) has to do with the Anselmian picture of love. In short, Stump thinks that the Anselmian requirement that God must punish sin or have some satisfaction provided prior to acting in love toward his fallen creatures is a travesty of divine love. Nor is Anselm able to countenance the prospect of forgiveness—though, on Stump's reckoning, love seems to require it.

But is that right? Suppose for the sake of argument that Christ's reconciling work is intended by God for the salvation of *all* fallen human beings. And suppose that this is brought about by Christ. Christ's satisfaction, being the work of the God-man, is also an act of mercy on God's part. God doesn't forgive human sin by means of Christ's satisfaction, strictly speaking; and God doesn't set aside human sin. Rather, God remits its consequences by means of satisfaction, which is itself a sort of reparative act on God's part. But if that act of reparation is universal in its intended scope (that is, the scope of salvation), and is an act of divine grace and mercy so that Christ as the God-man suffers on behalf of *all* fallen human beings, then it is less clear (to me at least) that Anselm's position is a travesty of divine love as Stump suggests. For on this way of thinking it is *God* who brings about the act of reconciliation where human beings cannot; it is *God* who provides the means by which satisfaction is obtained in his own human nature as the God-man; it is *God* who intends to distribute the benefits of this satisfaction to all humanity; and it is *God* who ordains that this reconciling act is sufficient in principle to redeem the whole of humanity. This may well reflect a different account of divine love than that preferred by Stump, one according to which God must act in a way consistent with the justice and honor of God as well as the love and mercy of God. But, I submit, a travesty it is not.[32]

32. This critique should not be thought to detract from the excellence of Stump's project. Her book is likely to remain the most important treatment of atonement for some time.

6

Problems with Penal Substitution

Thus far in part 2 we have considered moral exemplarism, ransom, and satisfaction as three classic accounts of atonement. Often, in treatments of this doctrine, satisfaction and penal substitution are conflated—even in recent accounts such as that of Stump. But, as the argument of the previous chapter showed, that is a mistake. Satisfaction and penal substitution have distinct accounts of the mechanism of atonement. The two doctrines, though undoubtedly bearing a family resemblance to each other, are different, as two cousins are similar and yet different. In this chapter we turn to look at penal substitution as an important and influential doctrine of atonement, even if it is also much maligned in the literature on the topic.

There are a number of contemporary defenders of penal substitution, many of whom are of an evangelical persuasion. Take, for instance, the late James I. Packer. In a widely referenced theological essay on the topic, he writes, "Christ's death on the cross had the character of penal substitution, and . . . it was in virtue of this fact that it brought salvation to mankind."[1] Similar sentiments have been expressed elsewhere in

1. See Packer, "What Did the Cross Achieve?," 11. I shall cite this version of the lecture in what follows. The literature on penal substitution is considerable. Notable recent treatments

recent times, most recently by William Lane Craig.[2] Yet, despite such defenses of the doctrine, penal substitution still faces significant problems. These problems are often alluded to in the literature on the subject and are common knowledge among historians of doctrine and theologians working in this area.[3] However, in this chapter I want to suggest that these problems have not been adequately resolved. More work needs to be done in order to demonstrate that they have been given the *coup de grâce*, in order to demonstrate that penal substitution is a viable doctrine of the atonement.

In this chapter, I will address what seems to me to be five systemic problems for the logic of penal substitution. I do not claim these are the *only* problems facing the doctrine, but I do think they are five of the most serious.[4] I will argue that, although some of these difficulties may be overcome by careful explanation, there are several interrelated issues that those wishing to shore up penal substitution still need to adequately address. The chapter begins by setting forth the assumptions that lie behind the traditional penal substitutionary account of the atonement. Then, in the second section, we shall consider the doctrine proper and the five criticisms of it, before closing with some remarks about the significance of this analysis for contemporary versions of the doctrine.

include Holmes, "Can Punishment Bring Peace?"; Lewis, "Do We Believe in Penal Substitution?"; Porter, "Swinburnian Atonement"; Thurow, "Communal Penal Substitution"; Strabbing, "The Permissibility of the Atonement"; G. Williams, "Penal Substitution"; Woznicki, "Do We Believe in Consequences?"; and Woznicki, "'One Can't Believe Impossible Things.'" But the most sustained recent defense of the doctrine is from Craig, *Atonement and the Death of Christ*, and his abstract of that work in Craig, *Atonement*.

2. See Craig, *Atonement*; and Craig, *Atonement and the Death of Christ*.

3. See, e.g., Franks, *Work of Christ*. They have also been discussed in the recent philosophy literature (e.g., Murphy, "Not Penal Substitution but Vicarious Punishment").

4. One important objection to penal substitution that I will not tackle here is that it implies that God is violent because God is appeased by the torture, crucifixion, and death of Christ. This criticism has been the subject of considerable debate in the recent literature. I have elected not to include a discussion of this concern here for two reasons. First, because (I judge) it would require a separate treatment to do it justice, and second, because it seems to me that even if we set aside worries about divine violence, which some defenders of penal substitution have waived away, the problems besetting penal substitution are significant and systemic. In other words, even if defenders of penal substitution can address modern worries about divine violence, they must still face conceptual problems with the view—problems that are, as it were, baked into the doctrine of penal substitution. I have dealt with the concerns raised by divine violence in *Approaching the Atonement*. For a scathing critique of recent attempts to sidestep worries about divine violence in some extreme versions of penal substitution, see Farris and Hamilton, "This Is My Beloved Son."

Assumptions

J. I. Packer, in his influential essay on the logic of penal substitution, summarizes the doctrine in these words:

> The notion which the phrase "penal substitution" expresses is that Jesus Christ our Lord, moved by a love that was determined to do everything necessary to save us, endured and exhausted the destructive divine judgement for which we were otherwise inescapably destined, and so won us forgiveness, adoption and glory. To affirm penal substitution is to say believers are in debt to Christ specifically for this, and that this is the mainspring of all their joy, peace and praise both now and for eternity.[5]

The central idea is this: Christ atones for human sin by standing in the place of human sinners and taking upon himself the penalty of human sin in order to satisfy divine justice.[6] Put more expansively, we could say that penal substitution is the doctrine according to which Christ's atonement is (primarily) his work on the cross in which he takes the place of sinful human beings as a substitute in order to suffer the punishment that is due for human sin, or the penal consequences of that sin, so that the penalty of sin may be met and fallen human beings may be reconciled with God. On the first of these options, Christ actually *suffers the punishment* for sin in the stead of the sinner. On the second, Christ suffers only the *penal consequences* of sin that would, in the case of the sinner, constitute the harsh treatment of punishment. This distinction is important, because (as we shall see) the claim that Christ is punished in place of fallen humanity is much more difficult to defend than the claim that Christ suffers the penal consequences of human sin, primarily because it seems morally wrong to punish an innocent in place of the guilty.

But we begin to get ahead of ourselves. Let us begin by considering several assumptions that are common coin in the discussion of penal substitution

---

5. Packer, "What Did the Cross Achieve?," 35.
6. Packer's language of enduring divine judgment to win forgiveness is, I think, rather unhelpful though it is a common feature of much popular penal substitution theology. It is unhelpful because on the face of it, it seems strange to think that forgiveness is won *through* punishment, or at least through suffering a penalty. It seems intuitive to think that where punishment obtains there is no forgiveness. Instead, there is satisfaction of some legal requirement in order to remit the penalty due. Thus, forgiveness seems to be an alternative to punishment, not a consequence of it.

even if they are not always declared. These are (a) that *divine justice is retributive in nature*; (b) that *sin requires an infinite punishment*; and (c) that *satisfaction for sin must be made either in the punishment of the sinner or in the person of a suitable substitute*. These need some explanation before we may proceed to unpack the doctrine proper. We shall consider each of them in turn.

a. Regarding Divine Retributive Punishment

Although the precise shape of retribution as a justification for punishment is contested in the jurisprudence literature,[7] features commonly thought to be constituents of retribution are that it is backward-looking, depends on a notion of desert, and requires a concept of proportionality between punishment and crime, expressed in the idea that *the punishment must fit the crime*.[8] Retribution is backward-looking because it is concerned with crimes or sins that have been committed and are therefore punishable—as opposed to, say, consequentialist justifications for punishment, which are primarily forward-looking and about the implications of a crime. It typically includes a notion of desert because the thought is that the person who has sinned or committed a crime is normally (somehow) deserving of punishment if they are of sound mind in a sound body and can be held morally responsible for committing the crime or sin. And it includes a principle of proportionality because the idea is that the harsh treatment of punishment must be calibrated to the axiological or legal disvalue of the crime (or sin) committed. Disproportionate punishment is usually thought to be unjust even if it is motivated by retributive concerns, as is often the case with acts of vengeance.[9]

But, as I have argued elsewhere, there are two strengths to retributive justifications of punishment involved in a penal substitution theory.[10] The stronger of the two states that *divine justice does not permit forgiveness*.

7. The *locus classicus* is Cottingham, "Varieties of Retribution."

8. All of these are ideas contained in "pure retributivism," which we encountered in the previous chapter.

9. The literature on retribution in jurisprudence is vast. Although there is some evidence of pushback against retribution in the recent literature, it is still the most widely canvassed justification for punishment in criminal law. For a sophisticated recent defense of a retributivist approach to punishment, see Moore, *Placing Blame*. For a widely canvassed examination and critique of traditional justifications of punishment, see Boonin, *Problem of Punishment*.

10. See Crisp, "Divine Retribution."

The weaker version of the doctrine claims merely that *divine justice does not require forgiveness*. If divine justice does not permit forgiveness, then sin must be dealt with; it cannot be simply passed over or forgiven without a proportional punishment being meted out. There might be a number of reasons offered as to why this is the case. For instance, following Immanuel Kant, we might say that there is a categorical obligation to apply a certain penalty for a certain crime, and that not to impose such a penalty would be objectively morally wrong. Applied to divine justice, this would mean that God has a categorical obligation to apply certain penalties that must be imposed in order to remain a moral being. God has to punish sin according to the idea of proportionality just outlined; there must be a "fit" between crime and punishment, and God must ensure that the punishment matches the crime. It is not the case, on this view, that God could choose some other, alternative means of punishment or forgive the sin without any punishment being suffered by the sinner or by some penal substitute.

However, it seems to me that this poses considerable challenges for a right understanding of the divine nature. Even if one were to ground this moral obligation in the divine nature itself, rather than in some deontological moral standard external to God (thereby ameliorating some of the more obvious problems that would result from the application of the Euthyphro dilemma to this issue[11]), this still means that God has certain moral obligations that must be discharged. This is a problem if it is thought that God has no moral obligations, strictly speaking.[12]

Alternatively, one might say that God has to punish sin because there is something about divine justice that is inexorable. That is, divine justice must be satisfied. If this is the case, then it cannot be that God passes over or forgives sin without punishment on pain of God ceasing to be a moral being. For if God passes over or forgives sin, rather than punishing it justly,

11. The problems I have in mind here have to do with divine aseity—that is, the idea that God is psychologically and metaphysically independent of all that is created. We could put it in terms of a Euthyphro dilemma, like this: Does God act in particular ways because it is moral to do so, or are moral actions moral because they are enacted by God? If God's action is moral because it conforms to some external standard or property of morality, then this infringes divine aseity: God is dependent on some standard or property external to Godself. If moral acts are moral just because God does them, then this implies divine megrim: God simply decides what is moral, which is theological voluntarism. The traditional solution to this problem is to say God acts according to the nature of God, which is moral, grounding moral actions in Godself. For a useful overview of the issues, see Gould, *Beyond the Control of God?*

12. For a recent and accessible treatment of these issues, see C. Evans, *God and Moral Obligation*.

God would be acting contrary to God's own essentially just nature. In this matter I am assuming, for the sake of argument, that justice is something essential to the divine nature. If this justice is inexorable in its very nature, then God cannot remain essentially just and act contrary to that justice by, say, forgiving the sin of one of his creatures without punishment. For on this view, it is not in God's nature to do this. Obviously, this raises the question of whether divine justice is, in fact, inexorable. On the strong view of divine justice, the view that divine justice does not permit forgiveness, this would seem to be the case. Such a strong view of divine justice involves the following sorts of assumptions:

i. A person should not be treated any worse than they deserve.
ii. A person should not be treated any better than they deserve.
iii. One person should be treated in the same way as another for comparable crimes. That is, punishment should be fair.[13]

Fairness on its own need not mean justice is inexorable. It might be that a particular police force decides on a particular day that they will have an amnesty for illegal firearms. This means letting all people who possess illegal firearms hand in their weapons without fear of punishment for being in possession of illegal firearms on that particular day. This seems fair. No one person is treated differently from another with respect to handing in illegal firearms on that particular day. But this would mean that these people on this day are being treated better than they deserve (assuming they all deserve punishment for possession of illegal weapons). In this case, justice has given way to clemency, for the limited period of the amnesty. Human societies might allow this, but divine justice cannot (on this view), without violating (ii) of our tenets of justice. Similarly, if God decided that it would be fair to ensure that all those who possessed illegal firearms were hauled over hot coals for a thousand years, this might appear to be fair in that all those in possession of illegal firearms receive the same punishment. But it would violate the condition that persons are not treated any worse than they deserve (i). For surely no one deserves to

13. Adapted from Adams, "Hell and the God of Justice," 434. Paul Helm has pointed out to me that there are other concepts of fairness one could apply too, such as "outcome" fairness. A fiscal system with graduated taxation is said to be "fairer" than one that lacks this. However, the three aspects of fairness mentioned by Adams will suffice for the present argument.

be hauled over hot coals for a thousand years merely because they have been caught in possession of an illegal firearm!

These intuitions about divine justice dovetail with what has already been said about retributive punishment. As we have seen, among other things, retribution means the punishment must fit the crime. It must be fair; it must be proportional. So it cannot be too severe or too lenient, and (the thought is) it must be exercised against sin. If this applies to divine justice as the strong view of divine justice claims it does, then there does seem, *prima facie,* to be something inexorable about that justice. God, it would seem, has to punish sin rather than pass over it, or forgive it without punishment. It seems to me that many, perhaps most, theologians who have advocated some version of penal substitution or satisfaction theory of atonement have subscribed to the strong view of divine justice according to a retribution model of punishment. As we have already noted in passing in the previous chapter, this is the sort of view defended by Anselm in *Cur Deus Homo*:

> Likewise, if there is nothing greater and nothing better than God, then there is nothing, in the government of the universe, which the supreme justice, which is none other than God himself, preserves more justly than God's honour. . . . It is a necessary consequence, therefore, that either the honour that has been taken away should be repaid, or punishment should follow. Otherwise, either God will not be just to himself, or he will be without the power to enforce either of the two options; and it is an abominable sin to even consider this possibility.[14]

A similar line of thought about the inexorableness of divine justice can be found in some older textbooks of theology. One well-known example is Louis Berkhof:

> When man fell away from God, he as such owed God reparation. But he could atone for his sin only by suffering eternally the penalty affixed to transgression. This is what God might have required in strict justice, and would have required, if He had not been actuated by love and compassion for the sinner. As a matter of fact, however, God appointed a vicar in Jesus Christ to take man's place, and this vicar atoned for sin and obtained an eternal redemption for man.[15]

---

14. Anselm, *Cur Deus Homo* I.13, in Davies and Evans, *Major Works*, 286–87.
15. Berkhof, *Systematic Theology*, 375. Berkhof's work has been widely disseminated and is a kind of Anglicized digest of the work of the influential Dutch theologian Herman Bavinck.

Of course, one could take the weaker view of divine justice on a retributive model. To recap, this is the view that divine justice does not require forgiveness. God is not required to forgive the sinner without punishment, but God could do so. But then some justification would have to be offered for (a) why God does forgive some persons without punishment and not others, and (b) how it is that forgiving some but not others is consistent with the three tenets of justice just outlined above. For it does not seem fair to treat some sinners in one way, visiting divine justice upon them in punishment, and some sinners in another way, granting them the benefits of divine grace instead.[16]

In the modern literature, Richard Swinburne has defended the notion that divine justice does not require punishment.[17] Swinburne claims that atonement involves four constituents: repentance, apology, reparation, and penance. A guilty person should demonstrate repentance for a sin committed and apologize, seeking to make reparation where that is possible (and sometimes it is possible to make complete reparation). Finally, the guilty person should seek to demonstrate their penitence by a supererogatory act, which shows the offended party that they are truly sorry. Perhaps I am guilty of smashing your favorite vase. I can repent of this, apologize to you, and perhaps replace the vase with another, if it is replaceable. I may even give you a bunch of flowers to show how truly sorry I am and declare my sorrow privately and publicly. But perhaps it is a priceless Ming Dynasty vase. Then reparation is much more difficult (if reparation can be made at all), and a greater penance may be appropriate.

Swinburne applies this to the divine-human relationship in the following way. Human beings have acquired guilt through sin before God. This guilt is problematic because human beings are already obliged to render to God a moral life. God may deal with this guilt for sin in one of two ways. He could forgive the sin if the sinner is truly repentant and apologizes, with no further satisfaction required. In this way, divine justice does not require punishment for satisfaction. However, he could require

16. The difference between this view and the strong view of divine justice as applied to penal substitution is that on the strong view, punishment must be meted out before grace can be given. That is, punishment must be served either upon the sinner or upon a substitute, in order that the demands of justice are met, before grace can be offered. This need not apply on the weaker view.

17. See Swinburne, *Responsibility and Atonement*, 81–92, and chap. 10. In this respect he echoes the Thomistic tradition.

reparation and penance for the sin committed instead of this. Clearly, it is difficult for human beings to offer reparation for a sin committed against God, since they already owe God the fruits of a moral life. So it is good if God provides a means by which reparation and penance for the guilt of sin can be made (i.e., the work of Christ). When the sinner sincerely repents of his sin and apologizes to God for what he has done, pleading the work of Christ as a satisfaction for reparation and penance that the sinner himself cannot offer for the debt he owes God for his sin, then God will forgive that sin in virtue of Christ's vicarious work. Nevertheless, it remains true, on Swinburne's view of the atonement, that God could have decided that some action other than, say, Christ's crucifixion be the means of reparation and penance being made available to human sinners. But it seemed good to God that this was the means by which such reparation and penance was made.

It seems to me that Swinburne is right to suggest that atonement comprises repentance, apology, reparation, and penance with respect to human relationships. (The term "penance" may be unhelpful for some because of its theological associations. But I shall not take issue with that here.) However, defenders of a strong version of penal substitution and, it seems to me, an Anselmian view of satisfaction, maintain that this cannot apply *mutatis mutandis* to divine-human relationships for three reasons. First, the inexorableness of divine justice means that it is not possible for God to permit forgiveness without punishment because this would be contrary to the divine nature. Second, it is not possible, on this strong view of penal substitution, for human beings to offer adequate reparation and penance for their sinful condition (more on that in a moment). Third, it is not the case that God could have used any old means by which to ensure vicarious reparation and penance. As Steven Porter points out, this makes the cross an arbitrary choice for the satisfaction of sin.[18] And on an Anselmian view of things, the cross is anything but an arbitrary choice on the part of God.

b. Regarding Infinite Punishment

This brings us to the second assumption lying behind penal substitution: that only an infinite punishment provides the correct "fit" between

---

18. Porter, "Rethinking the Logic of Penal Substitution."

crime and punishment.[19] In brief, the central idea is that the dignity of God is infinite, which means that the seriousness of an offence committed against God is infinite, or infinitely surpasses that of other kinds. Assuming a retributive punishment thesis taken on the strong divine justice view, we could outline the following sort of (broadly Anselmian) reasoning:

1. God is worthy of infinite regard.
2. The gravity of an offence against a being is principally determined by that being's worth or dignity.
3. There is an infinite demerit in all sin against God, such that all sin is infinitely heinous.

This assumes that in the case of divine-human relationships the status of the person offended (God) is of crucial importance in determining the severity of the punishment to be meted out.[20] Sin against a being of infinite honor and worth has consequences that are themselves infinite for the sinner concerned. This sort of reasoning undercuts the Swinburnian thesis about divine justice. For, if it is cogent, then sin is so serious that it is not possible for God to merely forgive sinners without adequate reparation and penance being made.[21]

Whether God may forgive sin without punishment or not, there is another and related distinction here that it is worth pausing to consider before proceeding further. This is the distinction between the *absolute necessity* of atonement and the *hypothetical necessity* of atonement. This is a matter of whether it is in the nature of God to punish sin inexorably because of the heinousness of sin (hence, absolutely necessary), or whether God decrees that sin will be punished in this way, although he could have decreed some alternative (hence, hypothetically necessary).[22] The concern here is about the sort of necessity that motivates the atonement. Although

19. I have argued this point in more detail in "Divine Retribution."

20. I do not claim that this reasoning about the status of the individual offended applies to relationships between creatures, only that it applies to the special case of divine-human relationships.

21. Swinburne claims that this infinite punishment thesis constitutes "exaggerated talk" and that allocating a moral value to sin is "somewhat arbitrary," but he offers no substantive argument against the infinite punishment thesis. See Swinburne, *Responsibility and Atonement*, 154n10.

22. Turretin makes this point in *Elenctic Theology* 2:14.10, 418.

it looks superficially similar to the point about punishing or forgiving, it is in fact distinct. For it might be thought that God could have forgiven sin *tout court* and without any act of atonement. That is not the same as saying that God could have arranged for some act of atonement for human sin other than the one that he did in fact arrange, though some sort of arrangement was necessary in order for justice to be served, or for God to be satisfied. The distinction between what some scholastic theologians call the absolute and hypothetical necessity of atonement is really a distinction about whether *this particular* act of atonement is required for human salvation. It is not about whether an act of atonement is required as such. It is like saying a drowning person could be saved in several different ways, but one of those must be effectual if she is to survive. Some saving act is needed to bring about a successful rescue, even if it does not have to be the particular one that is, in fact, selected. In what follows I shall assume merely that God metes out infinite punishment for all sin on the basis of some sort of necessity, without adjudicating between "absolute" and "hypothetical" versions thereof.[23]

c. Regarding the Satisfaction of Punishment

The third background condition has to do with what traditional accounts of penal substitution often call the satisfaction of punishment—not to be confused with the Anselmian notion of satisfaction, which is an alternative to punishment. To clarify, suppose we think of satisfaction in broad terms as *an act by means of which the conditions of a moral or legal standard are met*—in this case, by a voluntary act of supererogation that generates merit of sufficient value to meet the requirement of divine justice. The act of supererogation in question could be a meritorious act that is not a punishment, as in the case of the Anselmian doctrine. Alternatively, it could be the suffering of a penalty in place of the sinner satisfying divine justice, as in the case of penal substitution. Thus, the language of satisfaction can be used broadly to categorize several sorts of atonement doctrine as they bear on the question of the satisfaction of divine justice or

23. I will not pause to consider related questions such as whether all infinite punishment is equal punishment (argued for in Crisp, "Divine Retribution") or the claim, made by Peter Geach, that God could mete out an infinite punishment for sin in a finite period. See Geach, *Providence and Evil*, 148–49. Though these are interesting questions, they would lead us too far from the present concerns.

divine honor, or more narrowly, to distinguish the Anselmian mechanism of atonement from that of penal substitution.

It seems that, according to classical theologians who defend penal substitution, divine retributive justice, taken on a strong view of divine justice according to an infinite punishment thesis, ensures that punishment for sin is distributed in order that divine justice is satisfied. This can be meted out in the person of the sinner, in hell, or in the person of Christ, as the one who is able to offer a sacrifice for sin which is of an infinite worth, and therefore is able to atone for the sin of those he has come to save (the elect). Satisfaction, construed in this penal-substitutionary way, depends upon the notion that a punishment is offered that is able to satisfy justice. Since this has to be an infinite, retributive punishment in order for there to be a "fit" between crime and punishment (on the basis of the argument for infinite punishment outlined earlier), this means that divine justice is satisfied either by the infinite punishment of the sinner in hell or by Christ taking on the punishment or the penal consequences of human sin, dying in order to satisfy divine justice. Some theologians, like Jonathan Edwards, have maintained that it is in the nature of God to display the justice and mercy of God, and that, as a result of this, salvation via penal substitution is particularistic. That is, Christ's atoning work is effective for a particular number of humans, less than the total number of humans.[24] This is a matter to which we shall return later in the chapter.

Penal Substitution and Its Problems

With these assumptions in place, we come to the substance of the doctrine of penal substitution. To begin with, it is important to see that punishment and atonement are not the same thing. Thus Swinburne writes, "Punishment is something imposed by the wronged party (in this case, God); atonement is offered voluntarily."[25] But this can be accounted for in a version of penal substitution:

1. All sinners are guilty and stand under divine judgment (this is consistent with our first and second assumptions, which were that *divine*

24. See Edwards, "Concerning the End," 530.
25. Swinburne, *Responsibility and Atonement*, 155.

justice is retributive in nature and that *sin requires an infinite punishment*).

2. God would be just if he punished all human sinners in hell infinitely (consistent with our third assumption, that *satisfaction for sin must be made either in the punishment of the sinner or in the person of a substitute*).

3. However, God could satisfy the perfect justice of God by punishing a substitute in the place of the sinner.

4. God will not punish the sin of all human beings in the person of a substitute since it is in the nature of God to display divine justice and divine mercy, thereby vindicating the nature of God before the created order (this is what we might call *the Edwardsian thesis* about the particularism of the extent of atonement just mentioned).

5. The sin of some (the elect) will be punished in the person of Christ, their substitute. The sin of others (the reprobate) will be punished in hell.

Anselm, of course, claims that Christ's work on the cross is not a punishment as such but a voluntary satisfaction offered up to God the Father. Thus, satisfaction in the narrow sense is not the same as penal substitution. For on penal substitution, Christ's work on the cross is not merely a voluntary satisfaction offered up to God (it is this, but it is not just this). It is also the voluntary taking up of the punishment of sin or the penal consequences of the sin of human beings, as a substitute for that sin.[26] So Christ voluntarily takes on the sin of elect human sinners in order to satisfy the requirements of divine justice. But this is not an offering made apart from the punishment or penal consequences of the actions of sinful humanity. It is an offering made in substitution for punishment or penal consequences, which distinguishes penal substitution from satisfaction. It is important to note here that Christ's substitutionary work on the cross is not a punishment for any sin Christ has done—for, strictly speaking,

26. In the previous chapter we noted that there is an important distinction between versions of penal substitution that imply Christ is punished in place of the sinner and those that imply Christ merely suffers the penal consequences that would be a punishment in the case of the sinner if the sinner served them. This historic distinction is also found in the recent literature—e.g., Craig's defense of a moderate penal-consequences version of penal substitution in *Atonement and the Death of Christ*.

Christ is guilty of no sin. However, as theologians say, he "becomes sin for us" (see 2 Cor. 5:21). Either Christ is punished in place of fallen human beings or he takes on the penal consequences of the sin of human beings, suffering instead of fallen human beings. This, according to L. W. Grensted, involves a "legal fiction."[27] Christ is treated as if he were guilty of our sin and punished in our stead, or at least is treated as an appropriate substitute who may suffer the penal consequences of our sin even if they are not his punishment, strictly speaking. But some theologians have claimed, in addition to this, that Christ literally takes on the sin of fallen human beings, as well as the guilt for that sin. However, this seems deeply problematic. It might be thought that Christ cannot become a penal substitute for us because this would involve him taking upon himself a debt that cannot be transferred from us to Christ (or from one person to another at all). If Christ takes on only the penal consequences of my sin, perhaps this problem can be ameliorated.[28] For it certainly seems less problematic to claim that Christ suffers the penal consequences of human sin rather than to claim that he suffers the punishment of human sin—given that he himself is without sin and, therefore, (plausibly) an inappropriate target for punishment.

The rationale for penal substitution raises a number of problems besides that pertaining to the claim that Christ somehow acts as a substitute for (elect) sinful human beings. The first of these has to do with whether the doctrine of penal substitution reduces the love of God to something arbitrary. This, it is alleged, is because the doctrine means God chooses to love only an elect few, less than the total number of humans, on no other basis than that God wills to do so. Hence, penal substitution seems to be open to the charge of voluntarism: God simply decides whom to save and whom to damn. And this smacks of divine megrim.

The second problem is that the doctrine means that God cannot forgive sin without some reparation being made for the sin committed that is of sufficient value so as to offset the sin committed in some way. It is not possible, at least on the strong version of penal substitution, for God to pass over sin, or forgive it, without reparation being made. Built into this understanding of atonement is the idea that God is "wroth with sin" and must deal with it according to his inexorable retributive justice in the

27. Grensted, *Short History*, 216.
28. This is Craig's claim in *Atonement and the Death of Christ*.

person of the sinner or a vicar. But this seems to limit God (is God *unable* to forgive sin?). And it has often been thought to make God a moral monster, extracting punishment from sinners who are born with original sin and cannot save themselves without divine intervention.

The last two problems are interrelated and pertain to the question of the transfer of sin and guilt from the sinner to Christ, and, in turn, the transfer of Christ's righteousness from Christ to the sinner in the imputation of sin and guilt, and Christ's righteousness, respectively. On the question of the transfer of sin, the following distinction needs to be observed. There are some debts that can be transferred from one person to another, and some debts that cannot. According to post-Reformation Reformed Orthodox theologian Francis Turretin, debts in the first instance are called "pecuniary debts."[29] So, if Smith owes a financial debt to Jones, his debt can be paid by Wayne, since what is required is that the financial penalty be met, nothing more. However, in the case of penal debts, the same conditions do not necessarily apply. A penal debt often involves more than the debt itself; it involves the person who has committed the crime that has generated the debt. So, if Smith has killed Jones, Wayne cannot take Smith's place and act as his substitute in the way he could with respect to Smith's financial debt to Jones. Smith's sin means *Smith* has to serve the punishment for his crime. For the thought is that there is something about the culpability accruing to Smith's crime that is inalienable and that can only be served by the person who has committed it. This is a problem for penal substitution if acting as a penal substitute entails the transfer of sin from the sinner to Christ, not just the transfer of the penal consequences of that sin from the sinner to Christ.

Similarly, if guilt is nontransferable, and the transfer of guilt is a constituent of penal substitution, then this would constitute a second sort of worry about penal substitution. Consider the case of Smith once more. In the first instance, the case of his financial debt to Jones, Wayne can step in and pay the money owed, thereby settling the debt. But she cannot take upon herself the guilt of Smith in so doing. Smith and Smith alone is the person guilty of incurring that debt, even if it is not Smith who pays the debt. Smith's guilt in this instance is not transferable to Wayne (or any other person who would seek to pay the debt he owes to Jones).

29. See Turretin, *Elenctic Theology* 2:14.10, 419.

This problem is even more pronounced in the case of Smith murdering Jones, which is the case of penal debt. Here Smith is guilty of the crime and nothing Wayne can do will mean that Smith ceases to be guilty of that crime. Even if Smith, Jones, and Wayne were living in a society where penal substitutes could take the place of a convicted criminal and serve the punishment of the person convicted, that, in and of itself, does not mean that the person taking upon themselves the punishment of another, in the act of taking on that punishment, takes on the guilt for that punishment too. It seems that the guilt accruing to a crime like murder is irremovable and nontransferable.

Responding to the Problems

Let us respond to each of these problems in turn.

a. Does Penal Substitution Make Sense?

First, can Christ be a penal substitute at all? As Berkhof puts it,

> All those who advocate a subjective theory of the atonement raise a formidable objection to the idea of vicarious atonement. They consider it unthinkable that a just God should transfer His wrath against moral offenders to a perfectly innocent party, and should treat the innocent judicially as if he were guilty. There is undoubtedly a real difficulty here, especially in view of the fact that this seems to be contrary to all human analogy.[30]

Traditionally, defenders of penal substitution have sought to avoid this problem by appealing to a concept of legal relaxation. God can "relax" the punitive requirement of divine justice so that a substitute can take on the penal consequences of the sin of another in the particular case of the atonement. This could take one of two forms. First, God could be said to relax the punitive requirement of divine justice by admitting that a substitute can, in certain circumstances, take on the penal consequences of another's crime where the substitute is not required to pay an equivalent penalty. That is, God can decide that, in the case of the substitute, God is willing to admit a punishment of inferior value to that required by strict

---

30. Berkhof, *Systematic Theology*, 376.

justice. As we noted in chapter 2, in scholastic theology this is called "acceptation." (A variation on this form of legal relaxation would be that Christ's work is not a satisfaction because of its intrinsic worth but only because God deigns to graciously accept it as a satisfaction for the crime committed, though God need not do so.[31]) Alternatively, God could relax the punitive requirement that justice be meted out only to the guilty party and allow a substitute to take the penal consequences of the crime instead of the guilty party. In this second form, the doctrine of legal relaxation has application only to the question of who serves the punishment, not, in addition to that, whether or not the punishment is served to the full. For on this second view, the punishment must be served to the full. So, in this second form of the doctrine, there is no relaxation of the requirements of divine justice. The only relaxation pertains to whether the perpetrator of the crime is punished, or whether a penal substitute suffers instead.

The first of these two views on legal relaxation is often attributed to Scotus and Grotius; the second, to those who defend a strong view of penal substitution, such as Owen or Turretin. (It does not particularly matter, for the sake of the present argument, whether these attributions are accurate or not. The point is these theologians are usually associated with developing these two versions of legal relaxation with respect to the atonement.)[32]

Let us apply this second form of the legal relaxation doctrine to penal substitution. Then, God, the one offended against, may be willing for Christ to take the place of the sinner and suffer the penal consequences of the crime of that sinner, as if Christ were that sinner. Here too, there are two ways in which this could be construed. In the first place, it might be thought that this arrangement cannot mean that the sinfulness of those human beings Christ came to save is actually transferred to Christ. Nor

31. See Hodge, *Systematic Theology*, 2:487, where this point is made. The difference between these two variations of this form of legal relaxation depends upon the way in which God accepts the penal substitution. In the first case, God decides to accept the inferior punishment. Here the substitute's satisfaction has an intrinsic worth, just not a worth equal to the satisfaction required for the crime committed. In the latter case, Christ's work does not have an intrinsic worth that makes it satisfactory; perhaps it is not satisfactory in the least, yet God graciously accepts it as if it were adequate, or satisfactory. But both defend the idea that there is a relaxation in the fact that a substitute is able to atone for the sin of another and that this satisfaction is not equal to the culpability of the crime committed.

32. For instances of these associations in the nineteenth century Reformed theological literature, see Shedd, *Dogmatic Theology*, 123; and Hodge, *Systematic Theology*, 2:487.

can it mean that the actual righteousness of Christ is really transferred to the sinner in place of their sinfulness. This is something that is, according to Berkhof, "utterly impossible."[33] The reason being, as we have already noted, that it is not possible for the sin and guilt of one person to transfer to another person. According to Berkhof, all that can be transferred from one agent to another is the guilt of sin as liability to punishment. The sinner remains the guilty party, and their liability to guilt does not transfer.[34] The sinner remains the one who has sinned, and the actual property of having committed this sin does not transfer. But that aspect of the guilt for the sin committed which renders the sinner liable for punishment is transferable, and Christ can suffer as a substitute for this liability to punishment, as an aspect of the guilt of sin. So, on this first view, all that is transferred from the sinner to Christ is the culpability for sin, not the sin itself, nor the fact that this particular person is guilty of having committed this particular sin. (In other words, not original sin as such, nor the whole of original guilt, but merely the culpability aspect of original guilt.)[35]

On the second view, we could apply the legal relaxation of penal substitution in the following way. God does transfer the guilt and sin of the sinner from the sinner to Christ. If this is the case, then God transfers the righteousness of Christ to the sinner. So, legally and morally speaking, the sinner is righteous. And, legally and morally speaking, Christ is the sinner and guilty for that sin, and therefore punishable for it. But it seems to me that, at the very least, the person who has committed a particular crime is guilty of having committed it, and that liability to guilt cannot simply be transferred from one individual to another individual (even if one believes that liability to punishment can be transferred from one person to another). Nor, it seems to me, can the sin itself, if it is a penal rather than merely pecuniary debt, be transferred from one person to another. If it is suggested that, though this is true in the case of creaturely legal transactions, it is not the case with the transaction between the Father and

---

33. Berkhof, *Systematic Theology*, 377.

34. This is the scholastic distinction between the *reatus culpae* (liability to punishment) and *reatus poenae* (liability to guilt), the two aspects of original guilt. I have discussed this in Crisp, "Scholastic Theology."

35. This raises a question about the justification of the sinner. How can someone who is still sinful and guilty for his sin be righteous in the sight of God? Presumably because the righteousness of Christ is imputed to the sinner just as the liability to punishment of the sinner is imputed to Christ. So here too, it seems, God treats one person as if he were another, the sinner as if he were Christ.

the Son in the atonement or in the covenant of redemption, this does nothing to alleviate the problem. It merely points out that it can only apply to this special metaphysical arrangement in the case of Christ's atonement. So, without some further argument to make sense of this view, it seems to me that it faces considerable conceptual challenges.[36]

Let us assume for the sake of argument that the second way in which the legal relaxation of penal substitution could be understood cannot work. Then we are left with the first way. This seems to be the way in which most defenders of penal substitution think of the transference of punishment from the sinner to Christ in the atonement. Take, for example, Calvin's exposition of this:

> To take away our condemnation, it was not enough for him to suffer any kind of death: to make satisfaction for our redemption a form of death had to be chosen in which he might free us both by transferring our condemnation to himself and by taking our guilt upon himself.

Moreover,

> Thus we shall behold the person of a sinner and evildoer represented in Christ, yet from his shining innocence it will at the same time be obvious that he was burdened with another's sin rather than his own. . . . This is our acquittal: the guilt that held us liable for punishment has been transferred to the head of the Son of God.[37]

Note that Calvin emphasizes the fact that Christ takes up the guilt of sinful human beings by transferring the condemnation of sinful human beings to himself. It is not his own sin with which he is burdened. He has transferred to himself the guilt that belongs to sinful human beings. Nor is it that this legal fiction involves anything more than the transfer of the penal consequences of guilt. So, it seems from this passage that Calvin's view is compatible with Berkhof's notion of liability to punishment (a

---

36. Perhaps a version of Augustinian realism can be used to make sense of the way of thinking of the atonement. If God makes the elect and Christ one metaphysical entity for the purposes of atonement, then the sin and guilt of the elect could pass to Christ as a part of the whole entity, and Christ's righteousness could pass to the elect in a similar fashion. This is the idea that motivates the realist version of the union account of atonement that I take up in chapter 8 and that I previously defended in *Word Enfleshed*.

37. John Calvin, *Institutes* 2.16.5.

notion Berkhof has culled from scholastic theology). It is this liability that Christ took upon himself in the atonement, according to this version of penal substitution.

Thus, the answer to how Christ can be a penal substitute at all involves a concept of legal relaxation that applies to Christ's atonement. Christ is able to be the substitute for sin because God decides that Christ's work satisfies the requirements for sin, and God is willing to accept Christ's work as a substitute for the sin of those human beings whom Christ came to save. Often defenders of penal substitution admit that there is no real precedent for this in human affairs.[38] But they typically appeal to the singular circumstances involved in Christ's atonement: the fact that it is God who decides whether to allow satisfaction to be made for sin; that God the Father covenants with God the Son to bring this satisfaction about; that no sinful human being could make this satisfaction; and that only the Son could achieve this satisfaction in the person of Christ. In taking on this role, the Son acts both as voluntary substitute, taking on the penal consequences of the sins of others, and as the one who is able to offer satisfaction for this sin. So both the penalty for the sin of human beings and satisfaction of divine justice are rendered in the one atoning act.

Of course, all this presumes that divine retributive justice is inexorable and must be satisfied, and that the legal relaxation of punishment in the case of the atonement is consistent with this divine justice. However, even if this is granted it still does not show that God is just in accepting the substitution of an innocent party (Christ) instead of the punishment of the sinner. That is, it still does not show how a penal substitute is a just substitute. Yet, as David Lewis points out in defense of the doctrine of penal substitution, we all allow penal substitution under certain circumstances. Although such double-mindedness about penal substitution is not an argument in favor of its application in a particular case, such as the atonement, it should give naysayers pause for thought. As Lewis puts it, "Those Christians who explain the Atonement as a case of penal substitution, yet do not in general believe in the principle they invoke, really are

38. Recently, in *Atonement and the Death of Christ*, Craig has tried to undercut this sort of worry by appropriating jurisprudential categories to make good on a penal-consequences version of penal substitution. Strabbing's recent argument in favor of penal substitutionary arrangements under certain circumstances in "The Permissibility of the Atonement" is also relevant in this regard. In some respects, her argument echoes the earlier work of David Lewis in "Do We Believe in Penal Substitution?"

in a bad way. Yet the rest of us should not be overbold in rebuking them. For we live in the proverbial glass house. All of us—atheists and agnostics, believers of other persuasions, the lot—are likewise of two minds about penal substitution."[39]

b. Does Penal Substitution Make the Atonement Arbitrary?

We come to the second problem for penal substitution: whether or not it makes the atonement arbitrary. Let us assume, for the sake of the present argument, that it is arbitrary. Why should this be a problem for the defender of penal substitution? Presumably because penal substitution means God chooses to save a limited number of humans rather than a greater number of humans, or even all humans. But if this is the problem, it is not a problem with the doctrine of penal substitution as such, but with a particular construal of this view along the lines of the doctrine of particular redemption (the notion that the atonement saves only a particular number of humans, those to whom Christ's saving work is effectively applied, rather than the totality of humanity). Penal substitution does not entail particular redemption. What is more, other accounts of atonement could be understood along particular-redemptionistic lines. So this sort of argument is not about penal substitution at all, but about particular redemption—which is a separate, although related, issue having to do with the scope of atonement rather than its nature. Its relevance depends on the theologian articulating a version of penal substitution that involves a commitment to a particular redemption.[40]

To make this clear, consider the fact that penal substitution could be combined with a version of universalism. It could be that God decides to save all of humanity through the penal-substitutionary work of Christ. Assume that God does decree this in such a way that Christ's saving work is effectively applied to all of humanity. It follows that no one (at least, no human) is damned; all humans are saved. I presume that far fewer

---

39. Lewis, "Do We Believe in Penal Substitution?," 207.

40. Of course, some theologians claim penal substitution entails particular redemption. (Garry Williams is a recent case in point.) But this is not obvious to me, and in any case, there are instances in the history of the doctrine of those who deny this, such as Jacob Arminius. The issue turns on the question (originally articulated by Peter Lombard) of whether penal substitution may be sufficient in principle or whether it must be effectual. It seems to me that it could be that Christ's penal substitution is merely in principle sufficient for all humanity, and not in addition effectual for all humanity.

contemporary theologians would have a problem with this application of penal substitution than they would with a particular-redemptionistic application of penal substitution, despite the fact that both versions of the doctrine depend on nothing more than God willing a course of action in salvation that effectually applies to a particular number of human beings.

So, it is not penal substitution as a doctrine of atonement that is in question here but the way in which it is applied: whether as a means to a particular redemption effectual for less than the total number of humans; as a means to the particular redemption of all of humanity, in a version of universalism; or some other view, such as the idea that the penal substitution of Christ makes the salvation of all humanity not necessarily actual but *possible*, because of the sufficiency of Christ's work of satisfaction. In this case, human beings need to exercise free choice in turning to Christ to appropriate the benefits of his saving work. (This sort of view is taken by some theological libertarians, such as the followers of Jacob Arminius.)

It might be thought that there is an optimal number of humans that God saves. Universalists might claim this, of course. But also, some who take a particular-redemptionistic view might maintain this.[41] One could argue that God saves a particular number of human beings less than the total number of humans (whatever that number might be) because just this number is the right number to display God's mercy and grace in salvation, and God's justice and wrath in damnation—along the sort of lines we saw Edwards advocate for earlier. For, it might be thought, it is in the nature of God to display both these attributes in his works optimally, and God has ordained that this optimal state of affairs obtains. (Both Edwards and Leibniz seem to say this.) So, a certain number of humans are saved and a certain number are damned (whatever the exact statistics may be). This may seem unpalatable to many theologians today, but it might appeal to those attracted to the combination of the concept of a best possible world and the notion of particular redemption. If this is the best possible world, and this world is a world where only some of humanity is saved by the atonement, then perhaps this is because this number of saved human beings is the optimal number (whatever that number may

41. Perhaps a theological libertarian might claim that there is such an optimal number and that God brings about a world in which an optimal number of humans freely choose salvation. For instance, some medieval divines seem to think that the number of elect humans that freely choose salvation replaces the number of angels that fell.

be). Why? Perhaps because it is in the nature of God to display his grace and mercy and justice and wrath and this particular-redemptionistic way is the optimal means to that end. I do not intend to argue for this claim, which seems deeply implausible to me.[42] I am simply pointing out that some Edwards-inspired theologians might be attracted to this sort of justification for believing that a particular-redemptionistic argument could be conjoined with a doctrine of penal substitution without conceding at the outset that this entails that the number of humans saved via the atonement is arbitrary. In a similar fashion, the universalist would claim that only the salvation of all humanity represents the optimal number of human beings saved because it is the objectively, morally best outcome. Moreover, if God is essentially benevolent, God will ensure that all humanity is saved because the salvation of all humanity is the objectively morally best outcome. So the number of the saved is not arbitrary on this view either. And, as we saw previously, universalism could be conjoined with penal substitution.[43]

So, the defender of penal substitution has to make a decision here. On the one hand, she could embrace the notion of particular redemption and state that Christ died for some elect, not the whole of humanity. This leaves two possible options: concede that the exact number of the elect is arbitrary as far as we can tell—after all, the secret things belong to God, as Deuteronomy 29:29 reminds us—or present an argument for the claim that the number of the elect is not arbitrary, perhaps along the lines I have suggested here. On the other hand, the defender of penal substitution could embrace the notion of universal redemption and state that Christ died for the whole of humanity, and that God ensures that all humanity is saved by this work (leaving to one side how this might come about). This also leads to two possible options: either concede that this divine decision to save all humanity is an arbitrary one or present an argument for the claim that it is not arbitrary—that this decision is, say, an objectively morally better state of affairs than the salvation of some number less than the

42. To spell it out, it seems deeply implausible to me that there is such a thing as an optimal number of humans for whom Christ died that is less than the total number of human beings.

43. I should add that the worry about arbitrariness really applies to theologically determinist accounts of salvation. Those who are theologically libertarian can always appeal to the fact that it is the response of the creature that yields the actual number of those saved, not God's predetermination of some particular outcome. This is typically thought to be a reason in favor of theological libertarian accounts of the scope of human salvation.

total number of humans. But it is also feasible for the defender of penal substitution to opt for the view that Christ's atonement is potentially universal, depending on the appropriation of its benefits via human free choice. This approach utilizes a sufficiency-efficiency distinction about the scope of atonement: Christ's work is sufficient to save all of humanity, but it is efficient (or effectual) only for those who appropriate it by faith in the exercise of libertarianly free choice. This is another way to avoid the charge of arbitrariness.

These different ways of thinking about the relationship between penal substitution and the arbitrariness problem are not exhaustive of all logically possible options. They are not intended to be. They are only intended as a sketch of some live options for contemporary defenders of penal substitution. So, penal substitution, understood in terms of universal redemption, does not raise an arbitrariness problem. Nor does particular redemption (whether of all or merely some of humanity) yield an arbitrariness problem, though this may be more surprising. God may have a reason for saving just the number God does, on this second sort of view. But what if God does not? What if one concedes that the number of human beings saved via the atonement is arbitrary? This question, as I have indicated, is broader than the doctrine of penal substitution. Other doctrines of atonement are also liable to this sort of criticism. This is, of course, merely *ad hominem*. If the defender of penal substitution embraces the claim that God ordains the salvation of a particular number of human beings via the atonement, without sufficient justification for this decision, then an arbitrariness problem does follow. But the theologian need not embrace this conclusion simply because they think penal substitution is true.

c. Why Cannot God Simply Forgive Sin without Punishment?

The force of this line of criticism has already been considerably reduced by the exposition of the assumptions behind penal substitution. If divine justice is both retributive and inexorable such that God cannot permit forgiveness without punishment or satisfaction, then it is not the case that God can simply forgive sin without some sort of satisfaction of divine justice being made. Of course, the critic could claim that this conception of divine justice is a travesty. But then some argument has to be offered as to why it is a travesty, and why some alternative conception of divine justice is preferable. I have already explained why defenders of this sort of penal substitutionary doctrine will claim that the notion that divine justice does not require forgiveness is not preferable to this. And, if the critic were to take the view that God must forgive sin without satisfaction because, say, the benevolence of God requires this, I think this is false. Divine benevolence only requires this if it is a constituent of divine benevolence that God loves all human beings equally *and savingly*. Even if we concede that divine benevolence does require that God loves all humanity equally and savingly, this does not entail that God cannot or will not require satisfaction for sin, only that God does not will the loss of any human being. It is perfectly consistent with this view of divine benevolence for God to save all humanity through the penal substitution of Christ.[44]

In any case, it seems to me that divine benevolence need not mean God has to love all humanity equally *and* savingly.[45] Divine benevolence is consistent with God loving all creatures but saving only some of them. Salvation is not dependent merely on divine benevolence but also on divine grace. God may love the sinner but hate the sin, and punish it in hell, just as the parent may love the child who is sentenced to life imprisonment for murder but approve of the punishment. So a distinction needs to be made between divine benevolence and divine grace in this respect: even if divine benevolence is an essential attribute of God, it does not follow that God has to save all humanity, because grace is not inexorable in the same way that justice is. From this it seems to me that the traditional view of divine retributive punishment as inexorable is not a travesty; it is coherent, even if it is unpalatable to modern theological tastes. So, this argument against penal substitution fails.

44. For that matter, it is consistent with this view that some human beings are ultimately lost if, say, some version of theological libertarianism is true—for presumably at least some theological libertarians think that God could will that no human being be lost and yet some humans reject salvation.

45. What if divine love includes the desire for the flourishing of the beloved and union with the beloved, as Eleonore Stump has claimed? Must God love all savingly then, if he desires union with the beloved? Not necessarily. It may be that humans have libertarian free will, in which case God's benevolence cannot be effectually applied to individuals without overriding their agency, and it may be that some human agents resist God's overtures and are punished in hell as a consequence. For a sophisticated discussion of this, see Stump, *Atonement*.

d. Can Sin and Guilt Be Transferred to Christ?

I shall deal with the problem of the transference of sin and the problem of the transference of guilt together. It should be clear from the foregoing that defenders of penal substitution have not usually been guilty of claiming that there really is a transference of properties from the sinner to Christ, or from Christ to the sinner, when it comes to sin, guilt, and Christ's righteousness. Rather, in the classical doctrine of penal substitution, God accepts Christ's satisfaction of the penalty due for sin as a penal substitute on the basis of a legal relaxation whereby Christ is able to take upon himself the liability to punishment. Nothing is transferred from the sinner to Christ beyond this legal fiction. Christ is treated as if he were the guilty party, though he is not, strictly speaking. The harsh treatment served is therefore not numerically the same as that owed by the sinner. It cannot be, because the sinner does not serve it; Christ does.[46] Nevertheless, the idea is that Christ suffers the harsh treatment that would be a punishment if it were served by the sinner, and that it is a punishment that is (somehow) qualitatively the same as that which would have been served upon the sinner had Christ not acted as substitute.[47] So, on this view, the punishment due for the guilt of sin may be transferred in an action of legal relaxation on the part of God. This, it is claimed by defenders of penal substitution, is just because it fits with the forensic nature of the atonement. But can the liability for penal debts be transferred from one individual to another? If a murderer were able to have the culpability for his crime transferred to another, surely we would think this would make a mockery of justice. Yet this is just what is involved in penal substitution. The murderer remains the one who has committed the crime. He remains the one guilty of committing the crime. But the penal consequences of the crime are transferred to a vicar who serves the punishment in his stead.

46. Alternatively, on the weaker penal substitution view, Christ serves the penal consequence of human sin, and not the liability to punishment strictly speaking.

47. How is Christ's punishment qualitatively the same as that suffered by the damned if he suffers on the cross for a matter of only some hours? There are several possible responses to this. One, following Peter Geach, is to say that Christ is able to suffer an infinite punishment in a finite period, where time is an infinitely dense continuum. The other is to say that Christ's death is a death of infinite significance and intensity, since it is the death of the God-man. An alternative is to deny that it is qualitatively the same as the infinite punishment of the damned and opt instead for the weaker view that God accepts some suitable substitution in the case of Christ that is not strictly speaking the same as the suffering of the damned. This is to return once again to questions about the *value* of the atonement.

This remains perhaps the most significant intellectual problem that defenders of penal substitution must address.[48]

Conclusion

Not all of the problems we canvassed seem insurmountable for the doctrine of penal substitution. The claim that God could just forgive human beings without punishment can be met given certain assumptions about divine justice and the divine nature, as can the claim that penal substitution makes God's action in election seem arbitrary. But whether it is possible for the sin and guilt of one individual to be transferred to another individual remains a real difficulty. Even if penal substitution means only that the penal consequences of sin are transferred from the sinner to Christ, there is still the worry that it seems unjust to inflict such harsh treatment on an innocent party instead of the guilty one. Perhaps God can relax his justice to the extent that he can accept a vicarious satisfaction of the infinite debt owed by human beings instead of punishing them,[49] even if it is a *sui generis* legal arrangement.[50] But these are not the only live options. There are alternatives open to those sympathetic to the sort of moral and theological intuitions that inform penal substitution but are concerned by some of the intellectual challenges faced by historic versions of the doctrine. One is to provide alternative arguments in favor of penal substitution—and such arguments are beginning to appear in the philosophical-theological literature.[51] The other is to opt for a version of Anselmian satisfaction theory instead, which might be thought of as a kind of theological "fall back" position. (The idea is this: if penal substitution raises more problems than it solves, perhaps a near relative of the doctrine that does not have these costs is a preferable alternative. Satisfaction is just such a near relative.)[52] As we saw in the previous chapter, satisfaction is a

48. For recent attempts to do just this, see Woznicki, "Do We Believe in Consequences?"; and Woznicki, "'One Can't Believe Impossible Things.'"
49. For a discussion of this, see Strabbing, "Permissibility of the Atonement."
50. In "Permissibility of the Atonement," Strabbing argues that one way around this is to claim that penal substitution may be permissible where there is no realistic possibility of the offender being able to provide adequate satisfaction for sin.
51. For instance, the arguments of Craig, Strabbing, Woznicki, and Thurow, which I have already mentioned.
52. This is the option favored in the recent literature by Joshua Farris and Mark Hamilton, whose constructive account of atonement is an updated and amended version of satisfaction

robust doctrine of atonement that delivers much of what penal substitution promises without some of the more problematic aspects of penal substitution having to do with transferring or imputing sin and guilt. But perhaps there is a middle way, somewhere in between these two. In the third part of this work, I will attempt to provide such an account, one which views the atonement as a work that is vicarious, reparative, and representational in nature but that is not a penal substitution.

---

that they call reparative substitution. See Farris and Hamilton, "The Logic of Reparative Substitution."

PART 3

Atonement and Salvation

We come in the third part to the constructive heart of the book. Matters are complicated by the fact that the argument offered here reflects a process of thinking on the topic of atonement and salvation that has been ongoing for over a decade. In the course of that time, I have written several books on the atonement as well as other books in which the doctrine features as a significant aspect. In earlier work, I developed what I called the "union account of atonement," and in particular a version of the union account that I called the "realist union account." In the same period, I was working on the doctrine of sin and came to revise my views on original sin in light of further reflection on the topic. Sin and salvation are, in many respects, two halves of one dogmatic whole. So the relationship between these two things is not incidental, theologically speaking. In the prequel to this volume, *The Word Enfleshed*, I also discussed the role of the Holy Spirit in union with Christ, and what that entails. Subsequent work in the broader doctrine of salvation has helped me to clarify some things here too, especially with respect to regeneration. Finally, as I have thought about the shape of salvation, it has become clearer to me that these different aspects of the arc of God's work in reconciling fallen human beings are just that, aspects of a larger whole, that whole being the work of bringing fallen humanity back into a participatory relationship with Godself.

These different ideas are all present in this final section. We begin in chapter 7 with an account of original sin. I argue for a corruption-only account of original sin. On this account, those chronologically downstream of our first aboriginal parents are born in a state of sin, with the moral corruption of original sin, which, like a kind of moral disease, excludes those who possess it from the presence of God absent atonement. But we are not born with Adam's guilt as well as the moral corruption that is consequent upon the primal sin. Thus, we have original sin but not original guilt. This view, or something very like it, was held by several of the early Reformers, including Zwingli and Calvin. I argue that this doctrine is defensible against several concerns and that it makes good sense of the biblical basis for the doctrine—especially the Adam Christology of Romans 5.[1]

In chapter 8 we turn to the nature of atonement—and, specifically, to the mechanism of Christ's reconciling work. In *The Word Enfleshed* I outlined an account of the nature of atonement that I called the "union account." In this chapter I first recap this previous work and some objections to that formulation of the doctrine. I then set out a second, related but distinct account of atonement. It too could be thought of as a union account, but central to this second account is a different mechanism of atonement. Whereas the first, realist union account utilized an understanding of atonement that was a species of penal substitution, this representational union account opts instead for a mechanism where Christ's atonement is a *vicarious, reparative, and penitential act of soteriological representation* whereby a "part" of humanity, Christ, may stand in for the whole of fallen humanity and act on behalf of the whole. Using some recent work in social ontology on the metaphysics of group action, I give an account of this mechanism as a *sui generis* act of representation ordained by God.

Chapter 9 focuses on the consequences of atonement—that is, on how the benefits of Christ's saving work are applied to the individual agent and to the new society that it forms, which is the mystical body of Christ. This falls into three parts. In the first, I give an account of the way in which

---

1. For earlier forays into this area, see the relevant chapters of Crisp, *Analyzing Doctrine*; Crisp, *Freedom, Redemption and Communion*; and Crisp, *God, Creation, and Salvation*.

God ordains the justification of the believer from eternity and the Holy Spirit applies the saving work of Christ to the believer in history. This is the calling and regeneration of the believer, which is entirely a work of divine condescension in which the uncreated grace of the Holy Spirit is infused into the believer. This in turn leads to consideration of the way in which the regenerate believer is united by the Spirit to Christ so as to be able to participate in the divine life. Then, in a third section, we consider the way in which the benefits of Christ's work generate the church from redeemed humanity. The church is to be understood as a group that is guided and directed by the Holy Spirit as a new society directed toward eschatological communion with God.

Chapter 10 provides a kind of synthetic snapshot of the sweep of soteriology, showing how the account of atonement set forth here sits within the broader doctrine of salvation. The thought here is this: atonement is a necessary condition for human salvation, but it is not sufficient taken in isolation from the other aspects of the order of salvation. This includes God's eternal decree to elect some number of human beings to life; the justification, calling, and regenerating of redeemed humanity in history; and the formation of the church as the mystic body of Christ formed for everlasting communion with God and participation in the divine life.

———————— 7 ————————

Sin and Salvation

W e have already noted in passing that one important theological constraint on any doctrine of atonement is an account of why it is that human beings are in need of salvation in the first place. Why, we might ask, is the reconciling work of Christ necessary for human participation in the divine life? One traditional answer has to do with the notion of sin. We read in the Pastoral Epistles that "Christ Jesus came into the world to save sinners" (1 Tim. 1:15). And Paul in particular is clear that human beings are sinners (Rom. 3:10), and that "the wages of sin is death, but the free gift of God is eternal life" (Rom. 6:23). The biblical picture seems to be one according to which human beings have fallen short of the glory of God (Rom. 3:23). This is not just a matter of proof texting. It seems to be part of the very fabric out of which the biblical material is spun. But it is one thing to fall short of a target or to fail to meet a particular marker or threshold. It is another thing to bear the kind of morally disordered nature consequent upon sin that is a constituent of many traditional doctrines of sin and original sin.[1]

---

1. This is also a traditional trope in subsequent theology. To give just one example, from Peter Lombard, the great medieval Master of *The Sentences*, "Christ is called mediator because, as intermediary between God and men, he reconciles them to God. He reconciles them by first removing the offences of men from God's sight, that is, by taking away the sins by which God was offended and we were his enemies" (*Sentences*, bk. 3, dist. 19, chap. 6, p. 82).

In beginning to give a constructive doctrine of atonement it seems appropriate to provide some notion of sin, and original sin in particular, in order that we have a clear idea of what it is that human beings are saved from by Christ's act of reconciliation. We will then be in a position to consider how it is that Christ provides the requisite act of reconciliation to deal with the moral condition in which fallen human beings find themselves.[2]

To this end, in this chapter I will give an account of original sin as it is related to human salvation. This is not the first occasion on which I have tackled the doctrine of original sin.[3] The version of the doctrine given here draws on my previous work in this area and attempts to meet some objections that have been raised in the recent literature to the kind of moderate Reformed doctrine of original sin that I have previously defended. We proceed as follows: To begin with, I shall set out the moderate Reformed doctrine and offer some explanatory gloss on each of the claims of the moderate Reformed doctrine of original sin, so as to flesh out its dogmatic claims. In the course of doing so, I shall also compare this moderate doctrine with relevant voices in the Reformed tradition, in order to show that it is, indeed, a legitimate expression of Reformed theology, even if some will think it represents a minority report in that tradition. In a second section I defend this moderate Reformed view against several criticisms. A short concluding section offers some reflections on the scope of this moderate Reformed doctrine of sin.

A Corruption-Only Doctrine of Original Sin

In this chapter I will set out and defend what I have elsewhere called the moderate Reformed doctrine of original sin. It is, as Thomas H. McCall

2. Some writers might question whether atonement should be thought of exclusively in terms of the remission of sin. My claim is that atonement is primarily about the remission of sin. It may also bring about other goods. But in terms of the biblical picture of salvation, it is sin that has estranged us from God and that leads to spiritual death. My own view is that the atonement makes reconciliation *possible*. It is made *effectual* by an additional divine work—that is, the secret work of the Holy Spirit, by whose agency we are united to Christ. I have discussed this issue in more detail in *Word Enfleshed* and "Regeneration Reconsidered."

3. See "On the Theological Pedigree"; "Scholastic Theology"; "Federalism vs. Realism"; "Pulling Traducianism out of the Shedd"; "Sin, Atonement and Representation"; "Sin"; "Retrieving Zwingli's Doctrine of Original Sin"; "On Original Sin"; *Analyzing Doctrine*, chap. 7; "On Behalf of Augustinian Realism"; "Moderate Reformed View"; and "Moderate Reformed Response," to which this chapter is a successor.

has recently pointed out, a corruption-only version of original sin.[4] By that he means it is an account of original sin that posits a corruption of human nature consequent upon a primal sin (perhaps the primal sin of our aboriginal parents), but not in addition to that the transmission of the guilt of that sin. We can outline the main constituents of this moderate Reformed doctrine of original sin as follows:

1. All human beings barring Christ possess original sin.
2. Original sin is an inherited corruption of nature, a condition that every fallen human being possesses from the first moment of generation.
3. Fallen humans are not culpable for being generated with this morally vitiated condition.
4. Fallen humans are not culpable for a first, or primal, sin either. That is, they do not bear original guilt (i.e., the guilt of the sin of some putative first human pair or human community being imputed to them along with original sin).
5. This morally vitiated condition normally inevitably yields actual sin. That is, a person born with this defect will normally inevitably commit actual sin on at least one occasion provided that person lives long enough to be able to commit such sin. (The caveat "normally" indicates that there are limit cases that are exceptions to this claim—e.g., infants that die before maturity and the severely mentally impaired.)
6. Fallen human beings are culpable for their actual sins and condemned for them, in the absence of atonement.
7. Possession of original sin leads to death and separation from God irrespective of actual sin.[5]

It seems to me that, taken together, these claims represent a moderate, and therefore defensible, version of the doctrine of original sin that is consistent with one strand of the Reformed tradition.[6] Because it is a moderate

4. See McCall, *Against God and Nature*, 201.
5. See Crisp, *Analyzing Doctrine*, chap. 7.
6. Specifically, a minority report in the Reformed tradition that stems from the work of theologians like Huldrych Zwingli and John Calvin. For discussion of this, see Crisp, "Sin," and Crisp, "Retrieving Zwingli's Doctrine of Original Sin." See also Allen's essay, "Calvin's Christ."

account, it may also be more promising for ecumenical rapprochement with other strands of the Christian tradition than some other versions of the doctrine of original sin that can be found within Reformed theology. Let us treat the numbered sentences of this moderate doctrine as dogmatic claims, considering and expounding each in turn.

Regarding 1

According to the first claim of the moderate Reformed doctrine, *all human beings barring Christ possess original sin*. Historically, many Christians have held that there was some primal sin by means of which original sin was introduced into the human race.[7] By *primal sin* I mean that first act of sin supposedly committed by our first parents, Adam and Eve, which led to all subsequent human beings being generated in a morally vitiated condition—the condition of original sin. The notion that human beings after the sin of our first parents possess original sin is relatively uncontroversial in the Western Christian tradition. Only those who, like Pelagius, deny the doctrine of original sin (and are therefore outside the bounds of theological orthodoxy) would be troubled by it. However, the notion that this affects all human beings is more controversial because many Roman Catholic Christians maintain that Mary *Theotokos* (that is, Mary the God-Bearer, the mother of Christ) was born without original sin by means of an immaculate conception. Those Christians who want to include Mary *Theotokos* along with Christ as being without original sin may make the relevant mental reservation in what follows. In any case, whatever we make of the moral state of Mary *Theotokos*, the notion that Christ is an exception to the humanity-wide condition of original sin is not theologically controversial in mainstream Western theology. It is an assumption of all Christians that Christ is without sin, though there are some theologians who have believed Christ's human nature was in some sense fallen, though he never committed sin. There is not space to enter into that debate here, but suffice it to say a person with a fallen human nature would already be

7. Many, but by no means all. A significant number of Christians have denied original sin as such. Here I am thinking of the Eastern Orthodox, who hold instead to the doctrine of ancestral sin, according to which our original parents sinned such that they wounded the human nature they passed on. Our natures need to be healed of that wound with the Balm of Gilead that is Christ. But this is not the same as a notion of original sin as a privation of a state of justice or even a corruption of human nature. For discussion of this, see Romanides, *Ancestral Sin*.

in a morally precarious state, one which would seem to disbar that person from being in the presence of God, whose eyes are too pure to look upon evil (Hab. 1:13). For what is it to be fallen if not to be in a morally vitiated state that inevitably gives rise to actual sin?[8] If Christ is God Incarnate, and God is incapable of sinning, then it is only a short, though crucial, step to saying that his human nature is without sin—in which case, it is difficult to see what to make of the claim that his human nature is fallen but not sinful. This seems like a distinction without a difference.[9]

So, the first claim of the moderate Reformed doctrine—that original sin is a condition all human beings barring Christ possess—seems fairly theologically secure, at least in the Western tradition. Few Latin Christians (whether Roman Catholic or Protestant) would deny it. However, the fact that this first dogmatic claim makes no reference to a primal sin, or an aboriginal pair, is much more controversial—for belief in some putative aboriginal pair from which all humanity is descended, and whose primal sin is (somehow) transmitted to all subsequent humans barring Christ, is a constituent of almost all historic Western Christian attempts to make sense of original sin. The moderate Reformed doctrine of sin does not require an original pair, nor does it require monogenism (the notion that we are descended from an original pair). However, it does not deny that there was an original pair from which we are descended either. Instead, it is a doctrine that prescinds from making a judgment about this dogmatic question. This, as we shall see, is an important consideration that marks what might be called a dogmatic minimalism that is part and parcel of the moderate Reformed view. By "dogmatic minimalism" I mean an approach to a particular doctrine (in this case, original sin) that attempts to affirm as "thin" an account as is doctrinally possible, consistent with wider theological and confessional commitments.[10] On the question of the etiology of original sin, the moderate Reformed doctrine is dogmatically minimalist.

Regarding 2

This brings us to the second dogmatic claim, which is that *original sin is an inherited corruption of nature, a condition that every fallen human*

8. For a recent discussion of this point, see Crisp, *God, Creation, and Salvation*, chap. 7.

9. I have discussed this in more detail in Crisp, *Divinity and Humanity*, chap. 4; and in Crisp, *God Incarnate*, chap. 6. See also Pawl, *In Defense of Extended Conciliar Christology*, chap. 6.

10. I have written about dogmatic minimalism elsewhere. See Crisp, "Desiderata."

being possesses from the first moment of generation. As is well known, the Reformed have a rather dim view of fallen human beings. The "T" of TULIP, the popular acrostic that summarizes the five points of Calvinism derived from the teaching of the Synod of Dort, stands for "total depravity." The idea is not that fallen human beings are as depraved as they could be but, rather, that fallen human beings are in bondage to sin, and this affects every area of human life. We could put it like this: Reformed theologians have traditionally taught that fallen human beings are morally corrupt, and that original sin itself is a moral corruption that we are generated with, and which affects us profoundly. There is also a distinction to be made between *original sin*, the morally vitiated condition that we are generated with, and *actual sin.* Actual sin connotes the sins we commit as moral agents. I sin because I am a sinner, born with original sin. But the sins I commit as a sinner are actual sins for which I am morally responsible. (We will return to actual sin in due course.)

Some Reformed theologians have argued that God immediately and directly imputes original sin from our first parents to all subsequent generations of humanity, and that on this basis we are reckoned to be guilty of original sin. But this seems a very strange arrangement, one in which the moral consequences of someone else's sin are transferred directly to me by divine fiat, yielding guilt in me for something I did not do. For one thing, that seems monumentally unjust, for then I have immediately transferred to me a sinful condition that I did not choose, rather like having someone else's debt immediately electronically transferred to my bank account, so that money is debited from my account as a result. For another, it implies a strange doctrine in which guilt can be transferred from one person (Adam) to another (me).

Other theologians reverse these claims, so that Adam's original guilt is said to be communicated to me by God because I am generated with the corrupt nature that is mediated to me by my forebears. So either God imputes Adam's sin and guilt to me prior to my existence or God ensures a corrupt nature is transmitted to me by natural generation and, as a consequence, guilt is imputed to me as well. Each of these traditional Reformed ways of thinking about the transmission of original sin and guilt are convoluted and not terribly intuitive.[11]

11. For a discussion of these matters, see McCall, *Against God and Nature*; and Murray, *Imputation of Adam's Sin.*

By contrast, the notion that original sin is an inherited moral condition, rather like humans can inherit physical conditions from their parents, seems plausible, and is not necessarily unjust.[12] Suppose a mother is a drug addict and she passes on her addiction to her unborn child because they share the same blood supply. The child inherits the addiction through no fault of her own. Similarly, suppose an ancestor sells himself into slavery and his heirs are then born in that state through no fault of their own. They inherit the moral burden their forebear has placed upon them.[13] We do not condone the mother's addiction or the ancestor's decision to sell himself and his heirs. Nevertheless, such arrangements are familiar and seem plausible, though reprehensible. Similarly, suppose that through some (collective) transgression a first human community is estranged from God. That estrangement, and any consequent moral disruption it causes, may be passed down the generations to later members of that community through no fault of their own. Whether we like it or not, our sinful choices often have effects on others around us. In cases like the addicted mother or the enslaved ancestor, one generation's choices have consequences that are inherited by the next. To commit some action that leads inexorably to one's own moral torpor is a terrible thing. To commit an act that adversely affects generations yet to come is much worse. Yet such actions are not unusual, as our two examples (of the addicted mother and the enslaved ancestor) suggest. Of course, if original sin is inherited like this, rather than being transmitted immediately and directly, then presumably it is transferred from one generation to another mediately, as certain congenital conditions are passed down from two parents to a child. It is not a condition that is picked up by imitation, as the Pelagians averred. On this way of thinking, it must be transferred by inheritance, like a genetic defect, rather than by immediate divine imputation.

Regarding 3

We come then to our third claim: that *fallen humans are not culpable for being generated with this morally vitiated condition*. With this in mind,

12. Here I draw on a strand of Reformed thought that can be found in various places, e.g., Edwards, *Original Sin*; and Shedd, *Dogmatic Theology*. Helpful context for this can be found in Evans, *Imputation and Impartation*.

13. This is an example used by other theologians, like Zwingli. For discussion, see Crisp, "Zwingli on Original Sin."

let us return to our earlier examples of the addicted mother and the enslaved ancestor. It is clear that the child born with an addiction because
her mother is an addict is not morally responsible for being born in that
condition. Similarly, the child born into a family of slaves is not responsible
for being born a slave. In neither case is the child concerned culpable for
the plight into which she was born. In a similar fashion, the child born
with the condition of original sin cannot be culpable for being generated
with that condition. How could she be? Culpability presumes some sort
of action on the part of the agent to whom it is ascribed, and the child
born with original sin is not in a position to have acted in a way that brings
with it the ascription of culpability.[14]

Regarding 4

This brings us to our fourth claim, which goes to the heart of the moderate Reformed view: *Fallen humans are not culpable for a first, or primal,
sin either. That is, they do not bear original guilt (i.e., the guilt of the sin
of some putative first human pair or human community being imputed to
them along with original sin).* One of the characteristics of much, though
by no means all, historic Reformed theology, has been the emphasis placed
upon the doctrine of original guilt alongside a doctrine of original sin.
Often the two notions are bundled together so that all human beings after
Adam and Eve are said to bear the moral corruption and guilt introduced
to the race through the first sin of our aboriginal parents.

The idea seems to be something like this: Adam and Eve commit the
first, or primal, sin. This brings about alienation from God and leaves humans with a morally disordered nature, one that lacks the moral structure
and integrity with which humanity was originally created. This condition
is then transmitted to subsequent human beings. But how are subsequent
generations of humanity guilty of Adam and Eve's primal sin? Historic
Reformed theology has two broad answers to this question. According
to the first, we are guilty of Adam's sin because Adam acts as our representative so that when he sins, his action has consequences for the rest of
humanity. There are many human analogs to this sort of arrangement,
such as diplomatic representatives acting on behalf of a nation, binding

---

14. Once again, this argument is made in the tradition by Zwingli and also by Anselm of
Canterbury. See Anselm, *On the Virginal Conception.*

that nation to certain international agreements. Similarly, our elected representatives in Parliament or on Capitol Hill represent our views and make political decisions on our behalf that bind us in certain ways—if, say, the decision becomes law. So the idea that Adam may represent us and that we may be bound by his action is a familiar one in other, mundane contexts. However, in the case of the diplomat and the politician, their roles as representatives depend on having a political mandate granted by the nation, or the voters, that they represent. There is no such arrangement with respect to Adam. We did not authorize our first parents, or some putative early human community, to act in this capacity. If someone represents us without authorization, we would normally think this unjust.[15] Perhaps it might be claimed that in the case of Adam, God authorizes his role as representative. Some may think this gives us reason to think that the arrangement is authorized. Nevertheless, it still seems unjust because it is not a decision to which we were party, or to which we could assent as moral agents. Surely God would not act unjustly?

The main alternative to representationalism is often called Augustinian realism, because it is supposed to have originated with Augustine of Hippo (though the matter of its ascription is, for our purposes, moot). Whether Augustine was an Augustinian realist or not, the idea is that I may be guilty of Adam's sin because I am somehow united with Adam in one metaphysical whole of which we are parts (hence, realism: we are really united to Adam as parts of one metaphysical whole object scattered across space and time).

Consider an analogy with an oak tree. Suppose we introduce a contagion into an acorn and plant it. What springs up is a sapling, then a young tree, and finally after many years, a full-grown oak. However, as it grows and matures the oak is misshapen and deformed because of the contagion introduced at the acorn stage of its life. Consequently, all the later stages of the oak as it grows and develops across time are marred by the contagion it bears. Now, the realist says that humanity is like the oak. Through his own deliberate fault, Adam introduces a contagion to humanity that is original sin. This has the consequence that all later stages of humanity are affected by the contagion so that they are morally deformed. Just as the

15. Is it unjust if Christ represents us without authorization? That is an interesting question. My view is that Christ is authorized by God, whereas Adam was not authorized to sin. So there is a relevant difference here.

later stages of the life of the oak may be said to share in the one life that began when the acorn was planted, so human beings living after Adam's first sin share in the life of Adam and therefore partake of his sin. If we are parts of one metaphysical whole that is fallen humanity, then perhaps the sin and guilt for that sin committed by Adam can be transferred to all the later stages of the life of humanity. (This is a matter to which we shall return in the next chapter.)

It seems to me that there is something to be said for the notion that Adam and his progeny are metaphysically united in the way that Augustinian realism presumes. However, it is not clear to me that this provides a good reason for endorsing original guilt as well as original sin. Consider Romans 5:12–19, which is arguably the most important biblical text for the doctrine of original sin, as well as being the putative basis for a doctrine of original guilt. This passage tells us that "sin came into the world through one man, and death came through sin, and so death spread to all because all have sinned" (v. 12). It also says that "death exercised dominion from Adam to Moses, even over those whose sins were not like the transgression of Adam, who is a type of the one who was to come [i.e., Christ]" (v. 14). What is more, "many died through the one man's trespass" (v. 15); indeed, "judgment following one trespass brought condemnation" (v. 16). For it is "because of the one man's trespass" that "death exercised dominion through that one" (v. 17). The passage concludes, "just as one man's trespass led to condemnation for all, so one man's act of righteousness leads to justification and life for all. For just as by the one man's disobedience the many were made sinners, so by the one man's obedience the many will be made righteous" (vv. 18–19).

Now, it is not at all clear to me that this passage implies original guilt. It may be consistent with something like the Augustinian realist picture of how sin is transmitted. It does seem commensurate with something like the inheritance of a morally vitiated condition. But it is difficult to see how it yields the notion that all human beings (barring Christ, and perhaps Mary *Theotokos*) are guilty of Adam's primal sin. The condemnation spoken of in the passage is surely most naturally coupled with the penalty of sin, which is death. In which case, the judgment following the trespass yields the penalty of death and condemnation, and nothing here implies that culpability is included in the judgment made, in the condemnation that is passed in consequence, or in the penalty that is applied to human beings as the upshot.

Happily, the notion of original guilt can be separated from the doctrine of original sin. One could be born with a condition of moral corruption inherited from some first ancestors and yet not be guilty of the sin of that ancestor—on analogy with being born with some genetic condition that is attributable to some distant ancestor, for which we bear no blame either. And such an arrangement may have important and unpleasant implications for the descendant of that ancestor. (Think of a genetic predisposition to a disease that is triggered by environmental conditions.) Nevertheless, some may worry that if this is to be a truly Reformed doctrine of original sin, some account must be given of the fact that original guilt is embedded in a number of the confessions of the Reformed churches.

For instance, we read this in the Westminster Confession: "They [our first parents] being the root of all mankind, the guilt of this sin was imputed, and the same death in sin and corrupted nature conveyed to all their posterity, descending from them by ordinary generation" (6.3). But there is no unanimous voice in the Reformed confessional tradition on this point. Some earlier confessions, such as the Scots Confession (1560) and the Belgic Confession (1561), elaborate a doctrine of original sin without original guilt. Nor is the doctrine of original guilt to be found in the writings of the fountainheads of Reformed thought. Neither Huldrych Zwingli nor John Calvin endorse it.[16] In fact, Zwingli denies that human beings are born guilty of sin, which he seems to regard as something like a disease passed on from one generation to the next.[17] Calvin writes about original sin as a contagion and corruption of human nature. He defines it thus: "Original sin, therefore, seems to be a hereditary depravity and corruption of our nature, diffused into all parts of the soul, which first makes us liable to God's wrath, then also brings forth in us those works which Scripture calls 'works of the flesh' [Gal. 5:19–20]. And that is properly what Paul often calls sin."[18] Earlier in the same passage, he writes, "Adam, by sinning, not only took upon himself misfortune and ruin but also plunged our nature into like destruction. This was not due to the guilt of himself alone, which would not pertain to us all, but was because he infected all

16. See Crisp, "Zwingli on Original Sin"; and Allen, "Calvin's Christ."
17. See, e.g., Zwingli, *On Providence and Other Essays*, 1–32.
18. Calvin, *Institutes* 2.1.8.

his posterity with that corruption into which he had fallen. . . . Adam so corrupted himself that infection spread from him to all his descendants."[19]

To sum up, original guilt does not rest on a strong biblical foundation. The main text used to defend the doctrine, Romans 5:12–19, does not appear to teach anything like a doctrine of original guilt. It is not a doctrine universally affirmed in Reformed theology—in fact, two continental fountainheads of Reformed theology deny it. And whether original sin is transmitted by imputation or by some realist doctrine (the two main alternatives in historic Reformed thought), original guilt need not be included in this arrangement. Thus, the rejection of original guilt seems consistent with at least one strand of Reformed theology going back to the Magisterial Reformers themselves, as well as with some of the early Reformed confessions.

Independent of these theological and traditional considerations, there is also a good philosophical reason (which has already been intimated in the foregoing) for setting original guilt aside: *guilt is nontransferable.* A person's guilt cannot become the guilt of her son or daughter, or of their sons and daughters, and so on. Even if that person is punished for her sin so that she is no longer culpable for it, she, and only she, is the one guilty of having sinned. Guilt is the inalienable property of the person who has sinned. This is due in large measure to the fact that guilt is intimately connected to a person's moral agency. We say that it was because Jones committed a particular moral action that she is the appropriate referent of this ascription of blame. Blame is ascribed to her because it was her action, and hers alone, and because she committed the act as a moral agent (not under the influence of a drug, or under duress, or because she was forced to do so, or whatever). Because she is blameworthy, she bears culpability.

If she does it together with some other person (as Adam did with Eve), then culpability, and thus guilt, may be shared. But that is because both moral agents participate in the same action. But clearly Jones's great-

19. Calvin, *Institutes* 2.1.6. Regarding the claim that fallen humans are subject to divine judgment through Adam's sin, he adds, "We are to understand it not as if we, guiltless and undeserving, bore the guilt of his offense but in the sense that, since we through his transgression have become entangled in the curse, he is said to have made us guilty" (2.1.8). Yet given his previous admission that we are not guilty of Adam's sin, and the qualification "*he is said to have made us guilty,*" I think the ascription of guilt here is best understood in a metaphorical sense, just as the child of a murderer may be said to be tinged with her father's guilt. We are not *literally* guilty of Adam's sin.

grandson who is removed by a great distance in time from Jones's sinful action cannot be said to be guilty of the sin committed by Jones because her great-grandson was not present when Jones committed the sin, and he did not approve it or participate in it. Consequently, Jones's great-grandson cannot be held accountable for her sins. But this is just what the doctrine of original guilt stipulates—that we are *guilty* of Adam's primal sin, though we were not present when he committed the sin and did not sanction it or participate in it. Yet this appears to be monumentally unjust. Since God cannot perform unjust actions, this gives us a strong independent reason (that is, a reason independent of appeals to theological authority or tradition) for thinking that there is something seriously amiss with the doctrine of original guilt.

Regarding 5

With this made tolerably clear, we can move on to the fifth theological claim of the moderate Reformed doctrine: *This morally vitiated condition normally inevitably yields actual sin. That is, a person born with this defect will normally inevitably commit actual sin on at least one occasion provided that person lives long enough to be able to commit such sin. (The caveat "normally" indicates that there are limit cases that are exceptions to this claim—e.g., infants that die before maturity and the severely mentally impaired.)*

Thus far we have seen that, according to the moderate Reformed doctrine of original sin, all human beings barring Christ are born with a corrupted nature. This means that we inherit a state of moral corruption. But we are not culpable for bearing this condition any more than the child of the addict is culpable for being born an addict, or the child of the slave is culpable for being born a slave. Now, on this account all those born with original sin will normally inevitably commit actual sin, for which they do bear responsibility. However, this is not true of all human beings. There are at least two sorts of limit cases salient to this aspect of the doctrine. The first encompasses those fallen human beings who do not live to an age at which they are capable of making the moral decisions that yield actual sin. The second includes those who are never in a position to commit actual sin because they never become fully developed moral agents due to some severe mental impairment.

Here I side with a minority report in the Reformed tradition. The nineteenth-century American Presbyterian theologian William G. T. Shedd argued that some fallen human beings are incapable of exercising faith and so they cannot be held responsible for failing to have faith in Christ.[20] He included infants before the age of moral responsibility and the severely mentally impaired in this category. On Shedd's way of thinking, such people are elected *en masse* and without the requirement of faith in Christ. I suggest that something similar be said of those who are born in a state of sin and who never reach a point at which they can commit actual sins—that is, actions of a moral nature that are sinful and for which they are morally responsible. Since children in utero and infants before the age of maturity are not fully formed moral agents and are incapable of making moral choices, they cannot be the subjects of moral responsibility. Similarly, those who are severely mentally impaired are incapable of making moral choices due to developmental deficiencies and cannot be the subjects of moral responsibility. They still possess original sin as a congenital-like moral condition, but they are not responsible for committing actual sins for which they bear guilt. In fact, it would seem that these two classes of individuals are not moral subjects, or cannot be counted as moral subjects, for the purposes of ascribing culpability for actual sin.

This does not necessarily mean that infants who perish before the age of discernment and the severely mentally impaired are elected as a class, as Shedd reasoned. Rather, the claim is only that such entities are not the proper subjects of moral responsibility because they are incapable of actual sin and not culpable for bearing original sin. However, it may be that God does elect these two sorts of individuals (infants before the age of reason and the severely mentally impaired) as a class, and without the requirement of faith. In fact, that is a view with which I am in sympathy. It is just that it is not part of the doctrine set forth here because it belongs to another topic—namely, to the doctrine of election.

Regarding 6

That brings us to our sixth claim: *fallen human beings are culpable for their actual sins and condemned for them, in the absence of atonement.* Earlier, in discussing the second dogmatic claim of the moderate

---

20. Shedd, *Dogmatic Theology*. See also Crisp, *American Augustinian*, chap. 7.

Reformed doctrine of sin, we distinguished between original and actual sin. Original sin is the condition that we inherit from our forebears; actual sins are those sins we commit as sinners. That is, being in a state of original sin, we commit actual sins—sins that are our own, rather than the moral state with which we are generated. Now, where a person is a moral agent and commits an actual sin, that person is normally culpable for that sin (provided she did it freely, without compulsion, was in her right mind, and so on). He or she is blameworthy for that sin, and guilt may be ascribed to the person as a consequence. Some Reformed theologians have argued that fallen human beings possess a double guilt: the guilt of Adam's original sin (that is, original guilt) and the additional guilt accruing as a consequence of the actual sins that a person goes on to perform as a moral agent. But since I have already given reasons for thinking that we do not have original guilt (in discussing the fourth dogmatic claim, above), it seems that the only sorts of actions for which a person can be held accountable are actions that they themselves perform, or to which they are party. It makes sense to think that such actions are ones for which we are blameworthy, just as it makes sense to think that virtuous actions are ones for which we are praiseworthy. And it is theologically uncontroversial among Christians committed to what Thomas Oden calls "consensus Christianity"[21] to maintain that, in the absence of atonement, these actual sins incur guilt, the upshot of which is condemnation.

Regarding 7

The seventh and final dogmatic claim of the moderate Reformed view of sin is that *possession of original sin leads to death and separation from God irrespective of actual sin.* Here the idea is that possession of original sin alone, without taking into account the guilt of actual sins, disbars a person from entering the presence of God without the application of the benefits of Christ's reconciling work. Imagine a man who is a leper being granted an audience with his prince. He is born with the condition through no fault of his own. Nevertheless, once it is discovered that the man has leprosy, he will be disbarred from the presence of the king. Such a medical condition prevents him from being ushered into the presence of his potentate because (at least historically) it was thought to be dangerous

21. See Oden, *Classic Christianity.*

and highly contagious. Similarly, on the moderate Reformed view of sin, fallen human beings are in a morally corrupted state irrespective of actual sin. Although they have inherited this corruption through no fault of their own, the presence of such corruption renders them unfit for the presence of God.

A similar view to this one can be found in the work of Zwingli. He writes, "Original sin, as it is in the children of Adam, is not properly sin ... for it is not a misdeed contrary to law. It is, therefore, properly a disease and condition—a disease, because just as he fell through self-love, so do we also; a condition, because just as he became a slave and liable to death, so also are we both slaves and children of wrath ... and liable to death."[22] Earlier we saw that Calvin writes of original sin as an "infection" that spreads from Adam to his progeny. The language of "disease" and "infection" used by these Magisterial Reformers should not displace the idea of original sin as an inherited corruption. Rather, like the case of the leper, they help to indicate why possession of original sin independent of actual sin renders a person unfit for the divine presence, through no fault of their own.

What, then, of those who possess original sin but never commit actual sin—our limit cases raised earlier, such as infants that die before the age of discernment and those who are severely mentally impaired? Are they disbarred from the divine presence just because they possess original sin, though they are not culpable for being in this moral state? It is certainly consistent with the logic of the moderate Reformed doctrine outlined thus far to reply in the affirmative to these questions. Perhaps those who fall under the description of these limit cases do indeed find themselves disbarred from the divine presence as a result. However, with William Shedd, I think this is a monstrous conclusion, one not worthy of God. We are told by the author of Ephesians to grasp "the breadth and length and height and depth" of the love of Christ (Eph. 3:18). Earlier in the same epistle, we read, "But God, who is rich in mercy, out of the great love with which he loved us even when we were dead through our trespasses, made us alive together with Christ—by grace you have been saved" (Eph. 2:4–5). But if, by sheer grace, God is able to make us alive in Christ while we are dead in our transgressions, why could God not save those "dead

22. Zwingli, *On Providence and Other Essays*, 40.

through [their] trespasses" because of original sin who have no capacity to exercise faith? Since the author of Ephesians tells us that faith itself is a gift of God, where that gift cannot be entertained because the person concerned is incapable of exercising faith, why would God not elect to save such people through Christ's atonement without faith? There is nothing to prevent God from doing so, nothing that can frustrate God in bringing this about. And, since God's grace and mercy are so great, God has the motivation to bring this about. God also has the means: the saving work of Christ. Although Scripture does not provide a warrant for thinking that God does save, through Christ, those born with original sin who are incapable of faith, it seems to me that it doesn't foreclose such a possibility either. Given what we know from Scripture and the tradition about the nature and purposes of God in salvation, and that God does not desire that anyone perish (2 Pet. 3:9), not even the wicked (Ezek. 18:23), there seems to be good reason to hope and expect that God does save such individuals as a class. These would be instances of persons with original sin rendered fit for the presence of God by having the benefits of Christ's work applied to them independent of the exercise of faith.

Some Objections to the Moderate Reformed Doctrine of Original Sin

This completes our exposition of the dogmatic claims that make up the moderate Reformed account of original sin. Having done this, we are in a position to consider some objections to this doctrine.

The first concern has to do with how this account is an improvement on the traditional Reformed doctrine that includes original guilt. For, on the face of it, it seems problematic to claim that fallen human beings are punishable for an inherited condition for which they are not culpable. However, as I have endeavored to argue, the idea that original sin is simply imputed by divine fiat to all human beings (barring Christ) is itself morally objectionable. Ascribing sin, and perhaps guilt, to one person on the basis of what some distant and long-dead ancestor has done seems monumentally unjust and immoral. Things are less objectionable where the arrangement is a realist, rather than merely a representationalist, one—that is, where Adam and his progeny are regarded, for certain purposes, as one metaphysical entity rather than where Adam is thought to merely stand in for, or represent, the rest of humankind. But a metaphysically realist arrangement also requires some explanation and is not without theological cost. These costs are not incurred by the more modest theological claim that original sin is an inherited moral corruption. We inherit all sorts of genetic oddities from our forebears. Perhaps we also inherit various traits and dispositions as well. The moderate Reformed view supposes that original sin is a kind of moral analog to these things. Like being born in a state of slavery, being born in a state of sin is a condition that is inherited from forebears, and it is a condition for which we are not culpable. As the person born as a slave is rendered unfit to be given the status and privileges of a citizen without some act of redemption, so also human beings in a state of original sin are rendered unfit to be given the status and privileges of citizens of the kingdom of God without some act of redemption. This explains why those in a sinful state may be barred from the presence of God though they are not culpable for being in the state into which they were born. It also explains why actual sin provides additional reasons for preventing us from entering the presence of God without atonement being made. Thus original sin is an inherited moral corruption for which fallen human beings are not culpable (though by it they are rendered unfit for the divine presence) to which is normally added actual sin, for which fallen human beings are culpable and worthy of condemnation in the absence of some act of atonement. This is clearly preferable to a doctrine of original sin that presumes I am guilty of Adam's primal sin.

A second concern is whether the moderate Reformed doctrine requires a historical Adam and Eve. I have already intimated in the foregoing that it does not have this requirement. In fact, the doctrine prescinds from making a judgment about whether human beings are descended from an aboriginal pair (which is monogenism) or from some larger population. So it is consistent with the view that there was a historical pair, Adam and Eve, whose offspring we are. But this is not a requirement of the doctrine. It could be that we are descended from a community of around ten thousand early hominins, from which early humans emerged, as scientists working in this area conclude to be the case. That view is also consistent with the doctrine. Where I have referred to Adam in the foregoing, this should be understood as a placeholder. The use of the names "Adam" and "Eve" does not indicate commitment to a historical aboriginal pair in a primeval garden, though the view expressed is consistent with these claims. In The Chronicles of Narnia, children from our world who cross over to that fair realm are often referred to by Aslan and natives of Narnia as "sons of Adam" and "daughters of Eve," though this appellation is, primarily, metaphorical. They are not literally children of Adam and Eve, but those who belong to the race of this fabled pair. By a similar token, someone today might be referred to as a child of Albion, or as being related to good old Uncle Sam. But we don't presume that this should be taken literally. Rather, we take such appellations metaphorically. In a similar manner, the use of the names "Adam" and "Eve" in the context of the moderate Reformed doctrine of original sin does not necessarily indicate commitment to a historical pair from whom the human race has sprung (though it doesn't foreclose that option either).

A third and closely related concern is whether this doctrine fits with some account of the evolutionary development of the cosmos and of humanity within it—with what is often called *evolutionary history*. Here too, the moderate Reformed doctrine stops short of a firm commitment one way or another. However, it is not consistent with just any old doctrine of evolutionary history. Many accounts of the evolution of the various species on our planet, and of the cosmos as a whole, are metaphysically naturalist in nature. That is, they presume that once the physical factors involved in evolutionary processes are accounted for, explanation is exhausted. On such accounts, there are no supernatural agents or powers in addition to physical processes and entities that need to be factored into the explanation of evolutionary processes. Thus, E. O. Wilson writes, "If humankind evolved by Darwinian natural selection, genetic chance and environmental necessity, not God, made the species."[23] Clearly, this sort of metaphysical naturalism is inconsistent with Christian doctrine as such, and therefore inconsistent with the moderate Reformed doctrine of original sin in particular. What is more, such metaphysically naturalist accounts of evolutionary history are nonteleological in nature. That is, they do not presume that there is some goal or outcome at which evolutionary processes aim. Such processes are said to be blind, the outcome of chance, inherently random. But any account of human sin that is truly Christian will be teleological in nature because Christianity is teleological in nature: Christians believe that a divine intelligence stands behind the cosmos, which is the divine intelligence's creature. The divine intelligence

23. Wilson, *On Human Nature*, xiii.

has created it, set it in motion, and overseen the physical processes by means of which human beings have come to exist, along with their sinfulness, which requires salvation.

So the moderate Reformed doctrine of original sin is commensurate with some accounts of the evolutionary history of the world, and human beings in it, although any such explanation would need to be teleological and metaphysically supernaturalist in nature. But the moderate Reformed account is not committed to some doctrine of evolutionary history; it is also consistent with the idea that God specially created the world out of nothing and fashioned human beings from dust and ribs. There are good prudential reasons for adopting this sort of approach to controversial theological topics. To this end, it seems to me to be a good thing for a doctrine that is proposed as an explanation for something as controversial as the origins, nature, and transmission of human sin that it be dogmatically minimalist in nature. The moderate Reformed doctrine prescinds from specifying a view on evolutionary history, and that is consistent with a dogmatically minimalist approach to original sin, deployed for prudential reasons. A diplomatic treaty commits the parties involved to language carefully selected so as to be acceptable to all signatories. Similarly, a dogmatically minimal account of original sin is likely to be acceptable to a wider range of those with a stake in the doctrine—both within the Reformed tradition and, perhaps, without. That, it seems to me, is a theological good worth pursuing.

A fourth and final objection concerns the Reformed *bona fides* of the moderate Reformed doctrine. In short, Is it really a Reformed doctrine at all? Elsewhere, I have attempted to provide reasons for thinking that the Reformed tradition tolerates more doctrinal breadth than is sometimes thought consistent with its confessionalism.[24] A similar sort of reasoning applies to the argument for the moderate Reformed doctrine of sin set forth here. That is, there is a range of views on this topic consistent with the Reformed tradition, and the view I have expressed here falls within that range. Some may worry that a view that represents a minority report within a tradition should not be preferred to the majority voice. But, as I have argued here, there is good reason to take the moderate Reformed view seriously, and

---

24. See *Retrieving Doctrine; Revisioning Christology; Deviant Calvinism;* and *Saving Calvinism.* Compare Stewart, *Ten Myths about Calvinism;* and Van den Brink, *Reformed Theology and Evolutionary Theory,* chap. 1.

good reason to worry about some important features of the sort of view more commonly regarded as the majority view in Reformed theology, which includes the notion of original guilt. But more fundamentally, perhaps, it is not clear (to me at least) that the views expressed here can really be written off as a minority report when they are very similar to ideas found in several early Reformed confessions and in the writings of two of the fountainheads of the Reformed tradition—namely, Zwingli and Calvin. Of course, I also think that the moderate Reformed doctrine, as a corruption-only doctrine, is more defensible than other Reformed accounts, and particularly more defensible than those accounts that include a doctrine of original guilt and commitment to a historical aboriginal pair. This is in part because it is a moderate doctrine; and doctrinal moderation is often a good thing. But, as I hope I have shown, it is also unambiguously a Reformed doctrine.

Conclusion

Some may worry that this reasoning seems almost entirely philosophical-theological and without detailed biblical exegesis. That is a good worry to have when doing Christian theology. But it is to mistake the kind of reasoning presented here. I am not offering in detail the biblical warrant for a particular doctrine of original sin, though I think the doctrine I have outlined can be supported from Scripture, and I have given some indication of this in my remarks about Romans 5 (see also the appendix at the end of this chapter). We might say that this chapter is a foray into doctrinal criticism, not in biblical theology or exegesis. To this end, I have attempted to provide a moderate account of original sin that is consistent with one strand of the Christian tradition (the Reformed tradition, broadly construed), though it is not the sort of view often reported as the Reformed doctrine of original sin. It is a minority report, though, as I have tried to indicate, not without theological support from at least two of the Magisterial Reformers (Calvin and Zwingli) and several Reformed symbols (the Belgic Confession and Scots Confession). I am also concerned with finding an account of original sin that avoids some of the significant drawbacks of those versions of the doctrine that presume original sin is imputed from Adam to us, and that we are guilty of Adam's sin—doctrines common among Reformed divines. This dovetails with my desire to isolate a doctrine that has ecumenical promise. Both Roman Catholic and Orthodox

accounts of the first sin do not include a doctrine of original guilt, and
they are privative in nature: the first sin is described as the privation of a
state of original justice or righteousness, or as the loss of some morally
exalted state with which the aboriginal human pair were created. The
doctrine outlined here is closer to this sort of view than to those versions
of the doctrine that conceive of original sin as a moral corruption that is
imputed to all humanity post-Adam along with original guilt. For those
concerned to find theological convergence between the different communions of the body of Christ, this may also be a reason for taking seriously
the argument I have presented.

Finally, as I have summarized it, the moderate Reformed doctrine with-
holds judgment about whether there is a specially created aboriginal human
pair from whom all subsequent human beings are descended. So it does not
presume monogenism (the view that we are descended from an aboriginal
pair), though it is consistent with it. It also prescinds from any judgment
about the origin of human suffering and misery, and about whether nature
is created "red in tooth and claw." In other words, the doctrine is consistent
with more than one story about creation and human origins, and that (it
seems to me) is a strength rather than a weakness.

With this moderate Reformed doctrine of original sin in place, we turn
next to a constructive account of the atonement, understood primarily as
an antidote to the corruption of original sin, and to the means by which
fallen humans may be reconciled and united to God so that they may
participate in the divine life.

Appendix on Romans 5:12–19

It is sometimes said that the traditional way of thinking about original sin
that dates back to Augustine depends in important respects on a faulty
reading of the so-called Adam Christology of Romans 5:12–19. This mistake stems from Augustine's failure to discern that his own Latin transla-
tion of the Bible misrepresented the actual Greek underlying the text.[25] A

25. For one recent discussion of some of the problems associated with Augustine's use of
Rom. 5, see Couenhoven, who points out that
Augustine's Scriptural evidence for the doctrine does not stand or fall with that one verse. In
particular, 1 Corinthians 15:22, "For as in Adam all died . . ." (cf. *Pecc.Mer.* I.8.8, III.11.19),

good recent example of this sort of objection to the Augustinian doctrine of original sin can be found in a recent essay by biblical scholar and theologian Joel E. Green. Green says that the phrase "ἐφ᾽ ᾧ πάντες ἥμαρτον" (*eph hō pantes hēmarton*) in Romans 5 does not imply that Adam is the one "in whom" all have sinned (as per the Augustinian misreading of this phrase). Rather, it should be rendered something like "since everyone has sinned," which, in the context of the whole verse, Green translates: "Just as through one human being sin came into the world, and death came through sin, so death has come to everyone, since everyone has sinned."[26] Set in the broader context of Pauline theology, Professor Green maintains that Paul's position is much milder than traditional Augustinians have thought. As a consequence of Adam's primal act, "sin as a hegemonic force was let loose in the world," so that "Adam's disobedience set in motion a chain of consequences, one sin leading to the next, not because sin is basic to the human condition but because Adam set the pattern for all humanity."[27] In this connection he (in my view, rightly) points out that Paul's concerns in this regard may not match our own. We should be wary of anachronism—that is, of reading into Paul a doctrine of original sin that is a later doctrinal development postdating Augustine.

Although I am sympathetic with much of what Professor Green says in his essay, I would register several caveats. First, we should be careful not to conflate the frequency with which a concept is mentioned with its importance in a particular tradition. The term "Trinity" appears nowhere in Scripture. And there is no clear, unambiguous statement of the doctrine of the Trinity in Scripture either. But I cannot imagine any serious Christian theologian claiming that for this reason we can excise the doctrine of the Trinity from the faith, because it is only clearly stated centuries after the New Testament was completed. It seems to me that something similar can be said with respect to sin and original sin in Scripture. Even if original sin is not mentioned by name in the text of Scripture, and the

---

is of the first importance for Augustine. Additionally, we must not forget that he does not simply base his views on a set of proof-texts; rather, he is convinced that St. Paul's contrast between type and antitype, Adam and Christ, leads logically to the ascription of the race's sinfulness in Adam, just as righteousness is solely found in Jesus Christ. Thus, the doctrine of original sin is based not only on the 12th verse of Romans 5 but on that whole chapter. ("St. Augustine's Doctrine of Original Sin," 363)

26. See J. Green, "Wesleyan View"; and J. Green, "Wesleyan Response."
27. J. Green, "Wesleyan View," 70.

doctrine is nowhere clearly stated, this does not mean it is a doctrine alien to the right understanding of the text.

Second, even if we concede that Professor Green and others are right about how to translate Romans 5:12, so that Augustine's rendering of the verse is mistaken, this does not necessarily defeat Augustine's claim that, as famously condensed in *The New-England Primer*, "In Adam's Fall, We sinned all." For as Romans 5:19, which bookends the Adam Christology of this section of the epistle, tells us, "Just as by the one man's disobedience the many were made sinners, so by the one man's obedience the many will be made righteous." The relevant phrase here is, "ἁμαρτωλοὶ κατεστάθησαν οἱ πολλοί" (*hamartōloi katestathēsan hoi polloi*)—that is, "the many were constituted [made] sinners." The sin of the one—Adam—constitutes the many sinners, just as the righteousness of the one—Christ—will constitute the many righteous. If that is right, then this verse seems to be much closer to an Augustinian reading of Paul's Adam Christology than Green's reading suggests. For the typology is such that something Adam does constitutes the many sinners, and something Christ does constitutes the many righteous in the sight of God. Although this is not the same as saying all sinned in Adam, it is significantly stronger than saying we have all sinned *like* Adam.

8

Representation and Atonement

There are many places in the New Testament in which Christ is said to be united with his people, the church. Many of these passages include organic analogies for this union that have been important in subsequent Christian thought, such as the vine and branches in the Fourth Gospel, or the members of a body and its head in 1 Corinthians. In the Pauline Epistles in particular, there is a significant emphasis on the related notion of participation in Christ's saving work of atonement.[1] For instance, in Romans 5:12–19 we read of Paul's so-called Adam Christology, in which the comparison between the two "Adams"—that is, Adam and Christ—is a way of distinguishing two groups: one made up of those who participate in the sin of Adam and one made up of those who participate in the benefits of Christ's reconciling work. Similar sentiments can be found in 1 Corinthians 15:22, which says, "For as all die in Adam, so all will be made alive in Christ." Such quotations could be multiplied.

1. Related, because it is commonly thought that the members of the universal catholic church (whose membership comprises the church across time visible and invisible, militant and triumphant) are either among those, or comprise those, for whom Christ's reconciling work is an atonement.

Thus, in 2 Corinthians 5:21 we read, "For our sake he made him to be sin who knew no sin, so that *in him* we might become the righteousness of God." And in Colossians 1:13–14: "He has rescued us from the power of darkness and transferred us into the kingdom of his beloved Son, *in whom* we have redemption, the forgiveness of sins."[2]

Such participatory language has not gone unnoticed in modern scholarship. In the middle of the twentieth century, the Oxford biblical scholar D. E. H. Whiteley observed,

> There is, of course, no passage in his [Paul's] writing where a substitutionary theory of Christ's death is stated explicitly and unambiguously, although there are several places where the thought of substitution cannot be excluded. On the other hand, there is a consistent strand of 'participatory' thought, and it is here, if anywhere, that we are to find St. Paul's theory of the *modus operandi* of the atonement through the death of Christ.[3]

Similar sentiments are expressed by more recent New Testament scholars as well. For instance, in the 1990s Morna Hooker, then Lady Margaret's Professor of Divinity in Cambridge, wrote, "It has long been my belief that Paul's notion of participation in Christ (conveyed in such phrases as 'in Christ' and 'with Christ') is the key to understanding his Christology." She goes on to clarify, "It is *not* that Christ and the believer change places, but rather that Christ, by his involvement in the human situation, is able to transfer believers from one mode of existence to another."[4]

More recently still, the American biblical scholar Michael J. Gorman writes, "As a fundamental category for understanding Paul, 'participation'—meaning participation in Christ, his crucifixion and resurrection, his story, and/or his present life—is now quite widely accepted." He continues, "For Paul, to be one with Christ is to be one with God; to be like Christ is to be like God; to be in Christ is to be in God. At the very least, this means

2. Emphases added.
3. Whiteley, "St. Paul's Thought on the Atonement," 255.
4. Hooker, *From Adam to Christ*, 5. This has been noticed by theologians as well. See, for example, Gorringe, *God's Just Vengeance*, 75. Tom Greggs also has a treatment of what he calls "participative ontology" in the first volume of his ecclesiology, but this focuses on the life of the church rather than on atonement. We will take up this theme in the next chapter. Interested readers should consult Greggs, *Dogmatic Ecclesiology*, chap. 3.

that for Paul cruciformity—conformity to the crucified Christ—is really theoformity or theosis."[5]

Scottish New Testament scholar Grant Macaskill, who has a rather different account of the nature of participation in New Testament theology than Gorman, nevertheless goes as far as saying that the New Testament as a whole—not just Pauline theology—provides "a remarkably cohesive portrayal of the union of human beings and God."[6]

Yet, though the participatory language in Paul is often noted, and has been discussed at length by biblical scholars,[7] until recently there has been little attempt by systematic theologians and philosophical theologians to assess whether this language can inform a particular model of atonement, and if it can, what such a model would look like. Happily, this is beginning to change, and there are several recent analytic-theological treatments of the atonement that draw upon participatory motifs in Paul in order to develop accounts of the atonement.[8]

This chapter is a contribution to the philosophical-theological literature on this topic. In it, I will provide a theological account of this Pauline participatory language of atonement that I call *the union account*. The argument is structured as follows: The first section sets up the union account. I begin by foregrounding some theological assumptions. I then set out a version of the theological just-so story I have used in previous iterations of the union account in order to give an overview of the view.[9] This I have called *the realist union account* for reasons that will become clear as we proceed. This is followed by some comments on the way in which I have previously construed this narrative, metaphysically speaking. There are several problems with the realist union account that have also been raised in the literature. These criticisms have led me to rethink the doctrine in several important respects. It is the task of the rest of the chapter to provide an overview of this revised version of the union account.

5. Gorman, *Inhabiting the Cruciform God*, 3, 4.

6. Macaskill, *Union with Christ*, 1.

7. See, e.g., C. Campbell, *Paul and Union with Christ*; Macaskill, *Union with Christ*; and Thate, Vanhoozer, and Campbell, *"In Christ" in Paul*.

8. See Bayne and Restall, "Participatory Model of the Atonement"; R. Collins, "Girard and Atonement"; and Hill, "'His Death Belongs to Them.'" The recent monograph by Khaled Anatolios, *Deification through the Cross*, is a welcome addition to the literature that attempts to weave participation into an account of atonement.

9. My previous iterations of the union account can be found, in order of publication, in *Word Enfleshed*; *Analyzing Doctrine*; and *Approaching the Atonement*.

I shall distinguish between the *nature of atonement*—and specifically, the mechanism by means of which human beings are reconciled to God—and the *consequences of atonement* in the broader category of the doctrine of salvation, or soteriology. With this distinction in mind, the second section of the chapter discusses the mechanism of atonement in more detail. After distinguishing key terms such as "vicarious atonement," "representation," and "substitution," I give the revised union account I will defend here, one that characterizes the atonement as a *vicarious, reparative, and penitential act of soteriological representation*. For short, I call this view the "representationalist union account." On this way of thinking, as a member of humankind, Christ is able to act vicariously on behalf of other, fallen humans. His work is reparative, penitential, and satisfies divine justice. Though it is a vicarious act, it is not a penal substitutionary act, strictly speaking. Borrowing some ideas from recent work in social ontology, I suggest that the redeemed are a special kind of *group* with Christ able to act on behalf of that group in atonement. This represents an important development in this iteration of the union account, which I had previously construed as a kind of realist doctrine of penal substitution, where the redeemed and Christ are one four-dimensional whole. The new iteration of the view does not require these claims and is, indeed, inconsistent with them. Nevertheless, both iterations are versions of a union account of atonement in which the idea of participation plays an important role. I close with some reflections on this revised version of the union account, summarizing it in a new theological just-so story of atonement.

This chapter completes what I want to say about the *nature* of atonement. However, it leaves the matter of the *consequences* of atonement unresolved. In the next chapter, I shall consider the relationship between the mechanism of atonement and the consequences of atonement in union with and participation in the divine life. Thus, the argument of this chapter is the first of two parts of the book focused on the nature of atonement and its consequences. Once we have these two things clear—that is, the mechanism of atonement and its consequences for participation in the divine life—I will provide a synthesis of the different strands of the argument set in the broader theological context of soteriology in a final, concluding chapter.

Approaching the Union Account of Atonement

a. Some Assumptions

Let us begin by making clear some assumptions. Like the New Testament scholars and theologians mentioned in the previous section, I assume that the participatory language of the New Testament, like some early patristic writing, should be understood in a realist manner rather than as mere metaphor or purely figurative.[10] That is, when Paul speaks of being "in Christ," or being "crucified with Christ," and so forth, he means to convey to his readers, by means of tropes and images, the idea that somehow believers are *really and truly* united to Christ and *really and truly* participate in his atoning work and attendant benefits. This extends to Paul's Adam Christology as well. When he writes in Romans 5 and 1 Corinthians 15 about the union of humanity with Adam and his sin on the one hand, and of those who are redeemed with Christ and his saving benefits on the other, he means his readers to take this with full seriousness as some arrangement that is real, not merely metaphorical or figurative. I am not suggesting Paul provides us with a *theory* about how we participate in Adam or in Christ. But what I am suggesting is that the sort of view he has in mind is one according to which the relation that exists between Adam and his progeny and between Christ and those for whom his reconciling work is effectual is a relation that implies real participation. The tropes Paul uses are an attempt to falteringly and partially gesture toward this reality, which is ultimately beyond our ken. *Somehow* we participate in Adam's sin, and *somehow* we participate in the saving benefits of Christ's reconciling work. Let us call this the *participation assumption in Pauline theology*, or just the *participation assumption*. Fleshing out what this might mean is a major task of this chapter.

To some readers this assumption will appear to stymie any further attempt at elucidating the matter in hand. For, so it might be thought, if the apostle Paul is not clear about the nature of the relation of participation in view, and he was bearing witness to divine revelation, then we have no real hope of making any further progress on this matter. For we are not in receipt of the kind of testimony to which an apostle is privileged: God

10. Here I have in mind the work of Irenaeus and Athanasius in particular, though other patristic authors might be cited. I have discussed both of these authors in more detail in Crisp, *Approaching the Atonement*, chaps. 1–2.

does not reveal himself to us as he does to Paul. However, this may be overhasty for at least two reasons. First, it presumes that we cannot know more about these matters than an apostle. Second, it presumes that the kind of tropes that Paul uses cannot generate further explanation. Neither of these presumptions are obvious, or obviously true.

Take the first. We do know more than the apostles about a lot of things, including matters of a theological nature. For instance, from his letters we can be confident that Paul did not have a clear idea of the two-natures doctrine that undergirds classical Christology, and neither did he have a clear idea of the Trinity as it was subsequently construed in conciliar documents.[11] Both of these things are now central and defining Christian doctrines. Yet they postdate Paul, being the product of further reflection by the church upon the deposit of apostolic teaching as a whole, as well as upon other Scriptures. So we know things of a theological nature that Paul did not—and not merely incidental matters, but matters central to the faith.

Second, it is feasible to build models that unpack or extrapolate from the kind of conceptual pictures one finds in the work of someone like Paul. This is a common practice in Christian theology. As an example, consider the way in which commentators and interpreters of mystical theologians seek to extrapolate from their writings ways of thinking about the nature of mystical union with God. Sometimes those mystical writers themselves engage in such commentary, as with St. Teresa of Ávila's famous image of the interior castle.[12] But the point is that the language of mystical prayer, which can sometimes be difficult and paradoxical and is littered with tropes, is subject to the attempts by interpreters to make sense of this language by means of explanatory apparatus.[13] That is analogous to

11. This is true whether one includes only some of the New Testament letters traditionally attributed to the apostle or all of them. Most New Testament scholars think Paul wrote seven of the letters attributed to him: Romans, 1 and 2 Corinthians, Galatians, Philippians, 1 Thessalonians, and Philemon. The remaining letters are thought to be deutero-Pauline—that is, not written by Paul though perhaps representing a kind of Pauline school of theology.

12. See Teresa of Ávila, *Interior Castle*. For an interesting analytic-philosophical attempt to model the notion of mystical union using Teresa's work in particular, see Pike, *Mystic Union*, especially chaps. 1–2.

13. For an overview of some major strands of interpretation in the Christian mystical tradition, see Nelstrop, Magill, and Oneshi, *Christian Mysticism*, especially chap. 1. A particularly noteworthy recent attempt to do just what I am talking about is Denys Turner's revisionist account of (mainly European male) Christian mysticism in *The Darkness of God*.

what we are after here with respect to the Pauline use of participation language regarding Christ's reconciling work.

A second and related assumption has to do with the *explanatory scope* of what I offer here. I am aiming for a fairly modest conclusion, conceptually speaking. What I want is the outline of a model of atonement in which participation features as a fundamental theme and that is consistent with the Pauline material. But I do not claim that what I set forth is the truth of the matter, strictly speaking. Rather, in keeping with the material first introduced in part 1 of this work, this is one plausible way of thinking about the atonement. It may not be the whole truth of the matter, given the proliferation of other atonement models in the recent (and historic) literature, as well as the now commonplace assumption among theologians and biblical scholars that no one model will be able to do sufficient justice to the complexity of the doctrine of atonement.[14] That said, I think that the view outlined here may be part of the answer to the question, *What is the atonement?* This is what theologians refer to as the question of the nature of the atonement (i.e., what the atonement is and what the mechanism of atonement amounts to) rather than the extent of the atonement (i.e., whom the atonement is for and the scope of those to whom it is applied).

A final assumption that is implicit in what I have said so far is that I presume philosophy, particularly analytic philosophy, may have useful things to contribute to our understanding of the atonement.[15] By that I mean useful arguments, distinctions, conceptual clarifications, and so on. But I also mean things like theoretical frameworks that might be used to underpin the superstructure of a theological argument, so to speak, such as those offered in contemporary analytic metaphysics. This is not so strange. The ambitions of systematic metaphysics in this regard are, in important respects, parallel to the ambitions of systematic theologians.

14. See, e.g., Baker and Green, *Scandal of the Cross*. See also J. Johnson, *Patristic and Medieval Atonement Theory*; and Crisp, *Approaching the Atonement*. Michael Rea is an example of a philosopher who thinks that there is insufficient scriptural data for privileging any of the New Testament images of salvation over the others for theory-building purposes. His view seems to be a kind of mysterianism about atonement models. See Rea, "(Reformed) Protestantism." By contrast, among recent atonement theologians, Khaled Anatolios is one who thinks there is one unifying account of the atonement that subsumes all others (see *Deification through the Cross*).

15. I do not say that analytic philosophy is the *only* kind of philosophy that has useful things to teach us, for that is plainly false. However, it is the philosophical tradition in which I have been schooled, which is why it features here.

Nevertheless, the role that philosophy has in this connection is, by my lights, ancillary to the theological task.

b. The Realist Version of the Union Account of Atonement

With these assumptions made tolerably clear, let us turn to the union account of the atonement. To begin with, I will rehearse the previously published version of the view, in a kind of atonement narrative or story, before commenting on its content. In order to distinguish it from the iteration of the doctrine I will be defending here, I will call this the *realist version of the union account* for reasons that will become clear presently. The story goes like this:

> God brings about an entity comprising Adam (from the fall onwards) and all of post-fall humanity barring Christ.[16] This is "fallen humanity" (see Rom. 5:12–19). Fallen humanity is a real entity that exists across time like the different stages of the life of one tree, from acorn to mature oak. I possess Adam's sin because I am a "part" of fallen humanity along with Adam, on analogy with the parts of my body and the whole of my body. Adam's sin is passed on to the later "parts" of this whole, extended across time, because he is the first human—just as a disease infecting the acorn (the first stage of the life of the oak) affects all the later stages of the life of the oak tree. Christ is the second Adam. He is the first member of a new humanity, one that is cleansed from sin and reconciled to God. Christ and those he comes to save are members of a second entity, which is called "redeemed humanity." As the hub between divinity and humanity, Christ is the intersection between God and humanity, and a fitting means by which humans may be reconciled to God. As the God-human, Christ is able to act on behalf of both God and humanity, communicating between them. Christ has a priority over other "parts" of redeemed humanity, although he exists later in time than some of them. For instance, he lives later than Abraham, although his work as the second Adam reconciles Abraham to God (Heb. 11:8–16, 39–40). Hence, those living prior to Christ can be proleptically incorporated into Christ's work as the second Adam. Christ is not guilty of sin; yet he acts vicariously, taking upon himself the penal consequences of the sins committed by the other members of redeemed humanity who are guilty of sin (and who are, therefore, also members of fallen humanity)

16. Roman Catholic and Orthodox readers may like to make the mental adjustment, "barring Christ and his mother, Mary *Theotokos*."

because they are "parts" of the same entity extended across time (2 Cor. 5:21). Christ's work atones for human sin, removing the obstacle of sin and reconciling members of fallen humanity to God. Through union with Christ by the power of the Holy Spirit, members of redeemed humanity begin a process of transformation into the likeness of God, becoming partakers of the divine nature. This process of transformation goes on forevermore. It is like a mathematical asymptote in that the human members of redeemed humanity draw ever closer to God in this process without ever becoming God or losing themselves in God.[17]

As I have already intimated, in previously published versions of the union account I construed the theological just-so story in a particular philosophical manner. This involved appropriating a four-dimensional construal of the doctrine of Augustinian realism, applied to both original sin and atonement. Historically, Augustinian realism was a way of spelling out how original sin is transmitted from Adam to his progeny. One standard objection to the doctrine of original sin is that it seems unjust that I am punished for the sin of an ancestor whose action I did not approve or condone. Augustinian realism provides one response to this objection. For on this view, Adam and his progeny (somehow) constitute one metaphysical whole such that the sin of Adam is truly my sin by virtue of the fact that I am in some sense one entity with Adam. (For instance, it may be that we were all seminally present in Adam when he committed the primal sin, or perhaps we all share a temporal part or stage with Adam at that moment.)[18] The realist version of the union account of atonement adopts this Augustinian realist theological framework and extends it, via the Adam Christology of Romans 5, to the atonement as well, so that (somehow) redeemed humanity comprises Christ and his elect, who are the members of the church. That, in short, was what was novel about the view. I set out both perdurantist and stage-theoretic (exdurantist) versions of the doctrine as a means of spelling out, in terms borrowed from analytic metaphysics, an Augustinian realist way of thinking about Adam and his

17. A similar account can be found in my earlier works *Approaching the Atonement* and *Word Enfleshed*, and in the conclusion to *Analyzing Doctrine*.

18. For historical discussion of Augustinian realism see, e.g., Augustine, *City of God* 13.14. For a theological recapitulation of this view, see Berkhof, *Systematic Theology*, 241–42. I have defended the doctrine against several common objections in Crisp, "On Behalf of Augustinian Realism."

progeny and Christ and his church.[19] To this was added a moderate penal substitutionary mechanism of atonement. As we saw in chapter 7, penal substitution is sometimes said to be the view according to which Christ is punished in place of the human sinner.[20] However, as I have argued in previous chapters, a more moderate, and more defensible, account requires only that Christ atones for human sin by taking upon himself the penal consequences for human sin.[21] The difference is this: suffering penal consequences does not necessarily imply that the intentional harsh treatment suffered is, in fact, a punishment. This avoids some of the more obvious, and problematic, aspects of penal substitutionary accounts of the atonement that have been the subject of critique in recent theology.

So, on this version of the union account, the mechanism of atonement is a combination of Augustinian realism applied to atonement as well as the transmission of sin. Christ acts as one temporal part or stage of a larger whole scattered through space and time so that he may take upon himself the penal consequences of the sin of other parts of this whole, which is fallen humanity. In performing this act, he generates a new whole, redeemed humanity, with respect to which he acts as the second Adam.

Clearly, this doctrine stands in continuity with a particular strand of the Christian tradition and seeks to draw upon historic views with respect to the transmission of sin in order to refurbish an old (and much maligned) account of the atonement. It also takes the realist interpretation of Pau-

19. Perdurantism and stage theory are two ways of construing four-dimensionalism. In this connection, four-dimensionalism is shorthand for a view about how objects persist through time. The idea is that objects that persist are four-dimensional entities, with time as the fourth dimension. Let us take the example of the philosophical crash-test dummy, Jones. The perdurantist says Jones persists through time from one moment to the next in virtue of being composed of numerous temporal parts that make up a temporal "worm" (that is, say, Jones from generation to somatic death). By contrast, the stage theorist says that the particular temporal stage is the relevant focus of attention, not the whole "worm," and that Jones persists in virtue of having one stage that is appropriately causally related to the next. The literature on this topic is large and technical, but a useful introduction can be found in Hawley, *How Things Persist*.

20. This is the way it is often construed in the historic literature as well. To take just one seventeenth-century Reformed Orthodox example, Johannes Wollebius writes that the satisfaction of Christ "consists, therefore, both of the bearing of punishment and of perfect righteousness" (*Compendium Theologiae Christianae* 1.18, p. 99).

21. This is the sort of view defended by William Lane Craig in his recent book *Atonement and the Death of Christ*. But Craig's position is not novel. It can be found in historical discussion of the doctrine as well. See, e.g., Denney, *Christian Doctrine of Reconciliation*, 266. Thanks to Danielle Ross for drawing my attention to this reference.

line Adam Christology seriously. The upshot is a species of participatory atonement doctrine.

c. Problems with the Realist Version of the Union Account

But as it stands, this realist version of the union account is subject to some important criticisms.[22] One line of objection centers on *problems of composition*. This iteration of the view implies that fallen humanity and redeemed humanity are real, four-dimensional objects composed of numerous temporally and spatially scattered parts. But what sort of entities are fallen humanity and redeemed humanity? Do they have moral properties? Are they agents? What could that even *mean* given that such gerrymandered entities do not have wills or the ability to act as a whole? A second sort of problem concerns the success of the view. One reason for positing the union account was to provide a story that makes sense of how Adam's sin is passed down to me, how the penal consequences of my sin are transferred to Christ, and how the benefits of Christ's atoning work are transferred to me as well. Call these *problems of transmission*. It may be that William Lane Craig has such problems of transmission in mind when he writes, "So-called realist accounts of the union, according to which humanity is one metaphysical entity (Crisp 2009, pp. 437–46), are utterly implausible and unavailing, being dependent upon a tenseless theory of time and implying a view of human personhood incompatible with divine punishment and rewards."[23]

Closely related to these problems of transmission are worries about injustice that the union account raises. This can be expressed as the concern that God transmits the sin of one person, Adam, to his progeny, who did not commit his sin and did not condone it, and the concern that God transmits the penal consequences of my sin to an innocent party, Christ. What is more, God also transmits the benefits of Christ's saving

22. I was not unaware of these problems, as the version of the union account discussed in Crisp, *Word Enfleshed*, makes clear. It is just that my philosophical colleagues have now taken up these concerns in subsequent publications, and, in the case of Stump, sharpened them.

23. Craig, *Atonement*, 81n30. I am trying to be charitable in my reporting of Craig's criticism. His first assertion about the tenseless view of time is made without argument (although he is a well-known critic of such views), and he does not expand upon his claims about human personhood. Nevertheless, he is clearly worried about the sort of view of transmission the realist union account presumes, though it would have been more helpful to know exactly why he thinks the realist view is "utterly implausible and unavailing." He repeats substantially the same objection in his more expansive account, *Atonement and the Death of Christ*.

work to me as an act of sheer grace. Call these *problems of injustice.*
Clearly, the problems of injustice supervene upon the arrangement presumed by the problems of transmission. Although she does not clearly
distinguish the problems of injustice from the problems of transmission
in this way, Eleonore Stump's recent criticism of the realist union account
gets at much of this concern:

> Crisp [argues] that Christ and human beings constitute one four-dimensional
> object and that in the case of such a corporate or perduring object the sins
> of some are the sins of the whole object, so that the punishment for the sins
> is suitably visited on the whole object as well. But this argument seems to
> me inefficacious to rebut the charge of injustice against a God who would
> proceed in the way proponents of the penal substitution theory propose.
> The sins that offend God are not sins of the whole four-dimensional object
> but of parts of it. As far as that goes, the whole four-dimensional object is
> capable of action only in a derivative sense, in consequence of the actions
> of some of its parts. That is because there is no one will which constitutes
> the will of this four-dimensional object, and any agency requires an act of
> will. For this same reason, there is no sin that could be committed non-
> derivatively by a four-dimensional corporate object of this sort, since any
> sin also requires an act of will. So even if it were true that Christ and some
> human beings constitute one four-dimensional object, it remains the case
> that when Christ is punished for sins committed by other human beings,
> those who willed the sin are not punished and someone who did not will
> a sin is punished. And therefore the charge of injustice is not rebutted.[24]

Now, versions of the problems of transmission and injustice are common coin in the atonement literature. Many theologians of the past have
worried about these concerns in connection with the mechanism of atonement. The problem of composition is a particular problem for the realist
union account given the metaphysical claims it implies. But it too is an
attempt to address a long-standing worry about how Christ may be said
to act vicariously on behalf of other human beings. So the fact that the
realist union account raises these problems is not strange or unexpected.
It is just that as it stands, the way in which the realist union account addresses these problems seems to some philosophical colleagues to raise
more problems than it resolves.

24. Stump, *Atonement*, 436n28.

d. Distinguishing Atonement and Its Consequences

So much for the previous iteration of the union account. In the face of these problems one option is to dig in one's heels and find resources with which to rebut the objections raised. That is feasible. There is a rich and sophisticated literature on matters that bear on this subject in both historic and contemporary philosophy that could be marshaled in defense of this iteration of the union account, not to mention the notable historic theological resources one could draw upon as well.[25]

An alternative involves regrouping with a variation on the view that attempts to address these worries in a version of the doctrine cast in a new argument. I choose this latter option. Partly this is motivated by a concern to avoid too many conceptual hostages to fortune. But more fundamentally, it is motivated by a sense that something about my previously published way of construing the union account was not quite right—that it fails to adequately track some of the relevant biblical and theological themes the view sought to incorporate.

So, suppose that we distinguish two elements of the doctrine of salvation. The first is the mechanism of atonement, whatever that may be. The second is a twofold unitive function performed by the Holy Spirit set against the backdrop of God's reconciling work that seeks to make redeemed human beings partakers of the divine nature. The first aspect of this is the application of the benefits of Christ's atonement to the believer by means of regeneration. The second aspect is the union of the believer with Christ. Note that these are aspects of one work by means of which the Holy Spirit unites the believer to Christ. They are not two distinct works conjoined together like different strands of a cord of rope.

Now, on this way of thinking, the unitive and participatory aspect of salvation is not just tied in with the mechanism of atonement. For there is a distinct work performed by the Holy Spirit in applying the benefits of Christ to the believer and in uniting the believer to Christ. This still leaves us the question of the nature of the atonement—of what sort of

25. I have in mind the recent work in applied analytic metaphysics in particular, such as that by Michael Rea and Hud Hudson, and Joshua Thurow, among others. There are also historic theological resources on which one could draw. For instance, the work of Jonathan Edwards, William Shedd, and Augustus Strong, as well as some aspects of the Mercersburg theologians like John Williamson Nevin, who was himself drawing on themes in Calvin. Interested readers may consult the bibliography for references.

act it is and how it is the means by which atonement obtains. But how we participate in Christ's atonement and how we benefit from it are now clearly distinguished as questions that pertain not to the atonement itself but to the consequences of it. On this way of thinking, strictly speaking, participation is an issue for the doctrine of soteriology more broadly rather than for the doctrine of atonement in particular. Although the nature of atonement is one aspect of soteriology, it is broader than the atonement because soteriology has to do with the whole of salvation—of how it is that God brings about the reconciliation of fallen humanity to Godself. Atonement is one central concern in this matter, having to do with the mechanism by means of which such reconciliation is made possible. But it is a constituent of soteriology, not the whole of it, just as a slice of bread is a part of the loaf, not the whole of it.

With this distinction in mind, let us turn to consider the mechanism of atonement afresh, in the context of the question of the nature of atonement. Then we will be in a position to reflect on the consequences of atonement with respect to participation and the broader sweep of soteriology in the next chapter.

The Mechanism of Atonement

Thus far we have recapped the previous iteration of the union account. It is now time to set out a revised version of the doctrine.

As we have seen in previous chapters, there is a family of atonement views in which Christ is said to offer a reparative act for human sin and alienation from God consistent with the demands of divine justice.[26] In the case of the doctrine of satisfaction, this obtains by means of an act that generates a supererogatory merit sufficient to meet the demands of God's justice or God's honor. It is, in other words, *an act by means of which the conditions of a moral or legal standard are met*—in this case, by a voluntary act of supererogation that generates merit of sufficient value to meet the requirement of divine justice. By contrast, in the case of penal substitution Christ satisfies the moral or legal standard by means of a specific kind of substitutionary act. He stands in the place of the sinner,

26. Here I am indebted to conversations with Carl Mosser and Danielle Ross, and to the work of Joshua R. Farris and S. Mark Hamilton. See Farris and Hamilton, "Logic of Reparative Substitution," esp. 64.

and he takes upon himself the punishment due to the sinner, or at least the penal consequences of the sin. But these are not the only two species of atonement doctrine that belong to this broad family of reparative views. Another member of this family is the governmental doctrine, where Christ is a penal example rather than a penal substitute whose work displays what God must do if sin is to be punished in a manner consistent with God's role as moral governor of the cosmos.[27] Yet another version is the kind of non-penal substitution envisaged by John McLeod Campbell and his followers, where Christ's reconciling act is a kind of vicarious penitence on behalf of fallen humanity (we shall return to this presently).[28]

Each of these traditional views brings something important to the table.[29] But it seems to me that none of them says exactly what needs to be said. Drawing on some ideas in Pauline theology, I want to suggest that the mechanism of atonement is better expressed as a *vicarious, reparative, and penitential act of soteriological representation*, whereby a part (Christ) may stand in for the whole (fallen humanity) and act on behalf of the whole. This shares much of the language and sensibility of satisfaction, penal substitution, the governmental view, and vicarious penitence—though it is, I think, distinct from each of these other views. However, not much depends on the claim of distinctness. If it turns out that the view is another iteration of one of these views, or a mash-up of them in the family of satisfaction accounts of atonement, so be it. My concern is not to produce an account that is *novel* (which has its own theological costs), but rather to try to get a clearer conceptual grip on the mechanism of atonement. Given that the atonement is a divine mystery and that what I

27. The *locus classicus* is Hugo Grotius, *Defense of the Catholic Faith*, though it is often said that Grotius was not a clear defender of the governmental account (a claim recently reiterated by Craig in *Atonement and the Death of Christ*). A clear nineteenth-century example of the doctrine is found in Miley, *Atonement in Christ*. I have discussed the view in Crisp, "Penal Non-substitution." For a critical account of the New England version of the doctrine that takes issue with my reading of the material, see Todd, *Moral Governmental Theory of Atonement*.

28. See J. Campbell, *Nature of the Atonement*. Another classic treatment indebted to a Campbellian approach is Mozley, *Doctrine of the Atonement*. I have discussed Campbell's doctrine previously in Crisp, "John McLeod Campbell and Non-penal Substitution." Both the governmental and the vicarious penitence views are also treated in Crisp, *Approaching the Atonement*, chap. 7.

29. These are indicative of the family of satisfaction views, not exhaustive of all variations within this family of views. Another recent example of a doctrine of atonement that draws on similar moral and theological sensibilities is Mark Murphy's vicarious punishment view. See Murphy, "Not Penal Substitution but Vicarious Punishment."

am aiming for is a kind of model of atonement, not necessarily the sober truth of the matter, a step toward greater clarity is an acceptable result.

a. Some Conceptual Distinctions

To this end, let us begin by setting out some conceptual distinctions. The first such distinction is between vicarious actions of different sorts. Often in the atonement literature insufficient attention is paid to the different ways in which an atoning act may be said to be a vicarious act. However, for present purposes, these differences are salient. So to begin with, let us say that a *vicarious action* is, broadly, *an act that is done for or on behalf of another*. There are all sorts of mundane acts that are vicarious in this way, from helping an aged person across the road to picking up a prescription from the pharmacy on behalf of a sick relative. What we are interested in is a subgroup of vicarious actions that are reparative in nature. A *reparative action* is one that *makes amends between two alienated parties*, or that *offers compensation for some wrong done*. A good example of this relevant to our concerns is paying for someone else's fine. This is the vicarious payment of a penalty, strictly speaking—sometimes, and perhaps mistakenly, called pecuniary penal substitution in the theological literature.[30] But the broader point is this: vicarious and reparative actions include acts that are instances of representation, substitution, and satisfaction.

Next, we might say that an act of *representation* is where *one individual acts or speaks on behalf of another person or another entity (such as a political state)*, bringing before the second entity the concerns of the first. For instance, the way in which a political or diplomatic representative acts on behalf of the people or the state of which they are a citizen.

Representation needs to be distinguished from *substitution*, however. A substitutionary act is an act whereby *one person or thing is replaced by another person or thing*. There are many mundane examples of this, such as the substitution of one player for another on the field in a game of rugby or football. Now, a substitute is not the same as a representative. When the prime minister or president represents a particular state, she or

---

30. Here I have in mind nineteenth-century theologians like Charles Hodge. I discuss his views in Crisp, "Federalism vs. Realism." It appears in the philosophical literature too. See, e.g., Lewis, "Do We Believe in Penal Substitution?"

he is not a substitute for that state. It is not as if the state is swapped out for the representative of the state. Rather, the representative has certain powers to act on behalf of the state in question. But the substitute does act in the stead of another. The substitute on the football field takes the place of the player coming off the field. The new player does not represent the rest of the team in playing. Rather, the new player takes the place of one of the members of the team who leaves the field of play to make way for the substitute. As New Testament scholar Simon Gathercole puts it, substitution "entails the concept of replacement, X taking the place of Y and thereby ousting Y: the place that Y previously occupied is now filled by X." This is different from representation because in representation "X does not thereby oust Y but rather embodies Y. Indeed, it is usually a presupposition of representation that X belongs to group Y, and so the representative is *part* of the body represented."[31]

But representation and substitution must also be distinguished from *satisfaction*, which, as we have already noted, is *an act by means of which the conditions of a moral or legal standard are met*. Christ's reconciling work is a satisfaction in this sense. As we saw when discussing Anselm's doctrine, on his way of thinking an act of satisfaction is not the same as an act of punishment. However, in principle a punishment might satisfy some moral or legal standard. So we might say, *pace* Anselm, that punishment may be an instance of satisfaction though it is not the only way in which satisfaction might be had. This is relevant for a discussion of atonement, and it explains why satisfaction and penal substitution are so often conflated in the literature, though they are in fact conceptually distinct. In the Anselmian sense, satisfaction is a voluntary vicarious act of divine grace whereby Christ acts so as to meet the moral standard that fallen human beings cannot, thereby providing an infinite merit that may be applied to those to whom the gift of faith is given. So, as we saw when discussing penal substitution, satisfaction has a broad sense—namely, the sense whereby the conditions of a moral or legal standard are met. But in atonement theology it also has a more narrow sense in which it refers to a given doctrine or model of atonement, usually associated with Anselm and his followers. In the broad sense it includes doctrines like penal substitution since it describes a kind of family of atonement views

31. Gathercole, *Defending Substitution*, 20 (emphasis original). I have already had cause to cite this passage earlier in the book, but it bears repeating here.

that share some sense in which Christ acts vicariously and reparatively in reconciling fallen human beings to Godself. But in the specific sense it describes a particular view of atonement which includes a mechanism of atonement that is distinct from that of penal substitution. In the case of the Anselmian view, the doctrine of satisfaction is in fact inconsistent with penal substitution because Christ's reconciling work is not, and cannot be, a punishment. Nor is it the suffering of the penal consequences of human sin borne by Christ. Rather, it is an act of supererogatory merit that meets the requirement of satisfaction laid down by divine justice.

With these distinctions in place we may turn to the way in which I want to construe the mechanism of atonement. This, I said, was as a vicarious, reparative, and penitential act of soteriological representation. The sort of view I have in mind is akin to the notion of synecdoche, which is a literary trope. In synecdoche one part of a thing stands in for the whole, as when in a game of rugby, we are told "Scotland won by a penalty." Here the Scottish rugby team stands in for the nation. In a similar fashion, in atonement Christ as the God-man stands in for the rest of humanity, representing and thereby providing salvation for humanity. This arrangement is not a fiction, nor is it merely a metaphor. It is not just a matter of imputation either. In this connection, imputation is the ascribing of a state in one thing to another, such as the ascription of one person's guilt to another in some traditional accounts of penal substitution. Rather, it is a representative and reparative act brought about by God on the basis of the union of Christ with humanity that obtains in his incarnation. It is because God the Son is united to a particular human nature that he may act on behalf of other human beings as a human being reconciling them to God. And it is because he is without sin that he may act on behalf of those who are human and sinful, and therefore incapable of saving themselves.

This sort of view also has some biblical warrant. Consider, for example, Romans 11:16. In this section, in which Paul addresses the election and rejection of Israel, he says, "If the part of the dough offered as first fruits is holy, then the whole batch is holy; and if the root is holy, then the branches also are holy." New Testament scholar D. E. H. Whiteley describes this notion as the *presupposition of the first fruits*. He explains that Paul "means, not that the sanctification of the first portion merely symbolises the sanctification of the lump, but that the sanctification of the first portion actually accomplishes that of the lump." This is somewhat obscure, which, in Whiteley's view, is "why this strand in St. Paul's theology has suffered comparative neglect; it has been distorted into substitutionary theories or partially understood as a theory of representative salvation."[32] But construing the presupposition of the first fruits in terms of a penitential and reparative act of soteriological representation may help elucidate the central Pauline claim at issue.

b. Group Action and Atonement

So how might we better understand this way of thinking about the mechanism of atonement? At this juncture we may turn for theological resources to the recent philosophical literature in social ontology. There is a sophisticated literature on group action.[33] Much of that literature is concerned with giving accounts of how it is that groups can be said to have moral responsibility or even act as agents.[34] But that cannot be the sort of thing with which we are concerned in atonement because neither fallen humanity nor redeemed humanity are agents or act as agents (which is a problem that was raised for the realist version of the union account). This is true even if we think that entities like fallen and redeemed humanity are real objects composed of numerous temporally and spatially scattered parts rather than being merely aggregates of agents, as I did in the previous iteration of the union account. One important reason for thinking that such entities or aggregates are not agents is that neither fallen humanity nor redeemed humanity are the appropriate subjects of moral predicates like reactive attitudes. That is, one cannot praise or blame an entity like fallen or redeemed humanity because such things are not the bearers of properties like moral responsibility.[35]

---

32. Whiteley, *Theology of St. Paul*, 132. This is an illuminating, but largely forgotten, study by an Oxford New Testament scholar of the mid-twentieth century.

33. A good introduction to this is Tollefsen, *Groups as Agents*. This has been brought into the sphere of theological discussion in the work of Joshua Cockayne in particular (see, e.g., Cockayne, "Analytic Ecclesiology").

34. See, for example, S. Collins, *Group Duties*. She sets out a tripartite model that attempts to distinguish ways in which different groups act collectively, including collectives that share common goals and have group-level procedures for decision making, such as nation-states.

35. Another concern, raised in the group ontology literature, is that at the group level fallen and redeemed humanity are not entities that have propositional attitudes, though the members of the two groups do. As Tollefsen puts it, "If you are a person who thinks that propositional attitudes are states only of phenomenally conscious beings, then group mental states are going to be a particularly difficult thing for you to swallow" (*Groups as Agents*, 53). Indeed.

Having said that, the presupposition of the first fruits, mooted by Whiteley in connection with Romans 11:16, suggests another way to think about the relation between Adam and his progeny, which make up fallen humanity, and Christ and those for whom his reconciling work ensures salvation in redeemed humanity. This involves the concepts of *representation* and *accountability*. The idea is that Christ may represent fallen human beings in his reconciling work and be held accountable for their sin. Note that holding a person accountable for an act is not the same as holding them morally responsible or even blameworthy for the act in question. We have already seen that an act of representation is a vicarious act, but not necessarily a substitutionary act. The agent who acts as a representative acts on behalf of another but does not necessarily stand in the place of another. Moreover, a representative may be held accountable for another without necessarily being held morally responsible for the action of another. Imagine a case where a young child finds the keys to the family car and manages to climb into the driver's seat, start the engine, and back the car into a neighbor's vehicle. The parent of the child would be held accountable for the action of the child, although she or he is not the one responsible for backing the car into the neighbor's vehicle.[36]

We might say that an agent is accountable for the action of another just in case the agent has *some liability to answer for the action of the other*. That is what the case of the parent and the child backing the car into the neighbor's vehicle addresses. The parent is accountable for her child's action. She has some liability though—crucially—she is not the one morally responsible for backing the car into the neighbor's vehicle. Thus, in this case, moral responsibility and accountability come apart. In other words, the parent bears the right sort of relation to the child to be held liable for the child's action, and to have to apologize and make reparations on behalf of her child. But she is not morally responsible for her child's action because she did not back the car into the neighbor's vehicle; the child did. By contrast, an agent is morally responsible for an act where, in addition to having some liability for the action in question, the agent is the appropriate subject of reactive attitudes with respect to the action. In such cases, we commonly think she or he is praiseworthy or

---

36. This homely example can be found in Tollefsen, *Groups as Agents*, 134.

blameworthy.[37] As J. R. Lucas points out, this is because desert is connected with action—with doing a thing. "Since desert is connected with doing, it is connected with responsibility. If someone is responsible for what he did, then we assess his desert in line with our assessment of his deed: if what he did was good, he deserves well, if bad, then he deserves ill."[38]

Now, let us apply this distinction between moral responsibility and accountability to the question of the mechanism of atonement, drawing on the Adam Christology of Romans 5 and 1 Corinthians 15. In these passages Paul suggests that there is some real sense in which we are "in" Adam, and bear sin as a consequence of this relation to our first parent, and "in" Christ, and bear redemption as a consequence of this relation to the savior. Recall that according to Paul,

> If the many died through the one man's trespass, much more surely have the grace of God and the free gift in the grace of the one man, Jesus Christ, abounded for the many. And the free gift is not like the effect of the one man's sin. For the judgment following one trespass brought condemnation, but the free gift following many trespasses brings justification. If, because of the one man's trespass, death exercised dominion through that one, much more surely will those who receive the abundance of grace and the free gift of righteousness exercise dominion in life through the one man, Jesus Christ. Therefore just as one man's trespass led to condemnation for all, so one man's act of righteousness leads to justification and life for all. For just as by the one man's disobedience the many were made sinners, so by the one man's obedience the many will be made righteous. (Rom. 5:15b–19)

And,

> Since death came through a human being, the resurrection of the dead has also come through a human being; for as all die in Adam, so all will be made alive in Christ. But each in his own order: Christ the first fruits, then at his coming those who belong to Christ. (1 Cor. 15:21–23)

37. There may be other important considerations to take into account in this connection, such as the notion, made famous by Susan Wolf, that ascriptions of moral responsibility involve the notion of a "real self," such that "an agent's behavior is attributable to the agent's real self . . . if she is at liberty (or able) both to govern her behavior on the basis of her will and to govern her will on the basis of her valuational system" (*Freedom within Reason*, 33). Though I think this is plausible, it takes us beyond what we need for the purposes of the present argument.

38. Lucas, *Responsibility*, 126.

There is an asymmetry between Adam (i.e., the first Adam) and Christ (i.e., the second Adam). Both act vicariously on behalf of some larger group. In the case of Adam, it is in part because he is the first human whose action is able to affect his own moral nature and be transmitted to all subsequent human beings via natural generation. Thus, we are all said by Paul to die "in" Adam. The same could not be said of a sin committed by, say, Seth or Methuselah because they are chronologically downstream of the first humans and, as a consequence, too late in time to be able to commit a sin that affects all (or almost all) instances of human nature. What is more, the aboriginal pair have a particular role as the first humans in covenant relationship with their maker that distinguishes them from all later human beings (see Gen. 2:15–17; 3:2).[39] As it has been traditionally understood in much Reformed theology, it is in virtue of the dereliction of this relationship in the breaking of the conditions of the covenant that they incur the penalty of sin and death (Gen. 3:16–24). Thus, there is an important covenantal dimension to the introduction of original sin. That is, the moral natures of the aboriginal pair are disordered in the act of primal sin (however we understand this), resulting in a moral corruption that is (somehow) transmittable, either through natural generation or immediately by divine fiat. I prefer the former explanation, which makes of the state of sin a kind of analog to a virus or congenital condition passed down the generations from Adam onwards.[40] But in either case, the corruption of original sin is transmitted from our aboriginal parents to all subsequent human beings, barring Christ.

In keeping with what was argued in the previous chapter on original sin, I have deliberately framed this way of thinking about the transmission of original sin in the language of the traditional way of understanding the primeval prologue for the sake of simplicity of explanation. But this is a placeholder, a kind of just-so story. If it turns out that there was no aboriginal pair as such, but an initial population or community from which modern human beings are descended, the story would need to be amended so as to reflect that. According to the aboriginal community version of the story, transmission obtains via a fault that is acquired by this

39. This is a traditional Reformed theological category. I do not propose to defend it here, but merely to use it.
40. See the discussion of the previous chapter. See also the discussion in Crisp, *Analyzing Doctrine*, chap. 7, and Crisp, "Sin in Reformed Theology."

initial community and then passed on to their offspring and so on down to the present. Readers who take this view are invited to make the mental adjustment in what follows and to bear in mind that talk of "Adam" does not necessarily imply commitment to belief in a historical Adam (though it does not exclude it either).

For present purposes, the main point to grasp is that, on the way of thinking I am outlining here, Adam is the natural head of the race in covenant relationship with his maker. (It is a covenant relationship because, so the primeval prologue in Genesis tells us, God made Adam and Eve and then placed them in the garden of Eden as caretakers on the understanding that they would not eat the fruit of the forbidden tree. Thus a *covenantal* relationship—that is, a relationship between two unequal agents, where the more powerful of the two sets the terms and conditions of the arrangement, like an ancient Near Eastern suzerainty treaty between a powerful state and a vassal.)[41] Fallen humanity, as I understand it, is just the group that comprises all those humans to whom original sin is transmitted plus Adam from the moment of his primal sin.[42] Adam is accountable and morally responsible for his primal sin.[43] He is accountable and morally responsible for introducing into human nature the corruption of original sin. But as we saw when dealing with the doctrine of original sin in chapter 7, fallen human beings are not culpable for being born with original sin. This is because, as I now understand it, there is no notion of original guilt piggybacking, so to speak, on the doctrine of original sin. Thus, the transmission of sin from Adam to his progeny incurs accountability and responsibility for Adam, but not for subsequent human beings. Fallen human beings do not bear accountability or moral responsibility for being born in the moral state they find themselves in, though they are culpable for actual sins they commit. Nevertheless, there is an important sense in which all humanity subsequent to the aboriginal

41. See, for example, Thompson, "Significance of the Ancient Near Eastern Treaty Pattern." The topic of covenant in the study of the Hebrew Bible is a vexed one, and I do not propose to enter the debate here. But see, e.g., Mendenhall, "Covenant Forms in Israelite Tradition"; Kline, *Treaty of the Great King*; Kitchen, *Ancient Orient and Old Testament*; and McCarthy, *Treaty and Covenant*.

42. Either Christ is not numbered among this group because he is not fallen, or he is numbered among this group because he immediately cleanses his human nature of sin upon assuming it. I have defended the latter view in Crisp, "On the Vicarious Humanity of Christ."

43. Recall that primal sin is the first, aboriginal sin of Adam and Eve. Original sin is the corrupt condition that results and that is transmitted to subsequent human beings.

pair *participates* in the sin of Adam because the morally vitiated condition brought about by Adam's primal sin has been transmitted to them. This does not mean we are somehow seminally or otherwise metaphysically present with Adam in his primal sin, as traducians believe.[44] But it does mean that Adam's sin is passed on to us and that we are generated in a morally corrupt state as a consequence of Adam's action. It is like saying of someone who inherits a congenital condition that she participates in the same condition as her parents.

The situation is rather different in the case of Christ and redeemed humanity. For Christ is not the first person in time to belong to the group he represents. He is chronologically downstream of many of those included in redeemed humanity, such as the Israelites of the Hebrew Bible. Yet they are included proleptically in his saving act (John 8:56; Heb. 11:13–15). So the logical or conceptual priority of Christ as the "New Adam" is theological not chronological in nature. By that I mean, Christ is the second Adam, but not because he is the first member of redeemed humanity in time, like the first Adam with respect to fallen humanity, but because he is the firstborn from the dead. We might say that redeemed humanity is organized *eschatologically* not *protologically*—that is, on the basis of the world to come and the order that God has prepared for it, not on the basis of the present world, in time, and its order from Adam until now. So, Christ is the second Adam in the sense that his priority is the priority of the firstborn among those living the resurrected life (1 Cor. 15). Redeemed humanity is constituted on the basis of the resurrected Christ, whose reconciling work makes possible human participation in the divine life in this world and the next.

How then may Christ be said to act vicariously and reparatively on behalf of fallen humanity, representing them in atonement? There are several components to this. First, there is the Anselmian argument for the conditional necessity of the God-man in *Cur Deus Homo*. Recall that, according to the Anselmian, Christ represents human beings by becoming a human being. Only as a human himself is he able to act on behalf of other humans. And only as a sinless human being is he able to act on behalf of

---

44. Put very roughly, traducianism is the doctrine according to which human beings are somehow metaphysically present "in" Adam at the moment of primal sin so that we literally participate in his sin. It is a correlate to Augustinian realism. I have discussed this in *An American Augustinian*.

other human beings in salvation, because fallen and sinful human beings already owe all that they are and all that they do to God as a debt—the debt of sin. But also, Christ must be divine because only a divine person can offer up a satisfaction of the right value. No mere human could provide satisfaction for the sin of all humanity, for no mere human is able to generate a merit of infinite value capable of satisfying divine honor and justice. Even if the details of Anselm's argument might be challenged, the central claim that post-fall human beings are incapable of saving themselves because they bear original sin seems theologically plausible, as does the claim that the value of Christ's work is infinite given the dignity and honor of the person who offers it, as was argued in chapter 2. Christ represents human beings as a human being, yet he must also be a human being without sin in order to represent humanity soteriologically. And he must be divine in order for the act to have the right kind of value requisite for the atonement. This is *the Anselmian representation requirement*.

Next, this vicarious act is *penitential* as well as representational. According to the *Oxford English Dictionary*, penitence is the "undergoing of a discipline or exercise as an outward expression of repentance and expiation of an offence, either voluntarily or as imposed by an ecclesiastical authority; a penance."[45] Christ's atonement is such an act. Specifically, it is an act of *vicarious penitence*, as the author of Hebrews makes clear (Heb. 5:7–10).[46] Christ's incarnation, life, death, and resurrection constitute one complex performative act by means of which he offers an apology on behalf of fallen humanity.[47] It may seem strange to think of Christ's atonement as an extended apology. Yet we often apologize on behalf of others where we bear an appropriate relation to the other in question. Thus, I apologize to my neighbor for my son who has backed the car into my neighbor's vehicle. Heads of state apologize on behalf of the nation for certain acts committed in the past, such as wartime atrocities. And leaders of organizations offer apologies for the actions of their representatives or

45. *Oxford English Dictionary*, s.v. "penitence," accessed March 14, 2021, https://www.oed.com.

46. This passage is an important source of J. Campbell's doctrine of vicarious penitence as well.

47. This is a point also made by Swinburne in *Responsibility and Atonement*, 84. Like Swinburne, I have in mind a kind of speech-act when I say that Christ's atonement is a performative action. These are acts by means of which particular states of affairs are brought about. In the case of atonement, it is reconciliation with God that is brought about.

members when they have misbehaved while acting on behalf of the organization or in its employ. I suggest that one reason why the idea of Christ offering an apology on behalf of fallen humanity seems odd at first glance, or even implausible, is because we tend to conflate the act of apology with related moral notions like culpability and blameworthiness. That is, we tend to think Christ cannot apologize on my behalf because he is not the one culpable for transgressing, and so is not blameworthy.

However, the cases of the apology made on behalf of my son backing the car into the neighbor's vehicle, or of the head of state or leader of an organization apologizing on behalf of the action of some of the members of the group they represent, should give us pause. Such examples show that in many circumstances we do think one person can act vicariously as a representative of a group in a penitential performative act. In these cases we do not ascribe culpability or blame to the person who acts in a representative manner. Rather, we hold them *accountable*. The parent is accountable for the actions of her child though she is not the one who backed the car into the neighbor's vehicle, and thus she is not culpable or blameworthy for committing the act. In certain circumstances, such as culpability for wartime atrocities, we might think that the head of state is accountable for the actions of citizens of the state even though he is not personally guilty of, or blameworthy for, the crimes in question. Similarly, Christ may be held accountable for the sin of humanity as the representative of humanity though he is not culpable for human sin nor blameworthy. The expression of this in a penitential act of atonement that comprises his incarnation, life, death, and resurrection does not imply that Christ is guilty of human sin, nor that the guilt of human sin is imputed to him. All it implies is that as a representative of humanity he may he held accountable for that sin. That is, he has some liability to answer for the action of the other. He may offer an appropriate performative act as a kind of apology on behalf of human sin, as well as a kind of penance for human sin.[48] Thus, a vicarious penitential act is (or at least can be) condign.

48. Compare the *Oxford English Dictionary* entry on penance as a noun, "The performance of some act of self-mortification or the undergoing of some penalty as an expression of sorrow for sin or wrongdoing; religious discipline, either imposed by ecclesiastical authority or voluntarily undertaken, as a token of repentance and as a means of satisfaction for sin" (s.v. "penance," accessed March 15, 2021, https://www.oed.com).

Now, in both the case of the parent and the case of the head of state, there must be an appropriate relation between the person representing and the agents represented. A parent can represent the son because she is his parent. The head of state can represent the nation because he is elected to that office. One way to understand this is as a relation between members of a group. The parent and child are members of a family, and the head of state and its citizens are members of a society or nation. In principle a member of a group may represent the group even if that person does not have a position of leadership in the group. For instance, a graduate student represents her institution at a conference, though she is not in an official position of responsibility as an office bearer in her institution and so does not formally represent the interests of that group. So representation can have fairly broad application to groups and their members. But group membership is a *sine qua non*. The graduate student represents the institution as a member of the institution, the parent can represent the interests of the child as a member of the family, and the head of state can represent the members of the state as a citizen of that state. In each case some kind of group membership is what makes it possible to invoke ascriptions of a representative sort that may imply accountability on behalf of the group. These are different sorts of groups, of course, and the relation borne by a parent to a child in a family is not the same as the relation borne by the president to the state or the graduate student to the university. Nevertheless, in each of these instances group membership determines whether the person in question may act in a representative role for the group. It is a necessary, but not sufficient, condition for such a determination.

Yet we have seen that, according to conditions of the Anselmian representation requirement, the same is true of Christ. Only someone who is a human can act on behalf of other humans because only a human bears the right relation to other humans—namely, being a member of Adam's race—that makes it possible to represent the concerns and needs of members of that race. And only one who is without sin is not already indebted to God and therefore capable of acting in this manner on behalf of another—that is, capable of an act of performative penitence that may be efficacious. What is more, only because Christ is a divine person is his vicarious act also an act that is of the right sort of value needed to bring about atonement for all humanity. Thus, Christ is uniquely placed to act as the representative of humanity. And, given that he is God and voluntarily takes upon himself this role in salvation as part of the gracious act of salvation ordained by the members of the Trinity in eternity—the *pactum salutis*—this arrangement is an appropriate one. For surely it is appropriate for God to arrange matters in this way with respect to his creatures. This is not an *ad hoc* arrangement. It is divinely ordained as an aspect of God's overarching aim in creation, which is to bring about reconciliation with alienated human beings in order that they may participate in the divine life everlastingly. Thus, Christ voluntarily takes upon himself the liability to answer for the sinful actions of fallen humanity. He consents to be accountable for atonement.[49]

In sum, the atonement is a vicarious, reparative, and penitential act of soteriological representation. Like the literary trope of synecdoche, Christ stands in for the whole of humanity in his act of reconciliation. But he is not a substitute for humanity, and he does not bear the punishment or guilt for human sin. Thus, penal substitution is excluded. His act does satisfy the standard of God's moral law. He does pay the penalty for human sin that includes death and alienation from God on the cross. But the payment of this penalty is an aspect of his penitential act on behalf of fallen humanity. Moreover, because he is the God-man, his vicarious action has the value sufficient to atone for the sin of all of humanity.

We are now in a position to provide a revised atonement narrative that supplants the version of the union account with which we began this chapter. In summing up this reparative, representational act of vicarious penitence that satisfies God's moral law, we can say this:

Taken together, Adam (from the fall onwards) and all of post-fall humanity barring Christ constitute a distinct group[50]—that is, "fallen humanity" (Rom. 5:12–19). Fallen humanity exists across time in a way analogous to

49. The fact that God ordains that Christ has this role makes this rather different from other accounts of mundane groups. Even those who, like Thomas Hobbes, think that "a multitude of men are made *one* person, when they are by one man, or one person, represented so that it may be done with the consent of every one of that multitude in particular," still hold that the group collectively *consents to* the representative (see *Leviathan* 1.16, 107). Not so in the case of atonement. Here it is *God* who ordains this state of affairs, and for a very good reason: human beings are incapable of saving themselves, let alone of banding together to authorize a representative to act on their behalf. For a discussion of this point, see Cockayne, "Analytic Ecclesiology," 108–10.

50. Roman Catholic and Eastern Orthodox readers may like to make the mental adjustment, "barring Christ and his mother, Mary *Theotokos*."

the different stages of the life of an organism, like a tree, from its beginning as an acorn to its maturity as an oak. Members of fallen humanity possess the moral corruption of original sin as a consequence of Adam's primal sin. It is passed from Adam to the later members of the group because he is the first human in covenant relationship with his maker. As such, his primal sin violates the conditions of the covenant with God and incurs the penalty of original sin, which is then passed down the generations to subsequent members of fallen humanity. In a similar manner, a chronic disease introduced to an acorn affects all the later phases of the life of the oak tree in a way that a disease introduced at some later moment developmentally downstream of the acorn would not.

Christ is the second Adam. He is the first member of a new humanity, one that is cleansed from sin and reconciled to God. Christ and those he comes to save form, together, a second group: "redeemed humanity." Christ is the interface between God and humanity and a fitting means by which humans may be reconciled to God. As the God-human, Christ is able to act on behalf of both God and humanity, communicating between them and acting as a conduit of divine grace to humanity, as a representative of humanity. Christ has a kind of priority or privilege over other "parts" of redeemed humanity, although he exists later in time than some of them, because he is the first of a new, resurrected humanity that is ordered eschatologically rather than (as with the first Adam) protologically. Thus, although he lives later than, say, Abraham, his work as the second Adam reconciles Abraham to God (Heb. 11:8–16, 39–40). In the purposes of God, those living prior to Christ can be proleptically incorporated into Christ's work as the second Adam. Christ is not guilty of sin; yet he acts vicariously on behalf of the other members of redeemed humanity who bear original sin and stand in need of reconciliation as members of fallen humanity. Christ's reconciling work (comprising his incarnation, death, and resurrection) removes the obstacle of sin and defeats death. He represents humanity before God and, as the impeccable God-man, is held accountable for the sin of other, fallen human beings. He atones for human sin through a performative act of vicarious penitence that culminates in his death and resurrection, which satisfy the demands of God's moral law and the penalty incurred by the primeval fall and curse. Through union with Christ by the power of the Holy Spirit, in regeneration, members of fallen humanity begin a process of transformation into the likeness of God as members of redeemed humanity, becoming partakers of the divine nature. This process of transformation goes on forevermore. It is like a mathematical asymptote in that the human members of redeemed humanity draw ever closer to God in this process, yet without ever becoming God or losing themselves in God.

This completes the constructive account of the mechanism of atonement. But one final concern remains. In the chapter on satisfaction we touched on Eleonore Stump's criticism of what she calls "the Anselmian view." One concern she raises that we did not tackle in detail there is that reparation for past acts is backward-looking and therefore insufficient for dealing with human alienation from God and with sins yet to be committed. Atonement must be more than the canceling of a debt; it must also put us in right relationship with God.[51] Stump's positive claim is well taken. But her criticism of reparative views of atonement is, I think, in need of correction. I take it that vicarious and reparative accounts of atonement hold that Christ's atonement includes within its ambit all the sins of the whole of humanity scattered through space-time—past, present, and future. We might put it like this: Christ's work atones for the sins of all humanity in all of history—past, present, and future—as seems obvious from the New Testament (e.g., John 1:29; Col. 1:20; 1 John 2:2).

Does atonement, then, merely remove obstacles to reconciliation, or does it bring about reconciliation? Here we must return to our earlier distinction between atonement and its consequences. The mechanism of atonement removes obstacles, making reconciliation possible. Union with Christ actualizes reconciliation via the gift of faith and the regenerating work of the Holy Spirit. Thus the act of atonement is one part of a larger soteriological whole. Only when the act of atonement and its consequences are seen together do we have a complete account of the reconciling work of Christ. And even then, we have only a partial account of soteriology. For the whole of salvation is not atonement or its mechanism, or union with Christ and regeneration. The whole of salvation is all these things realized in *theosis*—that is, in the culmination of God's intention to create a world of human creatures who participate in the divine life. We will need to consider the consequences of atonement in the next chapter. Then we will be able to offer a summary statement of soteriology that includes these two parts in a final, synthesis chapter.

51. See Stump, *Atonement*, chaps. 1–2.

Conclusion

In this chapter I have argued that Christ's reconciling work is a vicarious act of a particular sort. In it, he represents the members of fallen humanity to God, and he is held accountable for their sin. This is not so much a group action as it is an action by one agent on behalf of a group to which he belongs. The members of fallen humanity bear original sin. Those who live after Adam are not culpable for bearing this condition, though they are culpable for the actual sins they commit as bearers of this condition. Christ represents the members of this group in atonement. He is accountable for their sin. This arrangement is brought about by divine fiat, not on the basis of natural and covenantal factors as with Adam and the transmission of original sin. Nevertheless, although it is, in a sense, a legal arrangement (being dependent on divine fiat as a kind of positive law), it depends upon the real union of Christ with humanity in the incarnation. It is because of the incarnation that atonement obtains, and it is because of the incarnation that Christ is able to act as a mediator of salvation. God ordains this arrangement in what traditional Reformed theology has dubbed the "covenant of grace," or *pactum salutis*, whereby the persons of the Trinity are said to compact together to bring about human salvation through the reconciling work of Christ. Thus, God ordains human salvation, a salvation that obtains by means of Christ's incarnation. And in the person of the Son, God unites Godself to human nature. However, the incarnation has a double purpose in the eternal counsels of God. It is a soteriological act. But it has a logically prior aim, which is the union of divinity and humanity in one person so that he may be the conduit for union with God. One of the fundamental aims of creation is that creatures, particularly human creatures, participate in the divine life. God wishes to be united to created things because God loves God's creatures. God wants us to flourish. And God wants to be united to us so that we may participate in the divine life, everlastingly and asymptotically. The incarnation is a fitting means of bringing this about. Thus, incarnation serves these two purposes.

9

The Mystical Body
of Christ

In the previous chapter I distinguished between the nature of atonement and its consequences, and then I proceeded to outline two versions of a union account of atonement, opting for the second. This second and revised version of the union account characterizes the atonement as a *vicarious, reparative, and penitential act of soteriological representation.* I call this view, for short, the "representationalist union account." In distinguishing the nature of atonement from its consequences, I mean to keep apart (at least conceptually) the means by which Christ brings about the reconciliation of fallen human beings and the means by which the benefits of this saving work are applied to individuals. This is achieved via the secret work of the Holy Spirit in regeneration, though this work begins in eternity in the way in which God ordains the justification of those to whom God applies the saving benefits of Christ's reconciling work.[1] But in addition to justification and regeneration, which I take to be a divine act that terminates upon particular believers, transforming them, there is the manner in which the Spirit also unites the believer to Christ. These

---

1. I have discussed the notion of eternal justification in *Deviant Calvinism* and *Analyzing Doctrine.* And I have treated the notion of regeneration in *Freedom, Redemption, and Communion.* My comments here build on this previous work.

two things are, in fact, two aspects of one eternal divine act by means of which fallen human persons are enabled to partake of the saving benefits of Christ's atonement. Moreover, these consequences of atonement are, in turn, an aspect of the broader theological category of soteriology or the doctrine of salvation in which each of the divine persons of the Trinity is intimately involved. For, as catholic theology has traditionally presumed, *opera trinitatis ad extra indivisa sunt*.[2] It is as if in eternity God ordains the salvation of the fallen human beings he creates, and ordains the means by which that is brought about. The manner of salvation includes, on the one hand, the reconciling work of Christ in atonement and, on the other, the secret working of the Holy Spirit in transforming and healing the particular human person by the application of Christ's benefits and in uniting the human person to Christ. The objective, from a God's-eye point of view, is to reconcile fallen human beings to Godself in order that they may be able to participate in the divine life.

Yet in Christian theology salvation is not just about the reconciliation of the *individual* with God through Christ by means of the agency of the Spirit. Salvation is also concerned with the entity or group that is united with Christ in this act of reconciliation—that is, with redeemed humanity. For the members of redeemed humanity form the new society, the church, created by Christ's reconciling work.[3] The New Testament writings speak of the church variously in the language of organic metaphors as (among other things) the vine, the body, the bride of Christ, and the household of faith (e.g., John 15; Rom. 12:4–5; 1 Cor. 10:17; 12; 2 Cor. 11:12; Gal. 6:10; Eph. 5; Col. 1:24; 1 Pet. 2:5; Rev. 21:9).[4] It is not incidental that the reconciling work of Christ brings about the salvation not just of individuals but of the church as a whole. For the

2. That is, "the external works of the Trinity [in the created order] are indivisible." For a recent systematic treatment of this topic, see Vidu's monograph, *Same God*.

3. I presume that the church is coterminous with redeemed humanity. It may be that some members of redeemed humanity are not outwardly members of the church or do not have access to the sacramental life of the church. (For instance, a member of redeemed humanity may live in a country where there is no expression of the Christian church, or may be an adherent of another faith, or may have lived before the gospel was proclaimed.) Nevertheless, such persons, being members of redeemed humanity, are also members of the invisible church scattered through the centuries because they are united to Christ by the Holy Spirit and regenerate, even if they are not members of the visible church at a particular moment in history.

4. Joshua Cockayne notes that in "Scripture, there are at least 96 metaphors used to explain the nature of the Church" ("Analytic Ecclesiology," 103).

goal of Christ's soteriological work is not just the reconciliation of fallen human persons as a kind of collection or bundle of particulars. It is the formation of the church as a new society intimately united with Christ. The relation between Christ and the members of this group that is the church scattered through space and time is a kind of union formed by the Holy Spirit. Though we may go some way toward understanding this relation between God and his redeemed people, it is not something that we can fully fathom this side of the grave. For this reason, theologians have characterized the entity that is formed by the soteriological work of the divine persons as a *mystical* work, and the society formed by this work, *the mystical body of Christ*. In this connection a mystical work is one that has a certain symbolic or metaphysical significance that transcends human understanding. It is mysterious. Thus, one way to approach the question of the consequences of atonement in justification, regeneration, and union with Christ is as the means by which God forms the mystical body of Christ, the church. In this way, atonement and ecclesiology are linked through the agency of the Holy Spirit in his secret regenerating and unifying work.

This multifaceted act of salvation cannot be adequately analyzed in one chapter. Nevertheless, we can give an overview of some of its main lineaments, focused on the issue of the consequences of atonement. This we will do by dividing the discussion of this matter into three parts. In the first, I shall pick up where we left off in the previous chapter by discussing the way in which the saving benefits of Christ's reconciling work are applied to the believer, with particular reference to eternal justification as the ground of the work of the Holy Spirit in regeneration. Then, in the second part, I will turn to the manner in which the Spirit unites the believer to Christ so that she may begin to enjoy the benefits of Christ's saving work, and so participate in the divine life. In the third part, I will fold these two things, the application of Christ's benefits to the believer and the union of the believer with Christ, into the larger soteriological work of forming the mystical body of Christ, which is the church, drawing in particular on recent work in this area by Joshua Cockayne. Some of the elements of the first two sections of this chapter draw on my previous work in this area, applied to the present concern.[5] The third section takes

---

5. Particularly, *Deviant Calvinism*, chap. 2; *Word Enfleshed*, chaps. 8–9; and *Analyzing Doctrine*, chaps. 5–6, 10.

forward the discussion in a constructive way, and in conversation with the literature on social ontology.

Applying Christ's Reconciling Work

Suppose we think of the application of the benefits of Christ's atonement as a twofold action of the Holy Spirit. The first aspect of this action entails the moral and spiritual transformation made possible by Christ's reconciling work via the Holy Spirit in regeneration. The second aspect of this action involves the Spirit uniting the believer with Christ. We begin by considering the first, regenerative aspect of this divine act. It is predicated upon God's eternal decision to save a particular number of fallen humanity and to justify them by means of the reconciling work of Christ. In order to see this more clearly, let us turn first to the doctrine of justification from eternity. Then we will be in a position to consider the particular way in which this eternal act is applied to the believer in regeneration.

a. Justification from Eternity

The doctrine of justification has been a source of significant division in the Christian church, especially since the Protestant Reformation.[6] For many in the Roman Catholic tradition, justification is a process that begins with baptism and continues throughout the life of the individual. But for Protestants standing in the tradition of the Magisterial Reformation, justification is typically regarded as a kind of declarative act by means of which a person's status before God is transformed by the imputation of the alien righteousness of Christ brought about by atonement. What happens in life after the moment of justification is the ongoing sanctification of the justified person—not that person's continued gradual justification over time. The justification and transformation of the individual believer are two parts of what is usually known as the *ordo salutis*—that is, "the order of salvation."[7] As divines reflected further on these matters in post-

6. The standard scholarly history of the doctrine in English is McGrath, *Iustitia Dei*. For a useful snapshot of recent debate on this topic, see Beilby and Eddy, *Justification: Five Views*.

7. The *ordo salutis* is usually thought to comprise the following elements in Protestant thought: calling, regeneration, faith, justification, sanctification, perseverance, and glorification. The origin and development of the term is discussed in Muller, *Calvin and the Reformed Tradition*, chap. 6.

Reformation Protestantism, the shape of the *ordo salutis* was more carefully parsed, with some theologians providing sophisticated accounts of how the Holy Spirit works in the lives of believers.[8] The discussion was not just about distinguishing the different facets of the *ordo salutis* as it normally unfolded in the life of the believer. Rather, the order of salvation was also pushed back into eternity as it was brought into contact with the doctrine of divine election and the divine decrees more generally. What started as an attempt to describe the manner in which the sinner is transformed into a believer became a framework by means of which the whole sweep of human salvation could be viewed from the effectual calling of the believer by the Holy Spirit all the way through to glorification postmortem.

Our focus is constructive rather than historical. That is, I am interested in setting forth a view and defending it, rather than reporting on the development of a particular doctrinal trajectory in the history of doctrine. But of course, the two tasks are not unrelated. In high Reformed theology, as justification was viewed in its eternal aspect as one of the divine decrees of God in creation, the doctrine of God's eternal justification emerged. This is the idea that in the divine eternal purposes in creation, God ordains the justification of some number of fallen humanity consistent with his plans in providing effectual atonement for this number in the reconciling work of Christ.[9] What begins in eternity as God's decision to save that particular number, the elect, can be distinguished into the act by means of which this group is eternally justified in the purposes of God and the manner of securing the soteriological grounds for such justification in Christ's work of atonement.[10]

In earlier work in this area, I distinguished between two ways in which the doctrine of eternal justification could be construed. The first was

8. Consider, for example, the famous "golden chain" of salvation, which was a table of how God's plans in election are worked out, based on Rom. 8:28–30 and made popular in Reformed piety by William Perkins (see *Golden Chain*).

9. Notable Reformed theologians who have held versions of this view include William Twisse, prolocutor of the Westminster Assembly; John Gill; Tobias Crisp; and Abraham Kuyper. It is often, mistakenly, thought to imply antinomianism—the idea that we may "continue in sin in order that grace may abound" (cf. Rom. 6:1).

10. The assumption here is that God either cannot or does not simply declare righteous some group of humanity independent of some means by which that declaration is grounded in atonement. In other words, those justified are justified on the basis of Christ's atoning work, which is the means by which reconciliation with God is made possible. God does not simply declare some group of humanity righteous irrespective of a work of atonement. The two things are intertwined, the atonement being the ground and means by which justification is made possible.

justification in eternity, and the second was *justification from eternity*.[11] According to the doctrine of justification in eternity, God's declarative act of justification obtains at the eternal "moment" when God ordains it. What happens in history is that those who are eternally justified are made aware of their status when they are given the gift of faith by the susurrant working of the Holy Spirit. But importantly, on this view, the Spirit's secret work in the life of the believer does not transform the individual from a state of alienation to a state of justification. For the individual is already eternally justified. Rather, what happens is that an epistemic change takes place. It is like the case of King Arthur drawing the sword from the stone. In drawing the sword Arthur comes to understand that he is the heir to the throne and of royal blood, being a Pendragon. He does not *become* heir to the throne or a member of the royal line in the act of drawing the sword from the stone. The change is an epistemic one, not an ontological one. The same is true of the believer in the doctrine of justification in eternity.

By contrast, in the doctrine of justification from eternity, the transformation that takes place in the believer in time is completed, as it were, in history at the moment the individual comes to understand that they are justified by means of Christ's atoning work in the act of faith. This transformation is epistemic, but it is also legal and moral: the individual in question is changed from a state of alienation to a state of reconciliation. Although this is an act that is ordained in eternity in the purposes of God, it is completed at that moment in which the gift of faith is communicated to the believer by the secret work of the Holy Spirit. It seems to me that of these two versions of eternal justification, the doctrine of justification from eternity is preferable. For it tracks better with the sort of view one finds in the New Testament documents, as well as in subsequent tradition. We can express the justification from eternity view like this:

Justification from Eternity

1. God eternally decrees the number of the elect (that is, of redeemed humanity).
2. God eternally decrees that Christ is the mediator of salvation.

---

11. See the discussion in Crisp, *Deviant Calvinism*.

3. Christ is the ground of election (given that God the Son, the divine person who voluntarily assumes human nature, is a member of the divine Trinity) and the means by which election is brought about as the Elect One and mediator of our election.

4. God knows all those who are elect (that is, all the members of redeemed humanity).

5. God knows that all the elect (i.e., members of redeemed humanity other than Christ) will be saved through the work of Christ as mediator.

6. God knows that all the elect will be justified through the work of Christ by God's divine grace alone, according to God's will and purpose (Eph. 1:5).

7. It is eternally true that the members of redeemed humanity (other than Christ) are justified by Christ's meritorious work alone (not by their own merit).

8. The secret work of the Holy Spirit applies the benefits of Christ's work to each individual member of the elect.

9. This application normally obtains by means of the gift of faith, bestowed on the elect individual by the Holy Spirit, uniting that individual to Christ in regeneration.[12]

10. The application of faith to the elect individual completes the eternal act of justification; justification is an eternal act of divine grace that obtains in time at the very moment in which the Holy Spirit applies the benefits of Christ to the individual.

11. The application of faith to the elect individual enables that person to understand that she is included within the ambit of divine election and that she is justified.

12. The application of faith to the elect individual brings about an epistemic change to the person concerned.

13. The application of faith also brings about a moral and (perhaps) a legal change in the elect individual.[13]

12. The caveat "normally" provides some wiggle room for those who may be elect, and therefore members of redeemed humanity, but who are incapable of exercising faith—e.g., the severely mentally impaired and infants who die before the age of maturity.
13. Adapted from Crisp, *Deviant Calvinism*, 51–53.

Given that justification obtains on the basis of Christ's reconciling work, it is logically consequent to the atonement in the divine decrees. God desires that human beings participate in the divine life; God ordains Christ as the prototypical human, and as the means by which humans may participate in the divine life. In creating this world, God sees that human beings will need to be redeemed by means of an atonement, one provided by a God-man.[14] Therefore, God ordains Christ as a kind of divine-human hub. Those God ordains to salvation on the basis of Christ's reconciling work are justified from eternity. And the way this divine act of justification is made effectual in the life of the believer is through the gift of faith, and through the transformation brought about by the secret work of the Holy Spirit in regeneration.[15]

b. Regeneration as Infusion

There are different ways in which the doctrine of regeneration might be characterized. One promising avenue of exploration is the *infusion model* that can be found in the work of Jonathan Edwards.[16] On this view, it is the Spirit himself who is communicated to the believer in regeneration, and who is said to indwell the believer, infusing into her a new disposition that rectifies the moral disorder brought about through the removing of the Spirit's presence and the introduction of original sin that occurred in the primeval fall. Edwards describes this divine act as infusing in the believer a new *spiritual sense*. He writes, "This new spiritual sense is not a new faculty of understanding, but it is a new foundation laid in the nature of the soul, for a new kind of exercises of the same faculty of understanding. So that new holy disposition of heart that attends this new sense, is not a

14. I have discussed the topic of Christ as the prototypical human in *Word Enfleshed* and supralapsarian Christology in *Analyzing Doctrine*. Readers are directed to those works for further elaboration of these matters.

15. Calvin thought that the efficient cause of salvation is the good pleasure of God. The material cause is Christ. The instrumental cause is faith, and the final cause is the praise of God's grace. See the discussion of this in Muller, *Calvin and the Reformed Tradition*, 172. Though I am not casting the order of salvation in the language of the fourfold Aristotelian causes, and though my view differs in detail from that of Calvin, there is clearly a family resemblance.

16. I have discussed this in more detail in "Regeneration Reconsidered." The infusion account is one version of what Adonis Vidu calls the uncreated grace model of divine indwelling, which can be traced back at least to Peter Lombard. See Vidu, "Indwelling of the Holy Spirit," 259–60. For a digest of historic Reformed thinking on this matter that reflects the uncreated grace model, see Heppe, *Reformed Dogmatics*, chap. 20.

new faculty of will, but a foundation laid in the nature of the soul, for a new kind of exercises of the same faculty of will."[17] This strikes me as a plausible way of thinking about the manner in which the transformative experience of regeneration applies the benefits of Christ's atonement and God's eternal justification to the individual. We might summarize it thus:

> **Regeneration:** The divine action by means of which the Holy Spirit is communicated to the believer, indwelling the believer, and *infusing* a new supernatural disposition or habit into a fallen human person that provides a spiritual sense by means of which the regenerate person may begin to live a life pleasing to God.

In keeping with a broadly Edwardsian sensibility about the manner of salvation, we may add to this infusion account of regeneration a proviso about the nature of this divine act. Like atonement and justification, in historic Reformed thought regeneration is regarded as entirely a work of divine grace from beginning to end—including the very gift of faith itself (Eph. 2:8–9). Fallen human beings are incapable of saving themselves absent divine grace so that even the exercise of faith itself is a product of God's enabling of fallen human beings to act in a particular manner. In this process, according to traditional Reformed teaching, the fallen human being, bound by sin, is incapable of placing herself in a soteriologically advantageous position. It is not even the case that fallen human beings may come to a point at which they cease to resist God and open themselves up to divine grace.[18] For, so the Reformed have thought, this too is a work of grace.[19] As the influential seventeenth-century Reformed divine William Ames puts it in his discussion of conversion as an aspect of God's calling of an individual in the *ordo salutis*, "The will is the proper and prime subject of this grace; the conversion of the will is the effectual principle in the conversion of the whole man."[20] What is more, it is not merely the

---

17. Edwards, *Religious Affections*, 206. Elsewhere in his writings, Edwards says, "There is no other principle of grace in the soul than the very Holy Ghost dwelling in the soul and acting there as a vital principle" (*Writings on the Trinity*, 196).

18. In recent theology, this sort of view has been touted by Eleonore Stump (see Stump, *Aquinas*, 389–404). See also the discussion of this in Kittle, "Grace and Free Will." I discuss Stump's view in Crisp, "Regeneration Reconsidered."

19. Useful discussion of this can be found in Muller, *Calvin and the Reformed Tradition*, chap. 6.

20. See Ames, *Marrow of Theology*, 159.

enlightening of the mind that brings about this change. Rather, says Ames, "the will in this first receiving plays the role neither of a free agent nor a natural bearer, but only of an obedient subject."[21] The reception of this divine grace is, he maintains, "an elicited act of faith."[22] Although it is the act of the individual human agent, it is only by means of divine grace in the provision of faith that this action is feasible.[23] Such a view might be characterized as *monergism*—that is, the singular work of God in the heart of the believer. It is typical of the sort of approach to this question favored by those in the Reformed tradition. We could put it like this:

> **Monergism:** The doctrine according to which the application of the benefits of Christ's reconciling work by the agency of the Holy Spirit in regeneration is wholly a work of divine grace; in this process the human agent is entirely passive, but not quiescent.

Union with Christ

By means of the infusion of uncreated grace, the Holy Spirit indwells the believer, regenerating her and providing a new disposition to live in a way pleasing to God. Yet this action also unites the believer with the meritorious cause of this reconciling work—namely, Christ. But how? How is union with Christ brought about? It is one thing to say that by means of the agency of the Holy Spirit the believer is transformed in the act of regeneration. For we can conceive, however dimly, the idea of God indwelling and changing us from the inside out, so to speak. Nevertheless, this leaves unexplained how this also brings about the union of the believer with Christ. This is the next thing we must consider, as the second aspect of the consequence of Christ's atonement. In order to do so we will need to take a step back from the particular issues raised by the calling of the believer and the act of regeneration to think about how God sets up the *conditions* by means of which union with Christ might obtain. For as we looked first at justification from eternity as the ground of regeneration in the believer, so here we will need to consider the way in which God ordains the incarnation as the conduit by means of which

21. Ames, *Marrow of Theology*, 159.
22. Ames, *Marrow of Theology*, 159.
23. Ames, *Marrow of Theology*, 159.

redeemed human beings may be "hooked up" to the divine so as to be united to Christ, and thereby participate in the divine life. We may then connect this to the notion of union with Christ in order to provide a more complete account of this relation.

Thus, to begin with, we will need to say something about Christ as the hub between divinity and humanity, or the interface between God and humans that makes union with God possible. We can put it like this: Christ interfaces between God and humans as the prototypical human being, the one in whose image all other humans are formed (2 Cor. 4:4; Col. 1:15; Heb. 1:3).[24] He is literally the "firstborn of all creation"—not as one who is merely a creature or angelic figure, as the Arians supposed, but as one who assumes creatureliness into his own divine life in order that he may interface with creaturely existence and unite it with Godself. Although the human nature assumed by the Son begins to exist at a particular moment in time in the womb of the Virgin, it was (so it seems to me) eternally ordained as the prototypical human nature on the basis of which all other human natures were created. An analog may help illuminate the point here. In contemporary transhumanism literature there is the aspiration to unite the organic and the digital by means of so-called "wet" interfaces—that is, implants that might enable suitably enhanced human beings to directly access data via digital superhighways. Analogously, the incarnation is a means by which God may interface with creatures. In fact, the human nature of Christ is ordained by God as the prototypical human creature that the Word may "interface" with, "uploading" himself into the human nature that is miraculously generated for him in the womb of the Virgin.[25]

But this interface between divinity and humanity is ordained irrespective of human sin. It is, we might think, because of God's desire to be united with human creatures that God forms the human nature of Christ. For by means of this hub between divinity and humanity, God enables other

---

24. I have argued for this claim at greater length in *Word Enfleshed*, chap. 4.

25. I elaborate on this account of the incarnation in more detail in *Divinity and Humanity*, chap. 2. Lest I be misunderstood, I want to keep distinct two things here. These are, first, a claim about the human nature of Christ being the prototypical image of God on the basis of which we all are made to image the divine and, second, the claim that the incarnation brings about an interface between divinity and humanity in the theanthropic person of Christ. I distinguish these two things in more expansive terms in *Word Enfleshed*, and I direct interested readers to the discussion there.

human beings to be united to God. Elsewhere I have likened this to the way in which an internet router may provide a connection to the World Wide Web by means of an interface one end of which is hardwired to a telephone connection, enabling the router to directly access the internet, with the other end calibrated to send and receive radio signals from particular laptop computers that may be wirelessly connected to the router via Wi-Fi technology.[26] The laptops send and receive the radio signals that connect the user to the internet by means of the router. This is a common enough feature of contemporary life. In a similar fashion, Christ, as the router between divinity and humanity, is "hardwired" to the divine nature and is able, via the secret working of the Holy Spirit, to connect individual believers to the divine nature by means of his human nature. We are, as it were, united to Christ by the Spirit, who acts like the radio signals connecting the laptop computer to the router, which is Christ. What is more, Christ unites us directly to the divine nature as we interface with his humanity by means of the Spirit's agency.

Of course, an internet router is only of use if the laptop *is able* to connect to it wirelessly. The laptop computer must itself be switched on and capable of such connection, and it must have the technology necessary to connect to the hub activated—usually Wi-Fi capability. If the computer is closed, or switched off, or if its Wi-Fi capability is inactive, it will not be able to access the internet via the router. This is true even if the router is active and ready to receive radio signals from the laptop in question. This points us to a further dimension of union with Christ: To be united to Christ the believer must be "activated"—that is, regenerated—by means of the secret work of the Holy Spirit. Once the believer is regenerated and in a position to send and receive the "signals" carried by the Holy Spirit necessary to be united with Christ, she may be joined with Christ in a spiritual manner, as the beginning of the work of sanctification that leads to ever greater union with God in Christ and to participation in the divine life through Christ.

Lest it be thought that this image of union with Christ is rather too strong, and even something that does not reflect the sort of views one finds in historic Reformed theology, consider the following passage from William Ames's *Marrow of Theology*. It is anything but quotidian:

26. See my discussion of this in *Word Enfleshed* and *Analyzing Doctrine*.

The relationship is so intimate that not only is Christ the church's and the church Christ's, Song of Solomon 2:16, but Christ is *in* the church and the church *in him*, John 15:4; 1 John 3:24. Therefore, the church is *mystically called Christ*, 1 Corinthians 12:12, and the Fullness of Christ, Ephesians 1:23. The church is metaphorically called the bride and Christ the bridegroom; the church a city and Christ the king; the church a house and Christ the householder; the church the branches and Christ the vine; and finally the church a body and Christ the head. But these comparisons signify not only the union and communion between Christ and the church but also the relation showing Christ to be the beginning of all honor, life, power, and perfection in the church. *This church is mystically one, not in a generic sense, but as a unique species or individual—for it has no species in the true sense.*[27]

Other Reformed divines have been even more emphatic in this respect. Consider, for example, Jonathan Edwards:

God's respect to the creature's good, and his respect to himself, is not a divided respect; but both are united in one, as the happiness of the creature aimed at is happiness in union with himself. The creature is no further happy with this happiness which God makes his ultimate end than he becomes one with God. The more happiness the greater union: when the happiness is perfect, the union is perfect. And as the happiness will be increasing to eternity, the union will become more and more strict and perfect; nearer and more like to that between God the Father and the Son; who are so united, that their interest is perfectly one. If the happiness of the creature be considered as it will be, in the whole of the creature's eternal duration, with all the infinity of its progress, and infinite increase of nearness and union to God; in this view, the creature must be looked upon as united to God in an infinite strictness.[28]

Just as the relation between Christ and those he comes to reconcile to Godself is a kind of *sui generis* representative atonement ordained by divine fiat, so also the mystical union brought about by Christ's work in the formation of the church is itself both mystical and unique. Because of

27. Ames, *Marrow of Theology*, 176–77 (emphasis added). Ames's views are representative of much Reformed thought on this matter, rather than eccentric, and were influential on a number of subsequent Reformed thinkers, rather than marginal.
28. Edwards, "Concerning the End," 533–34.

this, our groping after language and images that may express something of these matters is always going to be piecemeal and partial at best. That said, the image of the wireless hub (Christ), the radio signals (the Holy Spirit), and the laptop computer (the believer) connected to the internet gives us some conceptual grip on these matters, even if it is at best analogous.

Nevertheless, it would be helpful to have some more formal way of thinking about the relation of union with Christ. So, let us say this: the relation of union is *binary* (having two relata: the believer and God in Christ, communicated by the Holy Spirit, who is the medium or bond connecting the two relata[29]) and *symmetrical* (connecting the believer to Christ and Christ to the believer, by means of the Holy Spirit). But it is also *monergistic*. That is, it is generated and sustained entirely by divine agency—in this case, the agency of the Holy Spirit in uniting the believer to Christ and Christ to the believer. It is also true in much Reformed theology that this relation is sustained and strengthened through the use of the sacraments. Thus, as Calvin points out, in the celebration of the Eucharist the believer is mystically united to Christ by feeding upon the sacramental elements. The bread and wine also (somehow) facilitate the spiritual feeding of the believer on the benefits of Christ's saving work via the Spirit. He writes, "Now Christ is the only food of our souls, and therefore our Heavenly Father invites us to Christ, that, refreshed by partaking of him, we may repeatedly gather strength until we shall have reached heavenly immortality."[30] This "mystery of Christ's secret union with the devout is by nature incomprehensible,"[31] avers Calvin. And yet, not only does the sacrament remind us of the "wonderful exchange"[32] by way of the Son of God taking on human flesh for our salvation, it also nourishes the soul of the believer through the real presence of Christ. As he goes on to say,

> Even though it seems unbelievable that Christ's flesh, separated from us by such great distance, penetrates to us, so that it becomes our food, let us remember how far the secret power of the Holy Spirit towers above all our senses, and how foolish it is to wish to measure his immeasurableness by

29. In Calvin's memorable phrase, "the Holy Spirit is the bond by which Christ effectually unites us to himself" (*Institutes* 3.1.1).

30. Calvin, *Institutes* 4.17.1.

31. Calvin, *Institutes* 4.17.1.

32. Calvin, *Institutes* 4.17.2.

our measure. What, then, our mind does not comprehend, let faith conceive: that the Spirit truly unites things separated in space.[33]

The feeding of the believer upon Christ by the power of the Spirit is, for Calvin, a real union, and an outward means of strengthening the union with Christ by the means of grace—one that offers a real, though mystical rather than merely corporeal, communion with the body and blood of Christ. Plausibly, the sacrament of baptism performs a similar function. For it unites the one baptized to the visible church in faith, and in the expectation of a fuller union that will be actualized as the child baptized comes of age and owns that faith for herself.[34] In this way, the union with Christ is fortified by the sacramental life of the church, though it is, in origin, a work of grace consequent upon the calling of the believer and the secret work of regeneration.

The Mystical Body of Christ

Thus far we have examined how God ordains the justification of redeemed humanity in eternity, though this obtains in time at the particular moment at which a given individual is regenerated by the infusion of the Holy Spirit. This monergistic work is transformative and sets the believer on the path toward ever greater union with God in Christ that goes on into the world to come in theosis. Union with Christ is the means by which the believer is united to God via the saving benefits of Christ's atoning work. Thus there is a movement from God through the agency and reconciling work of Christ via the Holy Spirit to the believer in regeneration. At the same time, there is another movement from the believer via the Spirit in union with Christ, aided by the sacramental life of the church. This brings us to the question of the church as the mystical body of Christ.

Not only are there organic analogies for the church embedded in the New Testament witness; there is also a long tradition of theological reflection on these images, as well as attempts to express them in various models and doctrines of the church. Thus, for instance, in Reformed theology we can find substantive use made of these images in Calvin's humanist-imbued thought, in Edwards's empiricist-idealist understanding of the church, or

33. Calvin, *Institutes* 4.17.10.
34. See, e.g., Calvin, *Institutes* 4.16.20.

in nineteenth-century ways of thinking about the church as the body of Christ that are indebted to German idealism, such as the views expressed by the Mercersburg theologian John Williamson Nevin.[35]

Recently, the British Anglican analytic theologian Joshua Cockayne has weighed in on the discussion of these matters in an account of the ontology of the church that takes seriously the biblical and historical ways in which the church has been understood as the mystical body of Christ, and that explores the social ontology literature as providing material for modeling this. As we saw in the last chapter, the social ontology literature on group theory can be quite helpful for thinking about the nature of atonement. It is therefore not surprising that it would also be of assistance when reflecting on the shape of the church as well, given the close connection between these two ideas: the church and Christ as the head of the church—that is, the *totus Christus*.

In the last chapter, we distinguished between group theories that include the notion that groups have agency and those that do not. I argued (to some extent against my own earlier work) that group theories that include the notion of group-level agency are problematic and opted instead for a way of thinking about the nature of atonement that did not require the idea that the whole of fallen humanity or redeemed humanity was an agent, or could be described using the language of agency. There are legal and political ways in which such language is co-opted, and sometimes this is for very good reason. This is the case in situations where corporations are treated as entities that may be the subject of legal action, including the corporations' assets as parts of one complex whole.[36] But as we noted in passing in the previous chapter, political theorists have thought of societies in an analogous way too.[37] Such accounts may be said to be realist about certain kinds of entities, whether legal, social, or political. But as

35. See Nevin, *Mystical Presence*. I have discussed Nevin's views in Crisp, "John Williamson Nevin on the Church."

36. As an interesting historical footnote, according to Christian List and Philip Pettit, this sort of notion goes back to an edict issued by Pope Innocent IV: "The classical connection between corporate responsibility and personhood was made in a debate about the exposure of a group agent or *universitas* to excommunication. In 1246 Pope Innocent IV argued against the excommunication of any such corporate entity on the grounds that although it might be a person—this important concession was made in passing—it was a *persona ficta*, a fictional or artificial person, and did not have a soul" (List and Pettit, *Group Agency*, 153).

37. See, e.g., Hobbes, *Leviathan* 1.16, 107. This is also picked up by Cockayne, "Analytic Ecclesiology," 109.

Cockayne points out (following the broader social-ontology literature), in such cases we do not think of the entities in question as bearing agency as a collective or as a whole. The entities posited are thought to be real, but agency is not at the group level. Rather, it is a function of the collective will of the individuals that make up the group. For instance, in the case of Hobbesian monarchies, the society authorizes the monarch whereupon the monarch is able to act on behalf of the group as a kind of political body or "person" that he represents. These Cockayne describes as *redundant realist* groups because "while this model is realist about the ontology of groups, the explanation of how groups think, act, and deliberate is entirely explicable by giving an account of how the authorized individual thinks, acts, and deliberates."[38]

Those who opt for thoroughgoing realist approaches to groups that include some idea of group agency Cockayne categorizes into two genera. The first, more historical approach, involves positing some sort of unifying principle or spirit on the basis of which we may speak of some kind of group agency. These Cockayne characterizes as *animation* theories. Examples might include the sort of views expressed by the nineteenth- and early-twentieth-century British Hegelianism of philosophers like F. H. Bradley.[39] But one might just as easily look to theological forebears of this view, like Nevin, for whom the mysterious uniting principle is none other than the Holy Spirit himself.[40]

However, more recently, philosophers like Peter French, and subsequently, Mitchell Haney, Christian List, and Phillip Pettit, have ventured other thoroughgoing realist accounts of group agency that are *functionalist* in nature.[41] The distinguishing feature of functionalist accounts of mind is that "what makes something a mental state of a particular type does not depend on its internal constitution, but rather on the way it functions, or the role it plays, in the system of which it is a part."[42] According to List and Pettit, an agent can be a system that has representational states, motivational states, and a capacity to act on such states. A representational state is one that "plays the role of depicting the world"

---

38. Cockayne, "Analytic Ecclesiology," 109.
39. See Cockayne, "Analytic Ecclesiology," 110.
40. For useful discussion of this, see W. Evans, *Imputation and Impartation*, chap. 5.
41. See, e.g., French, "Corporation as a Moral Person," 207–15; French, *Corporate Ethics*; Haney, "Corporate Loss of Innocence"; List and Pettit, *Group Agency*.
42. See Levin, "Functionalism."

and a motivational state is one that motivates action.[43] It is the functional role that these states play that is the focus of their attention in thinking about group agency. Thus, a corporation may be a group agent in the relevant functionalist sense if it has ways of representing the world (e.g., in the scope of business conducted by the corporation), motivational states that enable the corporation to act in a particular way with respect to its clients and products, and the ability to act as a group toward certain ends. Naturally, in such groups the interaction of particular individuals in units and in the whole is vital, and certain individuals may be authorized to act in particular ways on behalf of the group—for example, a CEO or a board or a manager.

Cockayne does an admirable job of attempting to motivate the application of a functionalist account of group agency to the church, drawing on the work of List and Pettit in particular. He advocates a "modified functionalist model" of ecclesial group agency. On this way of thinking, "the Church is a unified group which functions as an agent with representation and motivational states and is capable of acting on these states. It is constituted by individual Christian disciples and is united by the internal promptings of the Holy Spirit . . . and the external commands of the Holy Spirit."[44] The Holy Spirit unites us to Christ, on his view, and communicates Christ's will to the church.[45] The Spirit shapes and guides the church in its relation to Christ. But the church can disregard or rebel against the secret work of the Spirit in this regard and sin. This is important for Cockayne, who worries that some accounts of the church are too idealistic or imply that God is sinful by tying God's agency too closely to that of the church and its members. But he also thinks that other existing accounts of group agency are either too strong in their realism (so that the collective—the church—becomes more "real" or more fundamental than the individual agents making up the church) or too weak (so that insufficient attention is paid to the corporate role of the church, and the church is seen more or less as a collection of individual agents). He summarizes his view like this:

According to MFM [the modified functionalist model], the Church is constituted by individual Christian disciples, who in turn, coalesce into gathered

43. See List and Pettit, *Group Agency*, 20–21; and Cockayne, "Analytic Ecclesiology," 111.
44. Cockayne, "Analytic Ecclesiology," 118.
45. Cockayne, "Analytic Ecclesiology," 118.

collectives. . . . The unity of the Church is brought about by the work of the Spirit, who through instruction and guidance made possible by the liturgies of the Church, and his indwelling the mind of each individual believer, shapes the actions of the individual constituent parts to form motivational and representational states, which meet the necessary conditions for agency. . . . The Spirit enacts this work in line with the will of Christ, the head of the Church. . . . Finally, since each constituent member of the Church can reject or act in defiance of the will of Christ made manifest by the Holy Spirit, the actions of gathered collectives and individual disciples can diverge from the purposes of God, thereby bringing about apparent disunity within a united whole.[46]

That seems right. There may be groups that are committed to collectively upholding a proposition even though not all members of the group are individually committed to it—as, for example, when a political group includes members who are disingenuous in their group affiliation (maybe they are closet Marxists, though they claim to support the aspirations of the liberal party of which they are members). In that case, members of the group may uphold a given group proposition even if they personally do not share it. Applied to the church, there may be members who are disingenuous, though they publicly uphold the creed and affirm the doctrine and practice of ecclesiastical life. So this account is able to accommodate the messiness of ecclesiastical life in the case of disingenuous believers in the "mixed multitude" of the visible church.

However, Cockayne's analysis of the ontology of the church in terms of group action does raise some important differences between the church as the body of Christ, on the one hand, with Christ as its head, and Christ as the one whose work atones for the sins of the members of redeemed humanity, on the other hand. Christ is authorized (by God) to act on behalf of redeemed humanity. He represents them in atonement. As I argued in the previous chapter, this is a *sui generis* relation that is divinely constituted.

46. Cockayne, "Analytic Ecclesiology," 120. This summary is set against a series of desiderata with which he begins his account of the nature of the church. These are (1) the church is constituted by individual Christians; (2) these individuals at times coalesce into gathered collectives; (3) these collectives and individuals that partially constitute the church are not united in practice, theology, or belief; (4) such disunity arises in part due to human sin; (5) the Spirit unites the constituent parts of the church to respond to God in worship through Christ; and (6) Christ has authority and headship over the church. (Adapted from Cockayne, "Analytic Ecclesiology," 103.)

By contrast, the church, which comprises the members of redeemed humanity, is joined together by the agency of the Holy Spirit in calling and regeneration, and in union with Christ. The Spirit is the agent that, as it were, binds the members of the church together. This much animation models of group theory applied to the church have gotten right. For the church is animated and bound together by the agency of the Spirit, which is a necessary condition for the existence of the church. But the church as such does not act by means of an authorized *merely human* agent or representative in communing with Christ. Rather, the different members of the church act together by means of a *divine agent*—that is, the Holy Spirit who calls and regenerates them individually and who unites them to Christ and to one another as members of the mystical body of Christ. So it seems to me that animation models of group action articulate something fundamental concerning the nature of the church that should not be set aside. Although I think that Cockayne is right about much of his analysis of the nature of the church, it seems to me to err too much on the side of the individual. He writes, "We do not need to appeal to any mysterious force to explain the unity of the whole [church]. Indeed, unlike the animation model, this unity is provided by means of the will of a person, or group of persons." His view "does not appeal to some metaphysically strange force which emerges each time groups are formed."[47] Instead, it is the will of the Trinity that is the "driving force of the Church's unity."[48] But how is this mediated to the church if not by the "mysterious force" of the Holy Spirit? And how is the church to act together if not by means of the same Spirit who calls and regenerates the individual believers and unites them to Christ? The church is significantly unlike a corporation or even a collective like a hive. The reason for this is precisely that there *is* a mysterious "force" at work uniting the different members of the church together in a whole—that is, the Holy Spirit, without whose agency the church would not exist as a group at all.[49]

---

47. Cockayne, "Analytic Ecclesiology," 119.
48. Cockayne, "Analytic Ecclesiology," 120.
49. To be fair to Cockayne, his views are developing (and he has a monograph on ecclesiology forthcoming with Oxford University Press, which will be an important treatment of the topic). In a more recent essay, "We Believe in the Holy Spirit," Cockayne provides a more nuanced picture of the agency of the Spirit in the life of the church. There he writes, "While there are clear similarities between the community of the church and other kinds of social community, it is important to see that the church's unity comes not from human structures and the externally imposed ideologies of politicians but only through the work of the one Spirit, who unites the

Of course, the church fails in important respects, as Cockayne points out in his comments about disingenuous believers. The very fact that the historic fabric of the one, holy, catholic, and apostolic church is torn and patched and misaligned in all sorts of ways reflects the fact that the church does not act in accordance with the will of God expressed in the reconciling work of Christ and with the salvific agency of the Holy Spirit. Nevertheless, it is in attending to this agency, and in the infusion of uncreated grace that comes in being a member of redeemed humanity, that the individual believer is united with other believers as members of the mystical body of Christ. If anything, it seems to me that the church should be thought of in what Cockayne calls *"redundant* realist" terms,[50] as a special case of a group that acts by means of an authorized agent, the Holy Spirit, who unites the members of the church to one another and to Christ as the head of the church.[51] The Spirit animates the church; without his agency there would be no church, though there may be a collective or a corporation. Although the church *qua* church does not have agency as such, it is able to act together by means of the agency of the Holy Spirit, as the members of the church seek to be conformed to the image of God in Christ, to whom they are mystically united.

Conclusion

In this chapter I have provided an account of what I have called the consequences of atonement—that is, of how it is that the benefits of Christ's reconciling work are applied to the believer and form the church as the new society of redeemed humanity. In some historic accounts of atonement, one is left without an indication of the consequences of atonement, so that it is not entirely clear how the reconciling work of Christ actually touches down, so to speak, in the lives of particular individuals, let alone in the life of the church as a group. A famous example of this is the work of the great *Doctor Magnificus*, Anselm of Canterbury. *Cur Deus Homo*

---

one church with Christ, the one Lord" (187). That seems to me to be a much more appropriately *pneumatic* account of the life of the church.

50. Cockayne, "Analytic Ecclesiology," 109.

51. The Holy Spirit is "authorized" for this work as God, not by members of the group. In this way, and in a manner similar to the account given of the atonement in the previous chapter, the Holy Spirit's agency in the church is both mysterious and *sui generis*.

is a powerful and (in many respects) persuasive account of the work of Christ as a satisfaction. But the reader is left to her own devices to figure out how this work outside of us (*extra nos*) is applied to the particular individual (*in nobis*). (For Anselm, the answer to this question has to do with attending to the sacramental life of the church, beginning with the regenerative act of the Spirit in baptism and continuing in the daily celebration of the Eucharist, and in the use of the other sacraments, such as what is now called the sacrament of reconciliation.) I have tried to ensure this sort of lacuna does not bedevil the present work.

The chapter was divided into three sections. In the first, I argued that those who are members of redeemed humanity are justified by an act of sheer divine grace from eternity. This is actualized in the work of regeneration that brings about what Jonathan Edwards called "a new sense of things" in the heart of the believer through the infusion of uncreated grace, and the reordering and reorientation of the fallen individual through the secret work of the Spirit. Then we considered the second aspect of the way in which the Spirit applies the benefits of Christ to the believer. This has to do with uniting the believer to Christ, and through Christ to the divine nature. In this way the believer is reconciled to God and enabled to begin the process of participation in the divine life that begins with justification, calling, and regeneration, and continues through the process of sanctification. But this only deals with the relation of the individual to Christ. It does not address the corporate aspect of this union, in the mystical body of Christ. This we tackled in the third section of the chapter. Using some ideas culled from recent work in social ontology once more, and filtered through the helpful recent work of Joshua Cockayne, I argued for a special case of a realist and pneumatic account of the church as the mystical body of Christ.

With the end of this chapter, the constructive section of the work is complete. All that remains is to provide a synthesis of the whole in a dogmatic overview of the reasoning I have offered here, setting them into the larger framework of God's fundamental aim in creation and redemption of ensuring that God's creatures, and (for our purposes at least) especially human creatures, participate in the divine life. That is the task of the final chapter.

10

Soteriological Synthesis

In this final summary chapter, I will provide a synthesis of the various strands of the doctrine of atonement I have outlined in the previous chapters, especially in this third section of the work. The idea is to set these different facets into a broader account of soteriology—that is, the doctrine of salvation that includes the doctrine of atonement. Because this work is part of a larger research project on the incarnation and atonement that now encompasses a number of different books, I will draw on previous work in order to furnish some of the soteriological context of which I speak. For, inevitably, some of the elements of this larger context have not been a significant feature of the argument of this volume, given its more narrow focus on the nature of the reconciling work of Christ.

In offering a soteriological synthesis like this, I will be engaged in what Scott MacDonald calls *philosophical clarification* rather than *philosophical justification*.[1] Philosophical clarification is about getting a clearer picture of a given view, its conceptual shape and implications, whether it is internally consistent and coherent, and so on. In philosophical justification, by contrast, the focus is on arguments in favor of the view in question—reasons to think the view is plausible or cogent. Both intellectual projects

1. See MacDonald, "What Is Philosophical Theology?"

are important. But it is philosophical clarification that we are interested in here, not justification.

Soteriological Context

With this caveat in mind, let us turn to explicating the soteriological context for the doctrine of atonement I have outlined in previous chapters. An important theological principle in soteriology has to do with the ends or goals God has in the act of creation. One fundamental question here is whether there is an overarching end at which God aims in creating the particular world that God creates. This sort of concern is encapsulated in what we might call the "intention-execution principle"—which is, *what is first in intention is last in execution*. In other words, what God takes ultimate aim at in creation—the final goal God intends for the world God creates—is the last thing to come about in time, though it is the initial intention of God in creating the particular world God creates. This seems intuitive. When an artist conceives of a work of art, that idea, which is the first thing the artist intends when conceiving the work, is the last thing to be brought about in the making of the artwork. Only upon completing the work is the original intention fulfilled. Just so with creation. Since this is a summary chapter, let us put this principle more formally, like this:

> **Intention-Execution Principle:** That which is first in God's intention in creation is last in execution, in the actualizing of that intention in the created order.

Now, it might be thought that God's first intention in creating the world is not something that depends on the atonement or even on Christ. Certainly, there have been theologians in the history of the church who would have claimed this. One influential historical example, clearly articulated in the work of the great New England divine Jonathan Edwards, is the notion that the ultimate end for which God creates the world is God's own glory.[2] On Edwards's way of thinking, God bends all works toward this ultimate end, the incarnation and atonement included. But it might be thought that the incarnation and atonement have more than an

2. See Edwards, "Concerning the End."

instrumental value in bringing about the ultimate goal of creation. Here is one such alternative to an Edwardsian proposal: Suppose we think that God's intention in creation is to create a world of creatures with whom God can be in communion, enabling the creation, and especially humanity, to enjoy God and to participate in the divine life forevermore. If God loves the creation, and conceives it as an act of love, this creative intention does not seem particularly strange. For, on at least one widely canvassed understanding of love, including divine love, in loving an entity we seek that entity's flourishing and union with that entity in a manner suitable to the kind of thing it is.[3] If God loves what God creates then God seeks its flourishing and union with it in a manner suitable to the kind of thing it is. In which case, on the supposition that God's intention in creation is to fashion creatures with whom God may be united in intimate communion, enabling such creaturely participation in the divine life will be a function of God's loving motivation to create the world that God creates. That is indeed what seems to me to be a fundamental aim of God in creating this world. God creates the world in order to bring creatures into a state in which they may enjoy the divine presence and participate in the divine life. This has a cosmic dimension, for the reconciliation of all things intimated in Colossians 1 in the New Testament surely includes the renewal of creation *in toto*, and not just of fallen human beings. Nevertheless, the Christian gospel does presume that God has a particular regard for human creatures with respect to the ultimate end of the world God creates. We can spell out this regard in a doctrine of theosis:

> **Theosis:** The doctrine according to which redeemed human persons are conformed to the image of Christ in his human nature. By being united to Christ by the power of the Holy Spirit, redeemed human beings begin to exemplify the qualities of the human nature of Christ and to grow in their likeness to Christ (in exemplifying the requisite qualities Christ's human nature instantiates). The process of transformation and participation goes on forevermore. It is akin to a mathematic asymptote.

Although theosis is a doctrine that is being rehabilitated theologically speaking, it is still something of which Protestant thinkers in particular

---

3. I have indicated in previous chapters that this Thomistic account of love has recently been championed by Eleonore Stump. A good summary of her view can be found in Stump, "Love, by All Accounts."

are often suspicious. But there are examples of notable Protestant theologians who have embraced such a doctrine (or something very like it), even if they have not used the language of theosis. This is even true of a number of theologically formative Protestant thinkers, such as John Calvin and (arguably) Martin Luther.[4] Once again, it is Jonathan Edwards, in his dissertation on God's end in creation, who provides us with a clear example of a doctrine of theosis in Reformed, evangelical theology:

> The creature is no further happy with this happiness which God makes his ultimate end than he becomes one with God. The more happiness [enjoyed by two entities] the greater union: when the happiness is perfect, the union is perfect. And as the happiness [shared between the elect and God] will be increasing to eternity, the union will become more and more strict and perfect; nearer and more like to that between God the Father and the Son; who are so united, that their interest is perfectly one. If the happiness of the creature be considered as it will be, in the whole of the creature's eternal duration, with all the infinity of its progress, and infinite increase of nearness and union to God; in this view, the creature must be looked upon as united to God in an infinite strictness.[5]

An "infinite strictness" indeed! Thus, the first thing we must say in soteriology concerns God's intention in creation, and it seems to me that the right way to construe that is in terms of a doctrine of theosis. This is what frames the soteriology of this study.

Next, it seems to me that a doctrine of creation is incomplete if it is not *christologically conditioned*. By that I mean, creation should be seen through the lens of Christ. For, as the author of Colossians tells us, Christ

> is the image of the invisible God, the firstborn of all creation; for in him all things in heaven and on earth were created, things visible and invisible, whether thrones or dominions or rulers or powers—*all things have been created through him and for him.* He himself is before all things, and *in him all things hold together.* He is the head of the body, the church; he is the beginning, the firstborn from the dead, so that he might come to have

4. A classic treatment of Calvin on theosis can be found in Mosser, "Greatest Possible Blessing." For the Lutheran doctrine of theosis, see Mannermaa's classic work, *Christ Present in Faith.*
5. Edwards, "Concerning the End," 533–34. I have discussed Edwards's doctrine of theosis in detail in *Jonathan Edwards on God and Creation.*

first place in everything. For in him all the fullness of God was pleased to dwell, and through him *God was pleased to reconcile to himself all things*, whether on earth or in heaven, by making peace through the blood of his cross. (1:15–20, emphasis added)

There is a long tradition of viewing creation through a christological lens in light of such passages in the later New Testament.[6] For our purposes, we need two christological claims that are relevant for the soteriology set forth here. Let us call these *the christological conditioning principles of soteriology*:

Christological Union Account of Incarnation: The incarnation is a fitting means by which God is able to provide an interface between divinity and humanity so that human beings may participate in the divine life. This state of affairs would have obtained independent of human sin.

Christological Account of the Image of God: Christ is the image of the invisible God. His human nature is the archetype of human nature. Human beings are ectypal images of God, made after the image of Christ, the archetypal image of God. Mere human beings bear the divine image in virtue of the fact that human nature is in principle created with the capacities and powers necessary and sufficient to be in hypostatic union with a divine person. Because of these capacities and powers human beings are in principle capable of union with God by means of Christ, the image of God.

Standing behind these two christological claims is a species of what is sometimes called the "incarnation anyway argument." This is the idea that the incarnation is not dependent on human sin—as if there would only have been an incarnation if human beings sinned and required reconciliation to God. Instead, incarnation is a function of God's desire to be united to God's creatures in love. If God desires union with human creatures, then one fitting way of bringing that about is by means of incarnation. (Note: I do not say this is the *only fitting* way. The thought is that this is condign, not that it is the only condign means of bringing about this end.)

6. Recent theologians who adopt something like this approach include Marc Cortez, Ian McFarland, Thomas F. Torrance, and Kathryn Tanner. But this sort of view has an ancient pedigree that can be traced back to some of the earliest patristic theology in the works of thinkers like Irenaeus and Athanasius.

So, God desires to create a world of creatures, including human creatures, with whom God wishes to be united in love. This involves the flourishing of the creature and a union appropriate to the kind of creature in question. In the case of human beings, God brings about such union by means of incarnation. The hypostatic or personal union of God with a human creature in Christ is an intimate form of union indeed. But the incarnation is also the means by which other human beings that are not hypostatically united to God may interface with the divine through the agency of the Holy Spirit, as we shall see in the doctrine of regeneration. But we begin to get ahead of ourselves.

Next, and in light of the christological conditioning of creation, we turn to God's intention in justifying those who compose redeemed humanity (Rom. 5:12–19). In chapter 9, I put it like this:

Justification from Eternity

1. God eternally decrees the number of the elect (that is, of redeemed humanity).
2. God eternally decrees that Christ is the mediator of salvation.
3. Christ is the ground of election (given that God the Son, the divine person who voluntarily assumes human nature, is a member of the divine Trinity) and the means by which election is brought about as the Elect One and mediator of our election.
4. God knows all those who are elect (that is, all the members of redeemed humanity).
5. God knows that all the elect (i.e., members of redeemed humanity other than Christ) will be saved through the work of Christ as mediator.
6. God knows that all the elect will be justified through the work of Christ by God's divine grace alone, according to God's divine will and purpose (Eph. 1:5).
7. It is eternally true that the members of redeemed humanity (other than Christ) are justified by Christ's meritorious work alone (not by their own merit).
8. The secret work of the Holy Spirit applies the benefits of Christ's work to each individual member of the elect.

9. This application normally obtains by means of the gift of faith, bestowed on the elect individual by the Holy Spirit, uniting that individual to Christ in regeneration.[7]

10. The application of faith to the elect individual completes the eternal act of justification; justification is an eternal act of divine grace that obtains in time at the very moment in which the Holy Spirit applies the benefits of Christ to the individual.

11. The application of faith to the elect individual enables that person to understand that she is included within the ambit of divine election and that she is justified.

12. The application of faith to the elect individual brings about an epistemic change to the person concerned.

13. The application of faith also brings about a moral and (perhaps) a legal change in the elect individual.

So God creates this world, and God ensures that the creation is christologically conditioned with the end goal of theosis in mind. God ordains that human beings—made in the image of Christ, who is the image of God—are capable of participating in the divine life. Given that the world God creates includes humans who fall into sin, God ordains the justification of some number of those humans, those who are members of redeemed humanity, whom God justifies from eternity and regenerates in time by the Spirit, uniting them to Christ.

The Tragedy of Sin

However, before saying something more about the means by which such regeneration is brought about in the reconciling work of Christ, we should say something more about the obstacle to reconciliation—namely, sin itself. Recall that as I have explained it here and in my previous work on the topic, the version of the doctrine of sin I am aiming at is a variant on a Reformed account. In particular, I am following a minority report in the Reformed tradition that can be traced back to the work of the Magisterial

7. The caveat "normally" provides some wiggle room for those who may be elect, and therefore members of redeemed humanity, but who are incapable of exercising faith—e.g., the severely mentally impaired and infants who die before the age of maturity.

Swiss Reformer Huldrych Zwingli in particular (though Calvin's view is not dissimilar in this regard). Zwingli's doctrine of sin does not include the notion that fallen human beings are guilty of Adam's sin (i.e., of original guilt). There are, I argued, good biblical and moral reasons for resisting the creep of original guilt into our account of human fallenness. It is also important to track how sin thoroughly corrupts human beings (on this way of thinking), so that they still require salvation even if they are not guilty of Adam's sin in particular. Here is the corruption-only account of original sin in outline:

Corruption-Only Doctrine of Original Sin

1. All human beings barring Christ possess original sin.
2. Original sin is an inherited corruption of nature, a condition that every fallen human being possesses from the first moment of generation.
3. Fallen humans are not culpable for being generated with this morally vitiated condition.
4. Fallen humans are not culpable for a first, or primal, sin either. That is, they do not bear original guilt (i.e., the guilt of the sin of some putative first human pair or human community being imputed to them along with original sin).
5. This morally vitiated condition normally inevitably yields actual sin. That is, a person born with this defect will normally inevitably commit actual sin on at least one occasion provided that person lives long enough to be able to commit such sin. (The caveat "normally" indicates that there are limit cases that are exceptions to this claim, e.g., infants that die before maturity and the severely mentally impaired.)
6. Fallen human beings are culpable for their actual sins and condemned for them, in the absence of atonement.
7. Possession of original sin leads to death and separation from God irrespective of actual sin.

This is the view of original sin to which the doctrine of atonement that I have defended here is a reply. However, it is possible to combine the union account of atonement with a different view of original sin (perhaps a version of the Reformed view that includes original guilt). Similarly, it is possible to combine the corruption-only doctrine of original sin just outlined with a different account of the atonement. That is, neither of these two views is entailed by the other. Once more, the relation between them is more of a question of "fit" than of something more stringent. Nevertheless, it does seem to me that there is a good fit between a corruption-only account of original sin and the union account of atonement. The idea is that although fallen humans are not guilty of Adam's sin, they bear original sin on analogy with a kind of disease that is passed down the generations from our first parents. This condition inevitably gives birth to actual sin if a person lives long enough to sin and is not mentally incapable of forming the intention to sin. It is this condition, and any guilt associated with actual sin committed by individual fallen human beings, that Christ's reconciling work tackles. If a person perishes before being able to commit actual sin, and thereby incur guilt, or is never in a position to commit actual sin (because, say, she or he is severely mentally impaired from birth), it is still the case that original sin places such a person in need of salvation. For, as I have argued, possession of original sin renders a person unfit for the presence of God absent atonement. Moreover, although I have not provided an independent argument for this claim here, in a manner consistent with the findings of the first methodological section of this study, Christ's work is an atonement sufficient for the salvation of all humanity.[8]

The Solution to Sin in Atonement

This brings us to the mechanism of atonement, which was the focus of chapter 8. At the heart of that chapter was a kind of just-so story about the atonement. This I called the "atonement narrative." It went like this:

> Taken together, Adam (from the fall onwards) and all of post-fall humanity barring Christ constitute a distinct group[9]—that is, "fallen humanity" (Rom. 5:12–19). Fallen humanity exists across time in a way analogous to the different stages of the life of an organism, like a tree, from its beginning as an acorn to its maturity as an oak. Members of fallen humanity possess

8. I discuss the sufficiency of Christ's atonement in "Anglican Hypothetical Universalism."
9. Roman Catholic and Eastern Orthodox readers may like to make the mental adjustment, "barring Christ and his mother, Mary *Theotokos*."

the moral corruption of original sin as a consequence of Adam's primal sin. It is passed from Adam to the later members of the group because he is the first human in covenant relationship with his maker. As such, his primal sin violates the conditions of the covenant with God and incurs the penalty of original sin, which is then passed down the generations to subsequent members of fallen humanity. In a similar manner, a chronic disease introduced to an acorn affects all the later phases of the life of the oak tree in a way that a disease introduced at some later moment developmentally downstream of the acorn would not.

Christ is the second Adam. He is the first member of a new humanity, one that is cleansed from sin and reconciled to God. Christ and those he comes to save form, together, a second group: "redeemed humanity." Christ is the interface between God and humanity and a fitting means by which humans may be reconciled to God. As the God-human, Christ is able to act on behalf of both God and humanity, communicating between them and acting as a conduit of divine grace to humanity, as a representative of humanity. Christ has a kind of priority or privilege over other "parts" of redeemed humanity, although he exists later in time than some of them, because he is the first of a new, resurrected humanity that is ordered eschatologically rather than (as with the first Adam) protologically. Thus, although he lives later than, say, Abraham, his work as the second Adam reconciles Abraham to God (Heb. 11:8–16, 39–40). In the purposes of God, those living prior to Christ can be proleptically incorporated into Christ's work as the second Adam. Christ is not guilty of sin; yet he acts vicariously on behalf of the other members of redeemed humanity who bear original sin and stand in need of reconciliation as members of fallen humanity. Christ's reconciling work (comprising his incarnation, death, and resurrection) removes the obstacle of sin and defeats death. He represents humanity before God and, as the impeccable God-man, is held accountable for the sin of other, fallen human beings. He atones for human sin through a performative act of vicarious penitence that culminates in his death and resurrection, which satisfy the demands of God's moral law and the penalty incurred by the primeval fall and curse. Through union with Christ by the power of the Holy Spirit, in regeneration, members of fallen humanity begin a process of transformation into the likeness of God as members of redeemed humanity, becoming partakers of the divine nature. This process of transformation goes on forevermore. It is like a mathematical asymptote in that the human members of redeemed humanity draw ever closer to God in this process, yet without ever becoming God or losing themselves in God.

This expresses the representational view of atonement that I defended in chapter 8. But doing so is only part of the story of reconciliation, as the final sentences of this narrative indicate. For Christ's atonement is a kind of *in principle* work that makes salvation available to fallen humanity. There is still the question of the consequences of atonement. That is, there is still the matter of how the benefits of this saving work are applied to particular individuals and to the life of the church as the new society that Christ's work seeks to establish. This was dealt with in the final constructive chapter of the book, chapter 9.

The Application of Christ's Reconciling Work

The application of Christ's reconciling work was divided into several parts, all of which are acts that are primarily *pneumatological* in nature. In the first, the action of the Holy Spirit involves applying the saving benefits of Christ to the believer in the transformative experience of regeneration, uniting the believer to Christ. I characterized regeneration thus:

> **Regeneration:** The divine action by means of which the Holy Spirit is communicated to the believer, indwelling the believer, and *infusing* a new supernatural disposition or habit into a fallen human person that provides a spiritual sense by means of which the regenerate person may begin to live a life pleasing to God.

This sat alongside a claim about divine and human agency in regeneration:

> **Monergism:** The doctrine according to which the application of the benefits of Christ's reconciling work by the agency of the Holy Spirit in regeneration is wholly a work of divine grace; in this process the human agent is entirely passive, but not quiescent.

Union with Christ

There is also the manner in which the Spirit unites the regenerate person to Christ, which is sustained through the use of the sacraments. We could summarize it thus:

Union with Christ: The binary, symmetrical, and monergistic relation established by the infusion of the Holy Spirit in the believer that unites the believer with Christ so that she may grow in grace, becoming a partaker of the divine nature in christological union. This union is enriched through the means of grace to be found in the sacraments.

The Church as the Mystical Body of Christ

This leaves the matter of the relation of believers to one another and to Christ in the new society formed by redeemed humanity, which is the mystical body of Christ—that is, the church. Using some work in social ontology and in recent analytic theology, I argued that the church is a group that has its reality via the agency of the Holy Spirit, who animates the members of redeemed humanity, uniting them. It is through *divine* agency that the church is formed and sustained, not through some spurious group agency over and above the agency of the members of the group. Thus, the church is formed into the body of Christ as it is more closely united through the secret working of the Holy Spirit. Where there is disunity and discord among the members of Christ's mystical body, this is a function of human sinfulness.

The mystical body of Christ is that group of redeemed humans who are the objects of God's desire in soteriology. The goal of creation is, in part, the union of the members of this mystical body with one another and with God in Christ through the agency of the Holy Spirit. Thus, atonement is a vital aspect—but only one aspect—of the reconciling work of God in creation. It is the means by which the redeemed are brought into the banqueting house of the bridegroom, over which is his banner of love (Song 2:4).

Bibliography

Abelard, Peter. *Commentary on the Epistle to the Romans*. Fathers of the Church Medieval Continuations. Translated by Stephen R. Cartwright. Washington, DC: Catholic University of America Press, 2011.

Abraham, William J. *Divine Agency and Divine Action: Systematic Theology*. Vol. 3. Oxford: Oxford University Press, 2018.

Adams, Marilyn McCord. "Hell and the God of Justice." *Religious Studies* 11, no. 4 (1975): 433–47.

Allen, R. Michael. "Calvin's Christ: A Dogmatic Matrix for Discussion of Christ's Human Nature." *International Journal of Systematic Theology* 9, no. 4 (2007): 382–97.

Ames, William. *The Marrow of Theology*. Translated by John Eusden. Grand Rapids: Baker, 1997 (1968).

Anatolios, Khaled. *Deification through the Cross: An Eastern Christian Theology of Salvation*. Grand Rapids: Eerdmans, 2020.

———. *Retrieving Nicaea: The Development and Meaning of Trinitarian Doctrine*. Grand Rapids: Baker Academic, 2011.

Anselm of Canterbury. *Cur Deus Homo*. In *Anselm: Basic Writings*, edited and translated by Thomas Williams, 237–326. Indianapolis: Hackett, 2007.

———. *Monologion*. In *Anselm: Basic Writings*, edited and translated by Thomas Williams, 1–74. Indianapolis: Hackett, 2007.

———. *On the Virginal Conception, and on Original Sin*. In *Anselm: Basic Writings*, edited and translated by Thomas Williams, 327–60. Indianapolis: Hackett, 2007.

———. *Proslogion*. In *Anselm: Basic Writings*, edited and translated by Thomas Williams, 75–98. Indianapolis: Hackett, 2007.

———. *S. Anselmi Cantuariensis Archiepiscopi Opera Omnia*. Tomus Primus et Tomus Secundus. Edited by F. S. Schmitt. Stuttgart: Friedrich Frommann, 1984 (1968).

Aquinas, Thomas. *Summa Theologica*. Translated by Fathers of the English Dominican Province. 5 Vols. New York: Benzinger Brothers, 1948 (1911).

Arcadi, James M., and James T. Turner Jr., eds. *T&T Clark Handbook of Analytic Theology*. London: Bloomsbury, 2021.

Augustine of Hippo. *City of God*. Translated by Henry Bettenson. Introduction by John O'Meara. Harmondsworth: Penguin Books, 1972.

Aulén, Gustaf. *Christus Victor: An Historical Study of the Three Main Types of the Idea of the Atonement*. Translated by A. G. Herbert. London: SPCK, 1931.

Baillie, D. M. *God Was in Christ*. London: Faber and Faber, 1961.

Baker, Mark, and Joel B. Green. *Recovering the Scandal of the Cross: Atonement in New Testament and Contemporary Contexts*. 2nd ed. Downers Grove, IL: InterVarsity, 2011 (2000).

Barbour, Ian G. *Religion and Science: Historical and Contemporary Issues*. San Francisco: HarperCollins, 1997.

Bavinck, Herman. *Reformed Dogmatics*. Vol. 3, *Sin and Salvation in Christ*, edited by John Bolt. Translated by John Vriend. Grand Rapids: Baker Academic, 2006.

Bayne, Tim, and Greg Restall. "A Participatory Model of the Atonement." In *New Waves in Philosophy of Religion*, edited by Yujin Nagasawa and Erik J. Wielenberg, 150–66. London: Palgrave Macmillan, 2009.

Beilby, James, and Paul R. Eddy, eds. *Justification: Five Views*. Spectrum Multiview Books. Downers Grove, IL: IVP Academic, 2011.

———. *The Nature of the Atonement: Four Views*. Downers Grove, IL: IVP Academic, 2006.

Berkhof, Louis. *The History of Christian Doctrines*. Edinburgh: Banner of Truth, 1969 (1937).

———. *Systematic Theology*. Edinburgh: Banner of Truth Trust, 1988 (1939).

Boersma, Hans. *Violence, Hospitality, and the Cross: Reappropriating the Atonement Tradition*. Grand Rapids: Baker Academic, 2004.

Boonin, David. *The Problem of Punishment*. Oxford: Oxford University Press, 2008.

Boyd, Gregory. "Christus Victor View." In *The Nature of the Atonement: Four Views*, edited by James Beilby and Paul R. Eddy, 23–65. Downers Grove, IL: IVP Academic, 2006.

Breiner, Nikolaus. "Punishment and Satisfaction in Aquinas's Account of the Atonement: A Reply to Stump." *Faith and Philosophy* 35, no. 2 (2018): 237–56.

Brooks, Thom. *Punishment: A Critical Introduction*. 2nd ed. London: Routledge, 2021.

Brown, David. "Anselm on Atonement." In *The Cambridge Companion to Anselm*, edited by Brian Davies and Brian Leftow, 279–302. Cambridge: Cambridge University Press, 2004.

Calvin, John. *Institutes of the Christian Religion*. Translated by Ford Lewis Battles. Edited by John T. McNeill. 2 vols. Philadelphia: Westminster, 1960.

Campbell, Constantine R. *Paul and Union with Christ: An Exegetical and Theological Study*. Grand Rapids: Zondervan Academic, 2012.

Campbell, John McLeod. *The Nature of the Atonement*. Grand Rapids: Eerdmans, 1996 (1856).

Cockayne, Joshua. "Analytic Ecclesiology: The Social Ontology of the Church." *Journal of Analytic Theology* 7 (2019): 100–123.

———. "The Imitation Game: Becoming Imitators of Christ." *Religious Studies* 53 (2017): 3–24.

———. "We Believe in the Holy Spirit . . . The Holy Catholic Church." In *The Third Person of the Trinity: Explorations in Constructive Dogmatics*, edited by Oliver D. Crisp and Fred Sanders, 183–200. Grand Rapids: Zondervan Academic, 2020.

Collins, Robin. "Girard and Atonement: An Incarnational Theory of Mimetic Participation." In *Violence Renounced: René Girard, Biblical Studies, and Peacemaking*, edited by Willard M. Swartley, 132–56. Telford, PA: Pandora, 2000.

Collins, Stephanie. *Group Duties: Their Existence and Their Implications for Individuals*. Oxford: Oxford University Press, 2019.

Cottingham, John. "Varieties of Retribution." *The Philosophical Quarterly* 29, no. 116 (1979): 238–46.

Couenhoven, Jesse. "St. Augustine's Doctrine of Original Sin." *Augustinian Studies* 36, no. 2 (2005): 359–96.

Craig, William Lane. *Atonement*. Elements of Philosophy of Religion. Cambridge: Cambridge University Press, 2018.

———. *Atonement and the Death of Christ: An Exegetical, Historical, and Philosophical Exploration*. Waco: Baylor University Press, 2020.

———. "Eleonore Stump's Critique of Penal Substitutionary Atonement Theories." *Faith and Philosophy* 36, no. 4 (2019): 522–44.

Crisp, Oliver D. *Analyzing Doctrine: Toward a Systematic Theology*. Waco: Baylor University Press, 2019.

———. "Anglican Hypothetical Universalism." Chap. 5 in Crisp, *Freedom, Redemption and Communion: Studies in Christian Doctrine*.

———. *An American Augustinian: Sin and Salvation in the Dogmatic Theology of William G. T. Shedd*. Paternoster Theological Monographs. Milton Keynes: Paternoster; Eugene, OR: Wipf & Stock, 2007.

———. *Approaching the Atonement: The Reconciling Work of Christ*. Downers Grove, IL: IVP Academic, 2020.

———. "Desiderata for Models of the Hypostatic Union." In *Christology, Ancient and Modern: Explorations in Constructive Dogmatics*, edited by Oliver D. Crisp and Fred Sanders, 19–41. Grand Rapids: Zondervan Academic, 2013.

———. *Deviant Calvinism: Broadening Reformed Theology*. Minneapolis: Fortress, 2014.

———. "Divine Retribution: A Defence." *Sophia* 42, no. 2 (2003): 35–52.

———. *Divinity and Humanity: The Incarnation Reconsidered*. Cambridge: Cambridge University Press, 2007.

———. "Federalism vs. Realism: Charles Hodge, Augustus Strong and William Shedd on the Imputation of Sin." *International Journal of Systematic Theology* 8 (2006): 1–17.

———. *Freedom, Redemption and Communion: Studies in Christian Doctrine*. London: T&T Clark, 2021.

———. *God, Creation, and Salvation: Studies in Reformed Theology*. London: T&T Clark, 2020.

———. *God Incarnate: Explorations in Christology*. London: T&T Clark, 2009.

———. "The Importance of Model-Building in Theology." In *T&T Clark Handbook of Analytic Theology*, edited by James M. Arcadi and James T. Turner Jr., 9–20. London: Bloomsbury, 2021.

———. "John McLeod Campbell and Non-penal Substitution." Chap. 5 in Crisp, *Retrieving Doctrine*.

———. "John Williamson Nevin on the Church." Chap. 8 in Crisp, *Retrieving Doctrine*.

———. *Jonathan Edwards and the Metaphysics of Sin*. Aldershot: Ashgate, 2005.

———. *Jonathan Edwards on God and Creation*. New York: Oxford University Press, 2012.

———. "Just Desert? An Assessment of Moderate Free Will Scepticism about Punishment." LLM thesis, University of Aberdeen, 2020.

———. "A Moderate Reformed Response." In *Original Sin and the Fall: Five Views*, edited by J. B. Stump and Chad Meister, 140–49. Downers Grove, IL: IVP Academic, 2020.

———. "A Moderate Reformed View." In *Original Sin and the Fall: Five Views*, edited by J. B. Stump and Chad Meister, 35–54. Downers Grove, IL: IVP Academic, 2020.

———. "On Behalf of Augustinian Realism." *Toronto Journal of Theology* 35, no. 2 (2020): 124–33.

———. "On Original Sin." *International Journal of Systematic Theology* 17 (2015): 252–66.

———. "On the Theological Pedigree of Jonathan Edwards's Doctrine of Imputation." *Scottish Journal of Theology* 56, no. 3 (2003): 308–27.

———. "On the Vicarious Humanity of Christ." *International Journal of Systematic Theology* 21, no. 3 (2019): 235–50.

———. "Penal Non-substitution." *Journal of Theological Studies* 59, no. 1 (April 2008): 140–68.

———. "Pulling Traducianism out of the Shedd." *Ars Disputandi* 6, no. 1 (2006): 265–87, https://www.tandfonline.com/doi/abs/10.1080/15665399.2006.10819933.

———. "Regeneration Reconsidered." Chap. 7 in Crisp, *Freedom, Redemption and Communion*.

———. *Retrieving Doctrine: Essays in Reformed Theology*. Downers Grove, IL: IVP Academic, 2011.

———. "Retrieving Zwingli's Doctrine of Original Sin." *Journal of Reformed Theology* 10 (2016): 340–60.

———. *Revisioning Christology: Theology in the Reformed Tradition*. Aldershot: Ashgate, 2011.

———. *Saving Calvinism: Expanding the Reformed Tradition*. Downers Grove, IL: IVP Academic, 2016.

———. "Scholastic Theology, Augustinian Realism and Original Guilt." *European Journal of Theology* 13 (2004): 17–28.

———. "Sin." In *Christian Dogmatics: Reformed Theology for the Church Catholic*, edited by Michael Allen and Scott R. Swain, 194–215. Grand Rapids: Baker Academic, 2016.

———. "Sin, Atonement and Representation: Why William Shedd Was Not a Thorough-Going Realist." *Scottish Bulletin of Evangelical Theology* 24, no. 2 (2006): 155–75.

———. "Sin in Reformed Theology." Chap. 2 in Crisp, *Freedom, Redemption and Communion*.

———. *The Word Enfleshed: Exploring the Person and Work of Christ*. Grand Rapids: Baker Academic, 2016.

———. "Zwingli on Original Sin." Chap. 5 in Crisp, *God, Creation and Salvation*.

Cross, Richard. *Duns Scotus*. Great Medieval Thinkers. Oxford: Oxford University Press, 1999.

Cyril of Alexandria. *On the Unity of Christ*. Translated by John Anthony McGuckin. Crestwood, NJ: St. Vladimir's Seminary Press, 1995.

Davies, Brian, and G. R. Evans, eds. *Anselm of Canterbury: The Major Works*. Oxford: Oxford University Press, 1998.

Denney, James. *The Christian Doctrine of Reconciliation*. London: Hodder and Stoughton, 1918.

Edwards, Jonathan. "Concerning the End for Which God Created the World." In *Ethical Writings*. Vol. 8 of *The Works of Jonathan Edwards*, edited by Paul Ramsey. New Haven: Yale University Press, 1989.

———. *Original Sin*. Vol. 3 of *The Works of Jonathan Edwards*, edited by Clyde A. Holbrook. New Haven: Yale University Press, 1970.

———. *Religious Affections*. Vol. 2 of *The Works of Jonathan Edwards*, edited by John E. Smith. New Haven: Yale University Press, 1959.

———. *Writings on the Trinity, Grace and Faith.* Vol. 21 of *The Works of Jonathan Edwards*, edited by Sang Hyun Lee. New Haven: Yale University Press, 2002.

Evans, C. Stephen. *God and Moral Obligation.* Oxford: Oxford University Press, 2013.

Evans, William B. *A Companion to the Mercersburg Theology: Evangelical Catholicism in the Mid-Nineteenth Century.* Eugene, OR: Cascade Books, 2019.

———. *Imputation and Impartation: Union with Christ in American Reformed Theology.* Studies in Christian History and Thought. Milton Keynes: Paternoster; Eugene, OR: Wipf & Stock, 2008.

Farris, Joshua R., and S. Mark Hamilton. "The Logic of Reparative Substitution: Contemporary Restitution Models of Atonement, Divine Justice, and Somatic Death." *Irish Theological Quarterly* 83, no. 1 (2018): 62–77.

———. "This Is My Beloved Son, Whom I Hate? A Critique of the *Christus Odium* Variant of Penal Substitution." *Journal of Biblical and Theological Studies* 3, no. 2 (2018): 271–86.

Farrow, Douglas. "Anselm and the Art of Theology." *Fellowship of Catholic Scholars Quarterly* 42, no. 4 (2020): 255–72.

Franks, R. S. "Acceptilation." In *Encyclopædia of Religion and Ethics*, Part 1, edited by James Hastings and John A. Selbie, 61–62. New York: Scribner's Sons, 1911.

———. *The Work of Christ.* London: Thomas Nelson & Son, 1962.

French, Peter. *Corporate Ethics.* New York: Harcourt, Brace, 1995.

———. "The Corporation as a Moral Person." *American Philosophical Quarterly* 16 (1979): 207–15.

Gathercole, Simon. *Defending Substitution: An Essay on Atonement in Paul.* Grand Rapids: Baker Academic, 2015.

Geach, Peter. *Providence and Evil.* Cambridge: Cambridge University Press, 1977.

Gorman, Michael J. *The Death of the Messiah and the Birth of the New Covenant.* Eugene, OR: Wipf & Stock, 2014.

———. *Inhabiting the Cruciform God: Kenosis, Justification, and Theosis in Paul's Narrative Soteriology.* Grand Rapids: Eerdmans, 2009.

Gorringe, Timothy. *God's Just Vengeance: Crime, Violence and the Rhetoric of Salvation.* Cambridge Studies in Ideology and Religion. Cambridge: Cambridge University Press, 1996.

Gould, Paul, ed. *Beyond the Control of God? Six Views on the Problem of God and Abstract Objects.* London: Bloomsbury, 2014.

Green, Adam. "Reading the Mind of God (without Hebrew Lessons): Alston, Shared Attention, and Mystical Experience." *Religious Studies* 45, no. 4 (2009): 455–70.

Green, Joel B. "Kaleidoscopic View." In *The Nature of the Atonement: Four Views*, edited by James Beilby and Paul R. Eddy, 157–201. Downers Grove, IL: IVP Academic, 2006.

———. "A Wesleyan Response." In *Original Sin and the Fall: Five Views*, edited by J. B. Stump and Chad Meister, 150–61. Downers Grove, IL: IVP Academic, 2020.

———. "A Wesleyan View." In *Original Sin and the Fall: Five Views*, edited by J. B. Stump and Chad Meister, 55–77. Downers Grove, IL: IVP Academic, 2020.

Greggs, Tom. *Dogmatic Ecclesiology*. Vol. 1, *The Priestly Catholicity of the Church*. Grand Rapids: Baker Academic, 2019.

Gregory of Nyssa. *Great Catechism*. In vol. 5 of *A Select Library of Nicene and Post-Nicene Fathers of the Christian Church*. 2nd series. Edited by Philip Schaff and Henry Wace. 14 vols. New York: Christian Literature, 1890–1900. Reprint, Peabody, MA: Hendrickson, 1994.

Grensted, L. W. *A Short History of the Doctrine of Atonement*. Manchester: University of Manchester Press, 1920.

Grotius, Hugo. *A Defense of the Catholic Faith: Concerning the Satisfaction of Christ against Faustus Socinus*. Translated by Frank Hugh Foster. Andover, MA: Warren F. Draper, 1889 (1617).

Gunton, Colin E. *The Actuality of Atonement: A Study of Metaphor, Rationality and the Christian Tradition*. London: T&T Clark, 1988.

Haney, Mitchell R. "Corporate Loss of Innocence for the Sake of Accountability." *Journal of Social Philosophy* 35, no. 3 (2004): 391–412.

Hart, H. L. A. "Positivism and the Separation of Law and Morals." *Harvard Law Review* 71, no. 4 (1958): 593–629.

Hawley, Katherine. *How Things Persist*. Oxford: Oxford University Press, 2004.

Helmer, Christine. *The End of Doctrine*. Louisville: Westminster John Knox, 2014.

Heppe, Heinrich. *Reformed Dogmatics*. Edited by Ernst Bizer. Translated by G. T. Thomson. London: Collins, 1950.

Hick, John. *The Metaphor of God Incarnate*. 2nd ed. Louisville: Westminster John Knox, 2005 (1993).

Hill, Jonathan. "'His Death Belongs to Them': An Edwardsean Participatory Model of Atonement." *Religious Studies* 54, no. 2 (2017): 175–99.

Hobbes, Thomas. *Leviathan*. Edited by Michael Oakeshott. Oxford: Basil Blackwell, n.d. (1651).

Hodge, Charles. *Systematic Theology*. Vol. 2. Grand Rapids: Eerdmans, 1940 (1845).

Holmes, Stephen R. "Can Punishment Bring Peace? Penal Substitution Revisited." *Scottish Journal of Theology* 58 (2005): 104–23.

Hooker, Morna. *From Adam to Christ: Essays on Paul*. Cambridge: Cambridge University Press, 1990.

Jersak, Brad, and Michael Hardin, eds. *Stricken by God? Nonviolent Identification and the Victory of Christ*. Grand Rapids: Eerdmans, 2007.

John of Damascus, *On the Orthodox Faith*. In vol. 9 of *A Select Library of Nicene and Post-Nicene Fathers of the Christian Church*. 2nd series. Edited by Philip Schaff and Henry Wace. 14 vols. New York: Christian Literature, 1890–1900. Reprint, Peabody, MA: Hendrickson, 1994.

Johnson, Adam J. *Atonement: A Guide for the Perplexed*. London: Bloomsbury, 2015.

———, ed. *T&T Clark Companion to the Atonement*. London: T&T Clark, 2018.

Johnson, Junius. *Patristic and Medieval Atonement Theory: A Guide to Research*. Illuminations: Guides to Research in Religion. Lanham, MD: Rowman & Littlefield, 2015.

Kelly, J. N. D. *Early Christian Doctrines*. 5th ed. London: A&C Black, 1977 (1958).

Kitchen, K. A. *Ancient Orient and Old Testament*. Downers Grove, IL: InterVarsity, 1966.

Kittle, Simon. "Grace and Free Will: Quiescence and Control." *Journal of Analytic Theology* 3 (2015): 89–108.

Kline, M. G. *Treaty of the Great King*. Grand Rapids: Eerdmans, 1963.

Kotsko, Adam. "Exemplarism." In *T&T Clark Companion to the Atonement*, edited by A. Johnson, 485–88. London: T&T Clark, 2018.

Krattenmaker, Tom. *Confessions of a Secular Jesus Follower: Finding Answers in Jesus for Those Who Don't Believe*. New York: Convergent Books, 2016.

Kvanvig, Jonathan L. *The Problem of Hell*. Oxford: Oxford University Press, 1993.

Levin, Janet. "Functionalism." In *Stanford Encyclopedia of Philosophy*, https://plato .stanford.edu/entries/functionalism/.

Lewis, David. "Do We Believe in Penal Substitution?" *Philosophical Papers* 26, no. 3 (1997): 203–9.

Lindbeck, George A. *The Nature of Doctrine: Religion and Theology in a Postliberal Age*. Louisville: Westminster John Knox, 1984.

List, Christian, and Philip Pettit. *Group Agency: The Possibility, Design, and Status of Corporate Agents*. Oxford: Oxford University Press, 2011.

Lombard, Peter. *The Sentences, Book 3: On the Incarnation of the Word*. Translated by Guilio Silano. Toronto: Pontifical Institute of Medieval Studies, 2008.

Lucas, J. R. *Responsibility*. Oxford: Oxford University Press, 1993.

Macaskill, Grant. *Union with Christ in the New Testament*. Oxford: Oxford University Press, 2013.

MacDonald, Scott. "What Is Philosophical Theology?" In *Arguing about Religion*, edited by Kevin Timpe, 17–29. London: Routledge, 2009.

Macquarrie, John. *Principles of Christian Theology*. Rev. ed. London: SCM, 1977 (1966).

Mannermaa, Tuomo. *Christ Present in Faith: Luther's View of Justification*. Minneapolis: Fortress, 2005.

McCall, Thomas H. *Against God and Nature: The Doctrine of Sin*. Foundations of Evangelical Theology. Wheaton: Crossway, 2019.

McCall, Thomas H., and Michael C. Rea, eds. *Philosophical and Theological Essays on the Trinity*. Oxford: Oxford University Press, 2009.

McCarthy, D. J. *Treaty and Covenant*. Rome: Pontifical Biblical Institute, 1982.

McFague, Sally. *Metaphorical Theology, Models of God in Religious Language*. Philadelphia: Fortress, 1982.

McGrath, Alister E. *Iustitia Dei: A History of the Christian Doctrine of Justification*. 4th ed. Cambridge: Cambridge University Press, 2020.

———. "The Moral Theory of the Atonement: An Historical and Theological Critique." *Scottish Journal of Theology* 38 (1985): 205–20.

McIntyre, John. *St. Anselm and His Critics: A Re-interpretation of "Cur Deus Homo."* Edinburgh: Oliver & Boyd, 1954.

Mendenhall, G. E. "Covenant Forms in Israelite Tradition." *The Biblical Archaeologist* 17, no. 3 (1954): 50–76.

Miley, John. *The Atonement in Christ*. New York: Philips and Hunt, 1879.

———. *Systematic Theology*. Vol. 2. Peabody, MA: Hendrickson, 1989 (1893).

Moore, Michael S. *Placing Blame: A Theory of Criminal Law*. Oxford: Oxford University Press, 2010.

Mosser, Carl. "The Greatest Possible Blessing: Calvin and Deification." *Scottish Journal of Theology* 55, no. 1 (2002): 36–57.

Mozley, J. K. *The Doctrine of the Atonement*. New York: Scribner's Sons, 1916.

Muller, Richard A. *Calvin and the Reformed Tradition: On the Work of Christ and the Order of Salvation*. Grand Rapids: Baker Academic, 2012.

———. *Dictionary of Latin and Greek Theological Terms*. Grand Rapids: Baker, 1985.

Murphy, Mark. "Not Penal Substitution but Vicarious Punishment." *Faith and Philosophy* 26, no. 3 (2009): 253–73.

Murray, John. *The Imputation of Adam's Sin*. Phillipsburg, NJ: Presbyterian and Reformed, 1977.

Nelstrop, Louise, Kevin Magill, and Bradley B. Onishi. *Christian Mysticism: An Introduction to Contemporary Theoretical Approaches*. Farnham, Surrey, UK: Ashgate, 2009.

Nevin, John Williamson. *The Mystical Presence: A Vindication of the Reformed or Calvinistic Doctrine of the Holy Eucharist*. Philadelphia: J. B. Lippincott and Co., 1846.

New-England Primer, The. Aledo, TX: WallBuilder, 1991. Facsimile of the 1777 edition (Boston: Edward Draper).

Oden, Thomas C. *Classic Christianity: A Systematic Theology*. New York: HarperCollins, 1992.

Packer, J. I. "What Did the Cross Achieve? The Logic of Penal Substitution." *Tyndale Bulletin* 25 (1974): 3–46.

Paul, L. A. *Transformative Experience*. Oxford: Oxford University Press, 2014.

Pawl, Tim. *In Defense of Extended Conciliar Christology: A Philosophical Essay.* Oxford Studies in Analytic Theology. Oxford: Oxford University Press, 2019.

Perkins, William. *A Golden Chain or Description of Theology, etc.* Edinburgh: Robert Walde-Graue, 1592.

Pike, Nelson. *Mystic Union: An Essay on the Phenomenology of Mysticism*. Ithaca, NY: Cornell University Press, 1992.

Porter, Steven L. "Rethinking the Logic of Penal Substitution." In *Philosophy of Religion*, edited by William Lane Craig, 596–608. New Brunswick, NJ: Rutgers University Press, 2002.

———. "Swinburnian Atonement and the Doctrine of Penal Substitution." *Faith and Philosophy* 21, no. 2 (2004): 228–41.

Quinn, Philip L. "Abelard on the Atonement: 'Nothing Unintelligible, Arbitrary, Illogical, or Immoral about It.'" In *A Reader in Contemporary Philosophical Theology*, edited by Oliver D. Crisp, 335–53. London: T&T Clark, 2009.

Rashdall, Hastings. *The Idea of the Atonement in Christian Theology, Being the Bampton Lectures for 1915*. London: Macmillan, 1920.

Rea, Michael C. "(Reformed) Protestantism." In *Inter-Christian Philosophical Dialogues*. Vol. 4, edited by Graham Oppy and N. N. Trakakis, 67–88. London: Routledge, 2017.

Romanides, John S. *The Ancestral Sin*. Ridgewood, NJ: Zephyr, 2002.

Schleiermacher, Friedrich. *The Christian Faith*. Edited by H. R. Macintosh and J. S. Stewart. Edinburgh: T&T Clark, 1999 (1830).

Shedd, William G. T. *Dogmatic Theology*. 3rd ed. Edited by Alan W. Gomes. Phillipsburg, NJ: P&R, 2003.

———. *A History of Christian Doctrine*. Vol. 2. Eugene, OR: Wipf & Stock, 1999 (1864).

Sonderegger, Katherine. "Anselmian Atonement." In *T&T Clark Companion to the Atonement*, edited by Adam J. Johnson, 175–94. London: Bloomsbury T&T Clark, 2017.

Spence, Alan. *The Promise of Peace: A Unified Theory of Atonement*. London: Bloomsbury, 2006.

Stewart, Kenneth J. *Ten Myths about Calvinism: Recovering the Breadth of the Reformed Tradition*. Downers Grove, IL: IVP Academic, 2011.

Strabbing, Jada Twedt. "The Permissibility of the Atonement as Penal Substitution." In *Oxford Studies in Philosophy of Religion*, vol. 7, edited by Jonathan L. Kvanvig, 239–70. Oxford: Oxford University Press, 2016.

Stump, Eleonore. *Aquinas*. New York: Routledge, 2003.

———. *Atonement*. Oxford Studies in Analytic Theology. Oxford: Oxford University Press, 2018.

———. "Love, by All Accounts." *Proceedings and Addresses of the American Philosophical Association* 80, no. 2 (2006): 25–43.

Swinburne, Richard. *Faith and Reason*. 2nd ed. Oxford: Oxford University Press, 2005 (1981).

———. *Responsibility and Atonement*. Oxford: Oxford University Press, 1989.

Tanner, Kathryn. *Christ the Key*. Current Issues in Theology. Cambridge: Cambridge University Press, 2010.

Teresa of Ávila. *Interior Castle*. Translated by E. Allison Peers. New York: Doubleday, 1961.

Thate, Michael J., Kevin J. Vanhoozer, and Constantine R. Campbell, eds. *"In Christ" in Paul: Explorations in Paul's Theology of Union and Participation*. Tübingen: Mohr Siebeck, 2018.

Thompson, J. A. "The Significance of the Ancient Near Eastern Treaty Pattern." *Tyndale Bulletin* 13 (1963): 1–6.

Thurow, Joshua. "Communal Penal Substitution." *Journal of Analytic Theology* 3 (2015): 47–69.

Thurow, Joshua, and Jada Twedt Strabbing. "Entwining Thomistic and Anselmian Interpretations of the Atonement." *Faith and Philosophy* 37, no. 4 (2020): 516–35.

Todd, Obbie Tyler. *The Moral Governmental Theory of Atonement: Re-envisioning Penal Substitution*. Eugene, OR: Cascade, 2021.

Tollefsen, Deborah Perron. *Groups as Agents*. Cambridge: Polity, 2015.

Torrance, Andrew B. "Can a Person Prepare to Become a Christian? A Kierkegaardian Response." *Religious Studies* 53, no. 2 (2017): 199–215.

Torrance, Thomas F. *The Mediation of Christ*. Colorado Springs: Helmers and Howard, 1992 (1983).

Treat, Jeremy. *The Crucified King: Atonement and Kingdom in Biblical and Systematic Theology*. Grand Rapids: Zondervan, 2014.

Turner, Denys. *The Darkness of God: Negativity in Christian Mysticism*. Cambridge: Cambridge University Press, 1995.

Turretin, Francis. *Institutes of Elenctic Theology*. Edited by James T. Dennison Jr. Translated by George Musgrave Giger. 3 vols. Phillipsburg, NJ: P&R, 1992–1997.

Van den Brink, Gijsbert. *Reformed Theology and Evolutionary Theory*. Grand Rapids: Eerdmans, 2020.

Vidu, Adonis. "The Indwelling of the Holy Spirit." In *T&T Clark Handbook of Analytic Theology*, edited by James M. Arcadi and James T. Turner Jr., 257–68. London: T&T Clark, 2021.

———. *The Same God Who Works All Things: Inseparable Operations in Trinitarian Theology*. Grand Rapids: Eerdmans, 2021.

Weaver, J. Denny. *The Nonviolent Atonement*. 2nd ed. Grand Rapids: Eerdmans, 2011.

Weber, Otto. *Foundations of Dogmatics*. Vol. 2. Translated by Darrell L. Guder. Grand Rapids: Eerdmans, 1983 (1962).

Westminster Confession of Faith, The. In *The Constitution of the Presbyterian Church (U.S.A.): Part 1, Book of Confessions*, 145–202. Louisville: The Office of the General Assembly, 2016. https://www.pcusa.org/site_media/media/uploads/oga/pdf/boc2016.pdf.

Westminster Shorter Catechism, The. In *The Constitution of the Presbyterian Church (U.S.A.): Part 1, Book of Confessions*, 203–21. Louisville: The Office of the General Assembly, 2016. https://www.pcusa.org/site_media/media/uploads/oga/pdf/boc2016.pdf.

Whiteley, D. E. H. "St. Paul's Thought on the Atonement." *Journal of Theological Studies* 8, no. 2 (1957): 240–55.

———. *The Theology of St. Paul*. Oxford: Basil Blackwell, 1970.

Williams, Garry. "Penal Substitution: A Response to Recent Criticisms." *Journal of the Evangelical Theological Society* 5, no. 1 (2007): 71–86.

Williams, Thomas. "Sin, Grace, and Redemption." In *The Cambridge Companion to Abelard*, edited by Jeffrey E. Brower and Kevin Guilfoy, 258–78. Cambridge: Cambridge University Press, 2004.

Wilson, E. O. *On Human Nature*. Cambridge, MA: Harvard University Press, 1978.

Winter, Michael. *The Atonement*. Collegeville, MN: Liturgical Press, 1995.

Wolf, Susan. *Freedom within Reason*. Oxford: Oxford University Press, 1990.

Wollebius, Johannes. *Compendium Theologiae Christianae*. In *Reformed Dogmatics*, edited and translated by John W. Beardslee III, 27–262. Grand Rapids: Baker, 1977 (1965).

Woznicki, Christopher. "Do We Believe in Consequences? Revisiting the 'Incoherence Objection' to Penal Substitution." *Neue Zeitschrift für Systematicsche Theologie Und Religionsphilosophie* 60, no. 2 (2018): 208–28.

———. "'One Can't Believe Impossible Things': A New Defence of Penal Substitutionary Atonement in Light of the Legal Concepts of Vicarious Liability and Respondeat Superior." *Scottish Bulletin of Evangelical Theology* 37, no. 1 (2019): 64–80.

Wright, N. T. *The Day the Revolution Began: Rethinking the Meaning of Jesus's Crucifixion*. London: SPCK, 2016.

———. *What Saint Paul Really Said: Was Paul of Tarsus the Real Founder of Christianity?* Grand Rapids: Eerdmans, 1997.

Zwingli, Ulrich. *On Providence and Other Essays*. Edited by Samuel Macauley Jackson. Durham, NC: Labyrinth, 1983.

Index